MEDITERRANEAN COOKING

THE HEALTHFUL WAY

Also by Marlena Spieler

MEDITERRANEAN COOKING

THE HEALTHFUL WAY

MARLENA SPIELER

PRIMA PUBLISHING

PRIMA PUBLISHING and colophon are registered trademarks of Prima Communications, Inc.

Illustrations by Diane Clark

Library of Congress Cataloging-in-Publication Data

Spieler, Marlena.
Mediterranean cooking the healthful way / Marlena Spieler.
p.   cm. — (Cooking the healthful way)
Includes index.
ISBN 0-7615-0387-0
1. Cookery, Mediterranean.   I. Title.   II. Series.
TX725.M35S65 1996
641.59'1822—dc20   96-29090
CIP

97 98 99 00 01 AA 10 9 8 7 6 5 4 3 2 1
Printed in the United States of America

NUTRITIONAL ANALYSES

A per serving nutritional breakdown is provided for each recipe. If a range is given for an ingredient amount, the breakdown is based on the smaller number. If a range is given for servings, the breakdown is based on the larger number. If a choice of ingredients is given in an ingredient listing, the breakdown is calculated using the first choice. Nutritional content may vary depending on the specific brands or types of ingredients used. *Optional* ingredients or those for which no specific amount is stated are not included in the breakdown. Nutritional figures are rounded to the nearest whole number.

HOW TO ORDER:

Single copies may be ordered from Prima Publishing, P.O. Box 1260BK, Rocklin, CA 95677; telephone (916) 632-4400. Quantity discounts are also available. On your letterhead, include information concerning the intended use of the books and the number of books you wish to purchase.

Visit us online at http://www.primapublishing.com

To Leah and Alan, for eating, tasting, and being enthusiastic;

My husband, Alan McLaughlan;

Georgia Hughes at Prima Publishing for commissioning this book and for her excitement about the project; and to Debra Venzke, who made editing almost painless;

Susie Morgenstern for being the best hostess and new friend anyone could want. And to her daughter, Dr. Maya, for saving my life in Nice and visiting me every day in the hospital;

Michael Bauer, M.A., Maria Cianci, Fran Irwin, and the rest of the Food Department staff at the *San Francisco Chronicle,* where many of these recipes first appeared. And Barbara Fairchild of *Bon Appétit* for sending a little package of the Mediterranean to my cold, winter-bound northern European kitchen;

Leah Spieler, Rev. Jon Harford, Gretchen Spieler, and Vanessa Welch for sharing our trip to the Languedoc, even when I got us stuck—*Jurassic Park*-style—in the bear enclosure of a French safari park;

M.A. Mariner, Richard and Rand Carreaga for a Mediterranean summer in the Oakland Hills;

Paul Richardson for visits to his Ibizan mountain home and for looking after our naughty dog;

Jerome Freeman and Sheila Hannon, who make any place, even in the dead of winter, seem as nice as summer in the Mediterranean; and to Sue Kreitzman, who can perform this magic in London's East End.

To friends, colleagues, and food lovers: Sandy Waks; Kamala Friedman; Dr. Esther Novak and Rev. John Chendo; Kathleen Griffin; Rosemary Barron for her evocative book *Flavors of Greece;* Helene Simpson; Paula Aspin; Fiona Beckett and Trevor Vibert (and their wonderful family); Ian Robertson and Marie Helly; Paul Corrigan of Graphic Office Supplies; Nigel Patrick and Graham Ketteringham; and Dan Ostrowsky for taking me to the market in Nice, introducing me to *Madame l'Artichaut,* and sharing his favorite *socca* spot. Thank-you to the British Hellenic Chamber of Commerce for rekindling my love affair with Greek olive oil;

To Rabbi Jason Gaber, a true friend; Amanda Hamilton and Tim Hemmeter for sharing life in their vineyard; Paul Aspin for wine-making tales of Verona; Peter Milne with thoughts of Venice and Nice; Fred and Mary Barclay; Vivien Milne, who loves to cook; "the dis-crete ones," Sid and Ivy Staddon, who didn't mind the storms on Crete; Stella and Louis for their hospitality at their traditional Cypriot taverna, To Porizin, in the village of Mesoyi near Paphos;

Grandmother Sophia Dubowsky ("Bachi" to all) for her love of good food, especially soup, and those Sunday suppers that began with breakfast;

My parents Caroline and Izzy Smith; Aunt and Uncle Estelle and Sy Opper; and my little cousins Melissa, Steven, Alison, and Lexie;

Freud, as always, a cat with the good taste to adore garlic and cilantro;

To the little beagle in the Languedocian village of Colombiers who was on our doorstep every morning, ready for breakfast.

Contents

Preface

FROM the moment the clouds parted and I first caught a glimpse of the blue, blue Mediterranean Sea from my airplane window, I was charmed. In the Mediterranean I discovered that colors were brighter, emotions were more volatile, and flavors tasted stronger. It was like living in a fauvist painting.

The markets enchanted me. I was struck by the dazzling variety of the fruits, vegetables, and fresh cheeses and by how very vibrant they tasted! Cafés and tavernas offered tables covered with little plates full of salads, olive oil-stewed vegetables, breads, olives, and pungent fresh herbs. How marvelous to spend an evening nibbling, sipping, and having a conversation as the parade of street life passed by.

In ensuing years I've spent months at a time in Greece, Italy, and the south of France from Catalonia to Provence, and have visited Spain often and lived in Israel. Always, I am captivated by the food—its freshness, its vitality, and by the fact that there is always something new and wonderful to discover.

Mediterranean food is not just one cuisine, but a rich tapestry of many. Yet all of the varied cultures and cuisines that make up this picturesque, brightly colored, vibrantly flavored food have much in common with each other. The lush fruits and vegetables—olives, citrus, garlic, chickpeas—that grow fat and flavorful in the hot sun, fresh cheeses, fermented milk and yogurt, legumes and grains, briny fresh fish, and small amounts of meat (usually lamb, sometimes chicken or game) make the basis for the cuisines of all the lands that touch the Mediterranean Sea.

Sometimes I feel that it is the flavor of happiness that defines the food of the Mediterranean: food strong in flavor, as bright as the relentless sun, as cooling as a dip in the sea. And as good for the body as it is for the soul, full of fresh vegetables and fruits, herbs and leafy greens, yogurts and fresh cheeses, grains and wholesome breads.

Part of the enchantment no doubt lies in the place that food and its cultivation hold in the cultures of these lands. Mediterranean peoples love to eat, drink, and entertain each other by the sharing of foods. Hospitality is huge, beloved, wonderful—often touching. Come upon a Greek family having their midday meal in a grove and you'll usually be bidden to join, and leave afterward bearing cucumbers, oranges, whatever they have to give.

The midday is a time for leisurely enjoying a meal rather than grabbing a sandwich as in northern Europe and the United States. Some say it is the heat of the day that makes a rest necessary. But the slow enjoyment, social interaction, and sharing of the meal are as nourishing as the vitamins and nutrients in the food.

Food in the Mediterranean is meant to be fresh. That pepper you eat for lunch, those peaches you slice up for dessert, the cheese you spread on your crusty bread—all will likely have been grown within a mile or two of your home. And wild foods, too, are not only gathered and cherished, but outings to the forest for mushroom gathering or berry picking are a fine weekend event. And whatever little patch of land you can get to is probably your vegetable garden; even city balconies will do—there are few without at least a pot or two of fragrant herbs.

Whether crusty French or Italian country-type bread, or flat breads like focaccia or pita, bread is eaten with every meal and usually bought twice a day from the local baker. When stale it is used for salads, soups, and casseroles. It might be rubbed with garlic and tomatoes then drenched with olive oil *(pamb y ambuet)* for a Catalonian breakfast, or grated into crumbs to toss with pasta for the Sicilian *le mollica*.

Everything is eaten in season, usually with great celebration: the first asparagus of March, thin slices of nutty raw artichoke, August's ripest red tomatoes or sweet tender peas, or autumn's multicolor carpet of wild mushrooms—once gone, they won't be in the market until next season, when they will be all the more delicious for the waiting.

With little grazing land, beef is eaten seldom or in small portions. Rather, sheep and goats are kept for their ability to graze on rocky hillsides and forage for whatever greens and grasses poke their way up through the rocks. Sheep's and goat's milk cheeses, therefore, are specialties of the entire area. They might be eaten fresh, light, and tangy or salted and pressed. Goat's and sheep's milk cheeses range from pungent, light, and mild to well-aged stinky. They might be coated with herbs or eaten with sugar and orange flower for dessert. Ricotta, pecorino, feta, *brousse, brin d'amour,* and *mizythra* are but a few of the varieties available.

Israel was the first place I ate yogurt: first with a thick layer of honey, then (when I got braver) with chopped onions and vegetables for *meze,* salads, and breakfast. In Greece I delighted over the little yogurt shops that dispensed their rich yogurt from earthenware bowls, rough on the outside, smoothly glazed on the inside.

Salads of raw and cooked vegetables—crisp cucumbers, juicy tomatoes, leafy greens and/or pungent herbs—

are always present, as is a bowl of olives: salty-fleshed, full of ancient flavor.

And each time I visit the region, I gasp in pleasure at my first glimpse of that sea; a sense of well-being permeates my entire soul. I long to get into the kitchen, crush some garlic, drizzle some olive oil, pour a glass of wine, and get ready for dinner.

My biggest problem in writing this book was in limiting the number of dishes to share, and also in deciding when to stop traveling to the Mediterranean long enough to spend a little time in the kitchen and at the computer. I think I've finally worked it out. But you know . . . this morning when I did my shopping, there was a sign on the window of the travel agent: Two Weeks in Tunisia: £199.

Introduction

THREE continents—Europe, Asia, and Africa—lie along the shores of the Mediterranean, embracing many countries and a cacophony of cultures and languages. Here there are three major religions, often at odds with each other, cultures that dictate differing goals and yearnings, social structures and mores that are strikingly different from each other.

At first glance the cuisines are many rather than one; they seem as different from each other as the countries they come from. Yet as you travel from region to region, languages blend into each other, cultures are shared, specialties acquire new names and accents, and you realize that they are as close as a family could be. All are based on the shared histories of conquests, rulers, pirates, wars, and settlements, going back thousands of years. In all, they are united by common strands: the sea itself, the mild climate, and the traditions that have been shared, transported, and adapted from the movements of history.

And their foods share common flavors, tastes, and colors, formed not only by the climate, soil composition, and history, but also by the mysterious forces that have contributed to making the Mediterranean temperament as lively as it is.

Based on wheat or rice, legumes, fresh vegetables, fish, and small amounts of meat and poultry, this food glistens with olive oil, reeks deliciously of garlic, and is (often) washed down with wine. Yogurt, chilies, and lemons add their zest, as do spices and herbs, rotating and changing as the regions of the Mediterranean change and blend into one another.

But culinarily, where exactly does the Mediterranean begin? Yes, it includes the lands of Spain and Italy, southern France and northern Africa, the coast of the former Yugoslavia and the lands of Greece, Israel, Turkey, Syria, Cyprus, Morocco, Albania, Monaco, Algeria, Tunisia, Egypt, Lebanon, and Malta. But the Mediterranean region is far more than the land that lies along the coast. Long before one sees the blue of the sea, suddenly the light changes. Olive trees and grapevines blanket the terraced hillsides, lemon trees and other citrus abound, and the food tastes of garlic and olive oil.

Western culture was born in the region around the Mediterranean where Pharaohs ruled long ago. Indeed, one of our first culinary writings is mentioned in the Bible in Exodus: as the Hebrews fled Egypt, there was a great lament for the garlic and leeks they left behind.

The Greeks, Phoenicians, and Romans colonized the area centuries before the Modern Era (B.C.E), establishing an agriculture based on olives, wheat, and wine. The climate, so similar from region to region—hot summers and mild wet winters—encouraged the growth of the same vegetables and fruit.

Although the Romans spread the art of cheesemaking, in the Mediterranean cheeses have remained zesty, sharp, and pungent, rather than unctuous and rich, as in cooler, northern climes. Mediterranean cheeses are usually made with goat's or sheep's milk rather than with cow's milk; in fact, it is said that the goat and the sheep are the poor person's cow: goats and sheep are able to graze the spindly weeds of the stony hilltops, unlike cows in their lush lowland pastures.

The love of yogurt spread through the region from Bulgaria and the Balkans, although with the exception of Sardinia (which has had a tradition of yogurt since the Roman Empire), yogurt is eaten mainly in the eastern Mediterranean and North Africa.

When Rome fell, so too did the glories of Roman cuisine. Food came to be in short supply and rather than thinking of ways to embellish it, people thought only of ways to get it into their stomachs. Hunger being the best condiment, they didn't need the finesse of inspired cooking. Some say that it was during those bleak hungry years after the fall of Rome that pasta eating gained in popularity, for it filled empty stomachs and was delicious with whatever could be found to go with it. This was the time that regional Italian cooking came into being, as the city-states developed their own cuisine and specialties depending on what grew best in their region.

In pre-Ottoman Turkey, yogurt and wheat dishes such as various breads formed the basis of much of the diet. Feasts and banquets were the main way of gathering for socializing and played a large part in developing social relations.

As Europe was ravaged by the darkness of the Middle Ages, the Arab and Ottoman cultures colonized the Mediterranean and brought with them the ingredients and flavors that formed the basis of the region's cuisine and way of eating. The Ottoman influence is evident in today's Greek cuisine as well as that of the eastern Mediterranean.

When the Moors—from what is now Morocco, Algeria, and Tunisia—worked their way through North Africa and into Spain, they brought Moslem culture, rituals, customs, and also new foods. When the Moors were pushed back to North Africa by the Christians, their 700 years of rule left behind distinctive tastes and dishes. Croissants, fruit jams, and marzipan are well-known examples of dishes that were introduced by Ottomans and/or Moors. North Africa was then settled by Spaniards, Jews, Turkish Moslems, and French, continuing the movement of cultures and flavors around the Mediterranean.

The return of New World explorers to Italy and Spain brought a staggering variety of fruits and vegetables to the table. Tomatoes, peppers, eggplant, and chiles; where would Mediterranean cuisine be without these? Chocolate was combined with the Moorish predilection for sweets and rapidly became a favored delicacy of Spain, spreading quickly to the rest of Europe.

Mediterranean cuisine today bears layers of history in its flavorings, yet the basics still remain. Eggplant, zucchini, tomatoes, garlic, lemons: most people eat one or more of these every day. Almonds and sweet flowers such as roses, orange flowers, and jasmine perfume many of the dishes from Spain to the eastern Mediterranean, North Africa, and southern France.

But enlivening the basic vegetables are flavors and seasonings that vary widely depending on where in the Mediterranean you dwell. Fresh herbs such as basil, parsley, chervil, borage, and sweet marjoram are favored from Provence through Liguria, while dried herbs such as oregano season much of the food from Italy's south through Greece and its islands. Dill, arugula, and coriander make their appearance in Turkey, and the fragrances of mint and cilantro permeate the salads, pilafs, and vegetable stews of the Middle East. Egypt perfumes much of its food with a whiff of cinnamon and cumin to balance the pungent cilantro; Tunisia favors a mixture of caraway, coriander, garlic, and hot pepper known as *tabil;* while Morocco seasons its foods lavishly, opulantly, often using a curry-like spice mixture called *ras al hanout,* rich with spices, flower petals, even the dried blister beetle known as Spanish fly. Spain enjoys fresh herbs in the spring and dried spices, especially saffron, in the summer when the heat is far too strong to grow delicate herbs.

Cooking Mediterranean food begins not in the kitchen but in the gardens and marketplaces. Wandering through the markets is exhausting, make no mistake, but there is no other way to learn the cuisine. The markets lie at the heart of the cuisine and culture: a riot of colors, smells, noises, the place to see what is in season and to find out the latest gossip. It's a great place to learn the language and perhaps even find a mate or a significant other, or at least a good recipe for tonight's dinner.

When I think of eggplant dishes I adore, I think back to the market in Iráklion where the seller explained to me how to make the best *Imam Bayildi* (page 192). To discover the true flavor of Nice, wander through Vieux

Ochre, yellow, and rust-colored stone houses topped with rose-tiled roofs, windows framed with green or turquoise shutters to keep out the heat of day.

Sounds muted by the herbs and grasses that cover the surrounding hills: toads croaking, dogs barking, a motorcycle revving its engine. A cock crows, church bells chime, sheep baa contentedly. Car horns beep occasionally as they negotiate the hairpin turns and 25 percent grades that wind through the hills, then suddenly fade. Mosquitoes buzz in the air, smelling dinner (most likely me).

High above us an airplane glides by, en route to Nice/Côte d'Azur. Smoke rises from the village almost vertically in the absence of breezes or wind. Lizards scurry over the still warm roof, across the stones of the terrace, and up the olive tree that shades our bedroom window.

Autumn *est arrivée,* with a vengeance. Persimmons and figs fall at our feet as

Nice, the old town, poking your way along the cobblestones, stopping at shops that specialize in pasta, pastries, fruits and vegetables, cheeses, coffee, and spices until you almost reach the sea. There is the Cours Selaya market, as picturesque as a Mediterranean market could be; sit in a café, drink a glass of chilled rosé, and nibble on inky black olives. I think about buying fresh pita from wheelbarrows in Jerusalem's Machane Yehuda, getting a lovely recipe for purslane and tomato salad in the marketplace in Perpignan, and sifting through piles of herbs and squash flowers in Venice's Rialto.

And as much as the type of foods eaten, cuisine in the Mediterranean is also defined by the way it is eaten: the sense of hospitality, the joy in sharing. I remember so many examples. Once when I arrived on a cold, damp autumn day to visit an olive pressing in Baena, Andalucia, I was handed a bowl of soup right away to sip as I warmed up from the journey. "It is our family tradition for many generations, to make this soup for people who have traveled to us," explained the olive grower. Another time, in Tuscany, we were invited into a monastery and ended up at the olive pressing, toasting bread and eating a garlicky *fett-unta (bruschetta).*

Most people who have visited Greece will have had the experience of being invited to join a wedding feast or into the fields to share a humble lunch under the olive trees. Most, too, will have had a cucumber, basket of tomatoes, or simply an orange pressed into their hands, or a bottle of wine brought to their table in a café, purchased by the table next to them. I've been invited into a Bedouin tent for thick sweet mint tea, been gifted with a bag of sweet juicy pears in the market in Ventimiglia, have had fellow passengers share their meals on trains in Italy, and villagers knock on my door in Greece bearing large pans of savory foods at holiday time so that we could share in their festivities.

Although many of the people who have extended their hospitality had very little, it is precisely this sharing that inspires and uplifts and not only makes me want to share my table, but has made me understand a fundamental element of this vivacious cuisine. And I firmly believe that it is not only the abundance of fruits and vegetables, the olive oil, grains, and red wine, but also these intangibles that so enhance life that make the Mediterranean diet one of the world's healthiest.

THE OLIVE

This fruit was known to the ancient Egyptians and Phoenicians. Mentioned in the Bible, it originated on the northern shores of the Mediterranean, probably in the region of Greece, then spread to the lands that dwell on the shores of this shallow sea. The Greeks brought the first olive trees to Provence at least 2500 years ago, and the Romans planted olive groves in Tunisia.

Olive trees grow easily in the Mediterranean but one must be patient: although they start bearing fruit around their sixth or seventh year, it's not until twenty-five years have passed that they really hit their stride and go on for centuries.

The fruit can never be eaten as is—it is far too bitter. Olives must be cured: either layered with salt or submerged in salty brine until their bitterness is leached out.

There are many, many different types of olives, ranging in size, flavor, the flesh-to-seed ratio, oil level, and so forth, combined with the vagaries of the weather and quality of soil. Olives start out green, but change color as they hang on the tree: a light brownish hue, then purplish, then black.

For oil, they are left on the tree until after they turn black. When they start to shrivel, usually around November, they are picked for pressing. When I lived in Israel, we walk beneath the trees; grapes and blackberries grow in profusion, their bushes lining the sides of the country lanes. There is a Provençal saying that wild food tastes best because it has struggled, and that struggle improves us all, even fruit and vegetables. And if we have a sudden downpour, there is a saying for that as well: today's rain brings tomorrow's olives.

At the top of the village is a factory that distills the scents for perfume and aromatic cooking extracts. It gives our lives a surreal, although very chic, quality. One evening you might find a cloud of Chanel No. 5 hanging over the valley, another wafts roses, jasmine, musk, or lavender. A gust of wind suddenly blows Fragonard through my room late at night, across the terrace and into the garden. At other times it is cooking scent, with little whirlwinds of vanilla, lemon, or almond cloaking the valley in a sweet cookie-like scent.

Always in the background are the sweet smells of Provençal life: bread baking in wood-burning ovens, garlic simmering in sauces, grass being cut, and blossoms blooming.

the local Arab women came house to house to pick the olives. Our agreement was that they could keep most of the yield, with the exception of several bottles of freshly pressed green oil and jars of tangy olives.

A note of practicality: for the best Mediterranean flavor, use the best olive oil you can find. This will usually, but not always, mean extra-virgin. The strong olive scent of a good oil is the very flavor of the Mediterranean. Don't skimp.

ONE

MEZE, ANTIPASTI, AND TAPAS

POMODORI ARROSTI, *Roasted Tomatoes with Garlic, Olive Oil, and Fresh Herbs*

HORTA VRASTA, *Spinach Dressed with Olive Oil and Lemon*

SALATA CAROTTA, *Tunisian Grated Carrot Salad with Diced Beets*

CIPOLLINI AGRO DOLCI, *Sweet-and-Sour Roasted Onions with Raisins, Cinnamon, and Cloves*

KOLOKITHAKI ME ELAIOLATHO, *Taverna Zucchini Salad with Lemon and Olive Oil*

COURGETTES BI CHERMOULA, *Zucchini Simmered with Moroccan Spice Paste*

VEGETABLES SERVED WARM

KOUSA, *Zucchini Stewed with Tomatoes and the Flavors of the Eastern Mediterranean*

PAPATES ME LIMONI, *Lemon-Mint Potatoes in Olive Oil from a Greek Taverna*

CHAMPIGNONS À LA MAROCAINE, *Sizzling, Spicy, Big Brown Mushrooms with Garlic and Cilantro*

ESTOFADA DE ESPARRAGOS Y ALCACHOFAS, *Wild Asparagus, Artichokes, and Peas from a Spanish Garden*

LES TOMATES AU FOUR AU GOÛT MAROCAINE, *Baked Tomatoes with Moroccan-Flavored Butter*

BROCCOLI AGLIO E OLIO, *Broccoli with Garlic and Olive Oil*

ZUCCHINI FRITTI, *Crisp Browned Zucchini Coins*

DISHES WITH BEANS OR RICE

SALADE DE FÈVES AU CUMIN, *Moroccan Fresh Fava Bean Salad with Cumin*

Ensalada de Judias Blancas y Zafferano, *Spanish White Beans with Saffron Vinaigrette*

Chickpea Salad in Tomato Vinaigrette from Santa Eulalia

Dolmathes (Dolmathakia), *Brown Rice-Filled Vine Leaves*

Salata bi Adas, *Lentil Salad with Spinach and Tomatoes*

Dishes Made from or with Bread

Pane con Ammogghio, *Bread with Sicilian Tomato Salsa*

Piadine con Rucola, *Flatbread Topped with Cheese and Arugula*

Focaccia al'Uovi, *Two-Grape Focaccia*

Crostini e Tartine

Crostini alla Pomodori e Caperi, *Tomato and Caper Crostini*

Crostini alla Fagioli e Rucola, *Crisp Garlic Toast with White Beans and Arugula*

Crostini alla Formaggio e Romarino, *Rosemary and Melted Cheese Crostini*

Crostini de Carciofi, *Artichoke Crostini*

Tartines au Chèvre et Tapenade, *Black Olive Canapés with Basil and Goat Cheese*

Crostini alla Formaggio di Caprina e Pomodori Secchi, *Tartina or Crostini of Goat Cheese, Sun-Dried Tomato, and Basil*

Dishes of Yogurt and Cheeses

Tzadziki, *Yogurt and Cucumbers with Garlic and Mint*

Labaneh bil Dukkah, *Yogurt Cheese with Olive Oil and Mixed Spice Topping*

Salata Filfil be Laban, *Roasted Red Peppers and Browned Eggplant with Yogurt and Mint*

LABANEH SALATEEN, *Egyptian Feta Spread with Mint and Cucumber*

BARLEY GRIT SALAD WITH YOGURT AND GARLIC

FROMAGE FRAIS AU CHERMOULA, *Pressed Tofu or Fresh Cheese in Chermoula*

SPIEDINI DI PEPERONI, *Rolls of Roasted Peppers Stuffed with Cheese and Aromatics*

SPREADS AND DIPS

PARSLEY SALATA, *Tahina, Parsley, Mint, and Cilantro Dip*

SPANISH PÂTÉ OF TOASTED ALMONDS, BLACK OLIVES, AND CILANTRO

AUBERGINE MAROCAINE, *Eggplant with the Flavors of a Moroccan Souk*

PATLICAN TAVASI, *Turkish Grilled Eggplant with Garlic-Tahina Yogurt Sauce*

SUBSTANTIAL APPETIZERS

PÂTÉ FORESTIER, *Wild Mushroom and Greens Pâté*

TORTILLA DE ANDALUZ, *Andalucian Olive Pressers' Tortilla of Potatoes, Red and Green Peppers, Tomatoes, and Herbs*

MUCKVER, *Turkish Fritters of Zucchini and Feta Cheese*

POLPETES ME DOMATES, *Dill-Scented Potato, Onion, and Cheese Patties with Tomato*

THESE little plates of savory mixtures, sometimes salty, sometimes spicy, always bright and invigorating, are nibbled slowly while you sip a glass of beer or wine, ouzo or raki, mineral water or cooling fruit juice.

More than a meal, throughout the Mediterranean this is an ancient way of living. At cafés in Cairo, mountain villages in Lebanon, tavernas in Greece or Turkey, or elegant restaurants in North Africa, you will often find your table set with a tantalizing assortment of little plates filled with savory tempting morsels. In Italy you will nibble from a table of *antipasti* or *stuzzichini* with your *apperitivi,* and in Spain it is *tapas* that fuel the long, sociable evenings.

Some cultures make a meal of them, others eat plate after plate then sit down to a complete meal. This array of tidbits is the most sociable of meals, little bites to help slow the progress of alcohol, to lubricate the conversation and stretch out the sharing of two friends, to discuss the day's happenings en route to home and family.

The first time I had *meze* was as a student in Israel: *hummous, salata Hatzilim,* pita bread for dipping. Our favorite café in Tel Aviv set out big seltzer bottles, which I thought the perfect liquid to both quench a summer thirst and help settle the spicy food.

When I visited Greece, *meze* appeared at the table, gratis, as soon as we ordered a glass of wine, beer, or ouzo. We quickly figured out that the more eaters we had in our party the larger the variety of tidbits and we became persuasive in our invitations. "We'd love to see you at the café tonight," we enthused, thinking that if we numbered eight or ten, who knew what delights Kostas would set before us—olives, lentil croquettes, little wedges of omelet, slabs of feta on bread, tendrils of pea greens sprinkled with vinegar, *tzadziki,* sliced beets, roasted potatoes.

By the time I got to Spain years later, I was ready. *Tapas* crawling would be easy, I had spent half my life priming myself. Roasted potatoes with sweet and hot red peppers, flambéed in brandy? I was ready! Wild asparagus softly scrambled with fresh eggs? Yes! Grilled beets and green onions with garlicky mayonnaise, salty fat olives, plates of pungent greens: I was ready for it all (although not understanding Spain's tradition of late night dining, I was not ready for the meal to follow as we neared midnight).

Recently, though, I have been reminded of how much I enjoy the tradition of dawdling happily over little plates: sitting in a small cobblestone piazza in Genoa, little tables set out on the stones, a glass of a bitter orange-scented *apperitivo* at my lips, plates of *stuzzichini* on the table. Restaurants wouldn't open for another hour, so we sat as the still-warm September day dwindled and chilled, sipping the deeply bittersweet drink and nibbling on wrinkly black olives and pickled peppers, *tramezzini*—little sandwiches of thin crustless bread, filled with a small amount of savory mixtures—and small chunks of cold spinach frittata. Around us groups of co-workers sat, en route between office and home, gossiping and relaxing; students met, plopped their books onto the tables, ordered *apperitivi,* and discussed their classes; two women greeted each other with kisses, inspecting each others' shopping bags and purchases. A young couple zoomed up on a Vespa, then sat hands and feet entwined, at their table, sipping drinks and feeding each other tidbits. Cats and dogs wandered underneath the tables, pouncing on dropped crumbs. And we sat, absorbing the atmosphere, languidly nibbling and drinking.

Pomodori Arrosti

ROASTED TOMATOES WITH GARLIC, OLIVE OIL, AND FRESH HERBS

Serves 4 to 6 as an *antipasto* or side dish

Roasting tomatoes brings out their sweetness and intensifies their flavor. Adding garlic both before and after cooking gives the dish a nice jolt of allium. Serve with chunks (rather than slices) of crusty bread to dip into the garlicky herb dressing and the tender, juicy tomatoes.

8 small to medium-size tomatoes, ripe and flavorful
 Pinch sugar, for sprinkling lightly
 Salt to taste
4 to 6 garlic cloves, chopped
2 tablespoons olive oil, or to taste
 Dash red wine (or balsamic) vinegar
 Fresh herbs, finely chopped, for sprinkling: sweet basil, oregano, mint, rosemary, thyme, or marjoram

Cut the tomatoes in half crosswise and arrange in a baking pan; ceramic is best, especially rustic round ceramic pans from Spain or Greece. Lightly sprinkle the tomatoes with sugar and salt, then with about half the garlic and olive oil.

Place in a 350°F oven and bake for 30 to 45 minutes, or long enough for the tomatoes to bake through and lightly brown but not become sauce. Check after 25 minutes and adjust the cooking time accordingly.

Remove the tomatoes from the oven and leave to cool. Before serving sprinkle with the remaining garlic and olive oil, and season with salt and red wine (or balsamic) vinegar to taste. Sprinkle with herbs and serve with juices from the pan spooned over.

68 CALORIES PER SERVING
5 G FAT
1 G SATURATED FAT
0 MG CHOLESTEROL
6 G CARBOHYDRATES
1 G PROTEIN
12 MG SODIUM

Horta Vrasta

SPINACH DRESSED WITH OLIVE OIL AND LEMON

Serves 4 to 6 as a *meze* or side dish

Any sturdy green may be used in this dish: chard, spinach, older arugula. Or do as they do in Greece: use a selection of whatever the garden or walk in the country has to offer that day.

The trick to this dish (besides cooking the greens until they are just tender and still bright green and full of flavor) is to squeeze the greens quite dry, and to crush a little garlic in a mortar and pestle and mix it with the olive oil dressing before tossing with the spinach.

2 pounds spinach or chard leaves (either red or white),
  cleaned; if using chard, remove the tough stalks
2 or 3 garlic cloves
  Salt to taste
2 to 3 tablespoons olive oil
  Juice of ½ lemon or a few drops of balsamic or red
  wine vinegar
  Garnish: 10 or so black olives

Cook the spinach/chard in small amount of boiling water until wilted and just tender. Remove from heat and drain (save liquid for soups or other dishes). When cool enough to handle, squeeze the spinach/chard dry (save liquid for another use). Cut coarsely; it will form a rough purée.

Crush the garlic with a pinch of salt in a mortar and pestle or food processor and mix with a tablespoon or so of olive oil.

Toss the cooked, cut-up spinach/chard with the garlic mixture to taste, then add the remaining olive oil and lemon juice or vinegar. Garnish with olives and serve at room temperature.

> 85 CALORIES PER SERVING
> 6 G FAT
> 1 G SATURATED FAT
> 0 MG CHOLESTEROL
> 6 G CARBOHYDRATES
> 5 G PROTEIN
> 226 MG SODIUM

Salata Carotta

TUNISIAN GRATED CARROT SALAD WITH DICED BEETS

Serves 4 to 6 as a *meze* or side dish

Cooked whole then grated coarsely, this salad brings out the best in the carrot, emphasizing its flavor and sweetness with a simple dressing of olive oil, lemon, onion, garlic, and spices.

The beets are slowly cooked until tender—nearly translucent—and sweet, then peeled, diced, and scattered ruby-like around the carrot salad. In North Africa and Europe, beets are usually bought already cooked.

2 medium-size beets, whole
1½ pounds carrots (about 10)
1 medium-size onion, preferably a sweet one such as a Spanish or red onion, coarsely grated
2 or 3 garlic cloves, finely chopped
Juice of 1 lemon
2 to 3 tablespoons olive oil
Pinch sugar
¼ teaspoon *each* cumin and paprika, or to taste
2 to 3 teaspoons white wine vinegar
Salt to taste

Cook the beets. I prefer baking: place the beets in a small baking pan and bake at 325°F for about 40 minutes, or until the beets are tender. Let cool, then slip off the skins and dice beets. Set aside.

Cook the carrots in boiling water or steam them until *al dente*, crisp-tender. Let cool.

Coarsely grate the cooked carrots, then combine with coarsely grated onion, chopped garlic, lemon juice, olive oil, sugar, cumin, paprika, vinegar, and salt. Taste for seasoning.

Arrange the carrot salad in the center of a serving plate and surround with the diced beets. Chill until ready to serve.

122 CALORIES PER SERVING
5 G FAT
1 G SATURATED FAT
0 MG CHOLESTEROL
19 G CARBOHYDRATES
2 G PROTEIN
97 MG SODIUM

Cipollini Agro Dolci

SWEET-AND-SOUR ROASTED ONIONS WITH RAISINS, CINNAMON, AND CLOVES

Serves 6 to 8 as part of an *antipasto* or as a side dish

This Italian dish of sweet-and-sour onions is rich with the caramelized flavor of roasting onions and tangy vinegar; thyme or marjoram gives a lovely herbal accent, cinnamon and cloves an exotic Moorish scent.

12 onions, peeled
 2 to 3 tablespoons sugar, for sprinkling
   Salt and black pepper to taste
 2 tablespoons olive oil
 2 tablespoons balsamic vinegar, or to taste
   Pinch *each*: finely chopped fresh thyme or marjoram
   leaves, cinnamon, and ground cloves
 1 tablespoon raspberry or red wine vinegar, if needed
 3 to 4 tablespoons black or golden raisins

Cut each onion in a criss-cross pattern, cutting almost but not completely through—the top will be cut but the bottom will still be attached. Place the onions in cold water for 30 to 60 minutes, so that the edges of the onions spread a bit and form flower-like shapes during baking.

Arrange the onions in a shallow baking pan large enough to accommodate them in one layer. Sprinkle with sugar, salt, pepper, olive oil, balsamic vinegar, thyme or marjoram, cinnamon, and cloves.

Bake the onions in a 375°F oven until they are nicely roasted, about 30 to 45 minutes, basting every so often with pan juices.

Remove the onions from the oven and sprinkle with raspberry or red wine vinegar and raisins. Taste the pan juices for salt and sugar; the juices should be quite sweet and sour.

Cool, and serve at room temperature.

150 CALORIES PER SERVING
4 G FAT
1 G SATURATED FAT
0 MG CHOLESTEROL
27 G CARBOHYDRATES
3 G PROTEIN
1 MG SODIUM

Kolokithaki me Elaiolatho

TAVERNA ZUCCHINI SALAD WITH LEMON AND OLIVE OIL

Serves 4 as a *meze* or side dish

Cooking the zucchini whole, then cutting it lengthwise before dressing it is a typical way of cooking zucchini for salads in Greek tavernas. It gives yet another dimension to the zucchini—the vegetable is firm yet tender, and subtly yet distinctly different from other zucchini preparations.

In our home, we always eat this with bread—rather than knives and forks—to scoop it up. It lasts up to about 5 days and becomes delightfully pickled as the days go by.

4 zucchini, trimmed but left whole
2 garlic cloves, whole
  Large pinch salt
1 tablespoon olive oil, or as desired
1 teaspoon white wine vinegar, or as desired
  Garnish: Handful (about ½ cup) black olives such as Niçoise or wrinkled black Italian

Cook the zucchini by boiling until just tender, about 7 minutes. Remove from water and leave to drain and cool. Meanwhile, crush the garlic with salt in a mortar and pestle or food processor.

Cut the zucchini first into halves or thirds, then cut each piece in half lengthwise. You will end up with half-cylinders, each 2 to 3 inches long.

Spread each zucchini length with a tiny bit of the crushed garlic, then drizzle with olive oil and vinegar. If there is any leftover garlic, dot it over the zucchini. Garnish with olives and serve.

Meze, Antipasti, and Tapas

**Yellow Squash and Green Zucchini Meze
with Mizythra Cheese**
Prepare the above recipe using half golden zucchini or
yellow squash, such as crookneck, instead of all green
zucchini. Garnish the dish with sliced or cubed mizythra
or feta cheese instead of olives.

```
83 CALORIES PER SERVING
5 G FAT
1 G SATURATED FAT
O MG CHOLESTEROL
8 G CARBOHYDRATES
3 G PROTEIN
106 MG SODIUM
```

Courgettes bi Chermoula

ZUCCHINI SIMMERED WITH MOROCCAN SPICE PASTE

Serves 4 to 6 as a *meze* or side dish

Chermoula is a Moroccan spice paste used to marinate all sorts of foods before they are cooked on the grill or simmered. Containing grated onion, garlic, and spices, it makes a spicy rich gravy while the zucchini simmer. I especially like this as a *meze,* or for lunch with a chunk of bread or alongside a bowl of couscous and yogurt, although I recently ate it alongside a goat cheese omelet and was very pleased.

The important thing is that the zucchini cooks until soft-tender, not just crisp-tender, so that the *chermoula* permeates the vegetable and it all cooks into an amalgamated dish.

   2 pounds zucchini, sliced
   2 small to medium-size onions, grated over the large holes of a grater
   4 to 6 garlic cloves, coarsely chopped
 1/2 teaspoon paprika
 3/4 teaspoon cumin
 1/4 teaspoon salt
     Large pinch *each:* black and cayenne pepper
 1/4 cup water
   3 tablespoons olive oil
     Juice of 1/2 lemon, or to taste
   3 tablespoons chopped fresh cilantro

In a large pot combine the zucchini with the onion, garlic, paprika, cumin, salt, black and cayenne pepper, water, and olive oil. Cover and simmer until the zucchini is just tender, then remove the lid and simmer another 5 to 10 minutes, until the liquid has been nearly absorbed and the zucchini is very tender.

Stir in the lemon juice and sprinkle with cilantro, then let cool to room temperature.

135 CALORIES PER SERVING
11 G FAT
1 G SATURATED FAT
0 MG CHOLESTEROL
10 G CARBOHYDRATES
3 G PROTEIN
96 MG SODIUM

Meze, Antipasti, and Tapas

Kousa

ZUCCHINI STEWED WITH TOMATOES AND THE FLAVORS OF THE EASTERN MEDITERRANEAN

Serves 4 as a *meze* or side dish

Kousa is at its best when made with the small, young, sweet zucchini of summer; out of season, or when the vegetable has grown large, it can be bitter and may require salting and rinsing to be as delicate as you'd like. The cinnamon stick gives a subtle scent; ground cinnamon does not give the same result, although it is nice, too.

You could serve this as a main course instead of as a side dish, accompanied by a crisp vegetable salad, chewy flat breads or crusty French bread, and a plate of feta or goat's milk cheese.

1 1/2 to 2 pounds young zucchini, sliced
   2 to 3 tablespoons olive oil, or as desired
   1 or 2 cinnamon sticks
   3 to 5 garlic cloves, finely chopped or crushed
   4 ripe tomatoes or about 1 cup diced ripe tomatoes
     Salt to taste, a pinch of sugar if needed
     Large pinch *each:* ground cumin and dried mint
     leaves, crushed
     Juice of about 1/4 to 1/2 lemon, or to taste

Sauté the zucchini in olive oil with the cinnamon stick(s); let the zucchini cook until lightly browned and crisp-tender.

Add the garlic, cook a moment, then add the tomatoes and cook another few moments until the tomatoes are saucelike (if using canned, this will be only a few moments; fresh will take a few minutes).

Season with salt, sugar (if needed), cumin, and mint, and remove from heat. Stir in the lemon juice and serve hot or at room temperature.

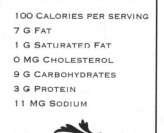

100 CALORIES PER SERVING
7 G FAT
1 G SATURATED FAT
0 MG CHOLESTEROL
9 G CARBOHYDRATES
3 G PROTEIN
11 MG SODIUM

Papates me Limoni

LEMON-MINT POTATOES IN OLIVE OIL FROM A GREEK TAVERNA

Serves 4 as a *meze* or side dish

The first winter I spent in Greece surprised me when it came to vegetables: how the Greeks loved their potatoes! Somehow I always associated the summer vegetables with Greece, forgetting that in the winter no sun ripens tomatoes or zucchini, no eggplant or cucumber grow in the heat of the day. Instead there are potatoes and cabbage and other cold weather vegetables, but treated with Mediterranean style and charm.

Often potatoes were served as part of our *meze* in the little taverna, Kosta's, whose terrace overlooked the village square, giving an excellent vantage point for nosy gossip gathering. (Unlike *ouzeris* in Athens and other big cities, in small towns and villages most tavernas and cafés bring the *meze* plates along with your drinks, gratis.)

Sometimes the potatoes were roasted over hot coals, served with a handful of wild herbs and greens in vinegar; at other times they were boiled and served with olive oil, lemon juice, and whatever seasonings were on hand or growing in the garden.

As for whether the Mediterranean diet works, let me add that our waitress was 93 years old (at the time), with a row of admirers that lined the wall of the café, few of whom were any younger than she.

1 1/2 pounds medium-size new potatoes, red or white
   3 to 4 tablespoons olive oil
      Coarse salt and black pepper to taste
      Juice of 1 to 2 lemons, freshly squeezed
      Crumbled mint to taste or fresh mint leaves, thinly sliced
  1/2 onion, finely chopped

Parboil the potatoes until they are half-tender. Drain and cool.

Rub the potatoes with a small amount of olive oil, then place over the medium-hot coals of a grill (at Kosta's they roasted them buried directly in the somewhat cooled coals, without parboiling). Cook until the skins are browned and crisp; the potatoes will be cooked through.

Slash open the potatoes and serve with a drizzle of olive oil, a sprinkling of coarse salt and pepper, a squeeze of lemon, and a scattering of mint and onion.

253 CALORIES PER SERVING
10 G FAT
1 G SATURATED FAT
0 MG CHOLESTEROL
38 G CARBOHYDRATES
4 G PROTEIN
8 MG SODIUM

❧ Champignons à la Marocaine

SIZZLING, SPICY, BIG BROWN MUSHROOMS WITH GARLIC AND CILANTRO

Serves 4 to 6 as an appetizer or side dish; Helene serves them for a delicious brunch

This recipe is from my friend Helene, who grew up in the French town of Nîmes, near Arles, although she has spent much of her adulthood in London. The cilantro gives the mushrooms an unexpected *frisson* of flavor and lends a decidedly North African feel to this pan-Mediterranean dish.

Portobello mushrooms are excellent for this recipe, or simply very mature mushrooms that have opened their fleshy caps and exposed their almost-inky gills.

The important thing is to make sure the oil is very hot, and to brown the mushrooms a little at a time so that they sizzle and brown rather than stew.

Serve with crusty bread to sop up the inky, garlicky juices.

2 tablespoons olive oil
1 small hot red pepper, cut into two pieces, or a pinch or two of red pepper flakes
1 pound large meaty mushrooms (such as portobello), cut into $1/2$- to 1-inch slices (about 4 per mushroom) or quarters
3 or 4 garlic cloves, finely chopped
2 to 3 tablespoons finely chopped fresh cilantro
Salt to taste

Heat the olive oil with the hot pepper until it smokes; if using a whole pepper cut into two pieces, remove and discard at this point. (Take care when frying the chili or pepper flakes not to inhale the fumes, which can irritate your lungs and bronchial tubes and result in a bout of coughing.)

Add the mushrooms, about a quarter at a time, and cook in the hot oil over medium-high heat until they brown and sizzle; remove to a plate.

When all of the mushrooms have been browned, return them to the pan, reduce the heat to low, add the garlic and cilantro, and cook a few moments together. Season with salt to taste and eat right away.

63 CALORIES PER SERVING
5 G FAT
1 G SATURATED FAT
0 MG CHOLESTEROL
5 G CARBOHYDRATES
2 G PROTEIN
4 MG SODIUM

Estofada de Esparragos y Alcachofas

WILD ASPARAGUS, ARTICHOKES, AND PEAS FROM A SPANISH GARDEN

Serves 4

Signs of a Spanish spring: gathering wild asparagus, harvesting the first artichokes and peas from the garden. We served them as a side dish, sort of a warm salad, dressed with olive oil and a dash of lemon. You could add balsamic vinegar instead, if you prefer.

Wild asparagus is spindly, slightly bitter, and full of strong asparagus flavor; if unavailable, use thin strands of ordinary cultivated asparagus.

You could eat this dish as a first course or appetizer with bread and maybe a chunk of goat cheese, or you could eat a big bowlful for dinner.

4 large or 6 small artichokes, each trimmed of its tough outer leaves and inner choke, down to all edible artichoke (or use 8 to 10 artichoke hearts, frozen are fine)
Juice of 1 lemon
1 bunch asparagus, tough ends trimmed
1 cup shelled young peas
1 garlic clove, finely chopped
2 tablespoons olive oil, or as desired
Sugar, salt, and pepper to taste
Garnish: Chopped fresh marjoram, thyme, or parsley

Cook the artichokes or artichoke hearts in boiling water with a teaspoon of lemon juice added to it. Drain and keep warm.

Meanwhile, cook the asparagus until crisp-tender, and cook the peas in water to cover with a pinch of sugar and salt until they are tender. Drain well.

20

Combine the warm artichoke hearts with the warm asparagus and peas, and toss with garlic, olive oil, lemon juice, and salt and pepper to taste. Garnish with the fresh herb of your choice.

Eat warm or at room temperature.

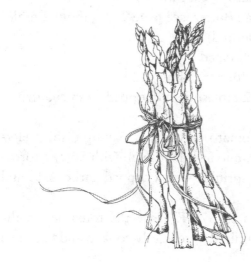

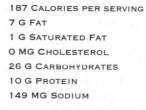

187 CALORIES PER SERVING
7 G FAT
1 G SATURATED FAT
0 MG CHOLESTEROL
26 G CARBOHYDRATES
10 G PROTEIN
149 MG SODIUM

Les Tomates au Four au Goût Marocaine

BAKED TOMATOES WITH MOROCCAN-FLAVORED BUTTER

Serves 4 to 6 as a *meze* or side dish

Slow baking of the tomatoes concentrates their sunny flavor; a dab of Spicy Moroccan Butter melts into the roasted tomatoes. It is unusually good and delightfully simple.

Accompany with crusty bread; for a more substantial dish, serve with slabs of grilled or broiled polenta.

8 to 10 ripe tomatoes, cut into halves
  Spicy Moroccan Butter (see page 283) (about 2 tablespoons or as desired)
3 garlic cloves, chopped
  Salt and sugar for sprinkling
  Garnish: 1 to 2 tablespoons chopped fresh cilantro

Arrange the tomato halves in a baking dish, preferably a round ceramic one. Dot them with Spicy Moroccan Butter, then sprinkle with chopped garlic, salt, and sugar.

Heat the oven to 375°F. Place the tomatoes in the oven and bake until they are lightly cooked and browned on top.

Remove them from the oven and spread with a little more Spicy Moroccan Butter.

Serve right away, sprinkled with cilantro if desired.

57 Calories per serving
3 g Fat
1 g Saturated Fat
6 mg Cholesterol
9 g Carbohydrates
2 g Protein
37 mg Sodium

Broccoli Aglio e Olio

BROCCOLI WITH GARLIC AND OLIVE OIL

Serves 4

Broccoli, steamed until just tender then run through the sauté pan with olive oil and garlic, is a quintessentially Italian dish, in Tuscany referred to as *broccoli alla Fiorentina*.

As a sort of trans-Mediterranean variation, add a shake of hot red pepper flakes for the flavor of Spain.

1 large or 2 small to medium-size broccoli heads
3 tablespoons olive oil
3 garlic cloves, chopped
  Salt and pepper to taste
  Juice of 1/2 lemon, or to taste

Trim the broccoli of its tough parts; peel the stem(s) and cut into bite-size pieces. Break the rest of the broccoli into florets.

Steam the broccoli until it is bright green, then remove from the heat and rinse in cold water to cool.

Combine the oil and garlic in a saucepan and warm until fragrant, then add the broccoli, salt, and pepper. Stir and cook for 5 minutes or so, add lemon juice to taste, then cook a few moments longer. Do not let the broccoli cook to a gray color; it should be tender but still green.

Serve right away, hot or at room temperature.

114 CALORIES PER SERVING
10 G FAT
1 G SATURATED FAT
0 MG CHOLESTEROL
5 G CARBOHYDRATES
2 G PROTEIN
19 MG SODIUM

Zucchini Fritti

CRISP BROWNED ZUCCHINI COINS

Serves 4

Tossing zucchini slices in a little flour, then browning them in a nonstick pan with just a touch of olive oil is simple enough, but the results are marvelous. I confess to adding the garlic; you can, too, if you like.

This recipe is courtesy of my friend, Sheila Hannon, who in true Mediterranean hospitality always has a bowl of the most succulent Greek olives from the corner deli for me.

4 zucchini, cut into coins
  Salt and pepper to taste
  Optional: 1 garlic clove, chopped
2 to 3 tablespoons flour, for dusting
1 tablespoon olive oil, or as needed

Toss the zucchini with salt and pepper (and garlic if desired), then with flour.

Heat a nonstick frying pan, then add half the olive oil and brown the zucchini in small batches, adding more oil as needed. Cook the zucchini until they are crisp and browned; as batches are cooked, remove them from the pan to a baking pan and keep them warm in the oven.

Eat as soon as they are all cooked through.

80 CALORIES PER SERVING
4 G FAT
1 G SATURATED FAT
0 MG CHOLESTEROL
11 G CARBOHYDRATES
3 G PROTEIN
8 MG SODIUM

Salade de Fèves au Cumin

MOROCCAN FRESH FAVA BEAN SALAD WITH CUMIN

Serves 4 to 6

Fresh fava beans are quintessentially Mediterranean. Throughout the area, from Spain to France, Italy to Egypt, and across North Africa, tender little green favas are eaten in salads, soups, rice dishes, pastas, omelets, and so forth. You'll find them as an appetizer or as a garnish—say, scattered atop fresh milky mozzarella, grilled fish or chicken, or tender pasta.

2 pounds fresh fava beans (about 3 cups shelled)
3 to 4 tablespoons olive oil
1 teaspoon cumin, or to taste
  Salt to taste
4 tablespoons chopped fresh parsley
3 or 4 garlic cloves, finely chopped or crushed in a
  mortar and pestle with a pinch of salt
  Juice of ½ lemon

Cook the fava beans in boiling water until just tender, about 10 minutes. Do not overcook. Drain the beans and, when they are cool enough to handle, peel them.

Dress the warm beans in the olive oil, cumin, salt, parsley, garlic, and lemon juice, adding more oil, lemon, cumin, and salt as desired to taste.

145 CALORIES PER SERVING
8 G FAT
1 G SATURATED FAT
0 MG CHOLESTEROL
11 G CARBOHYDRATES
9 G PROTEIN
100 MG SODIUM

Ensalada de Judias Blancas y Zafferano

SPANISH WHITE BEANS WITH SAFFRON VINAIGRETTE

Serves 4

A delicious Spanish *tapa* of white beans awash in saffron vinaigrette.

Saffron, with its slightly bitter, almost medicinal scent and flavor, is the most expensive spice in the world. It is harvested from crocus flowers—each flower yielding only a few strands of spice; hundreds and thousands of the flowers are needed to make a pound of spice. No wonder it is so costly.

Some find saffron almost unpleasant tasting. Others insist that its contribution lies chiefly in its ability to turn all it simmers to a sunshiny hue, and suggest that turmeric can be used for such dye jobs. Don't listen to them: turmeric does in fact color foods a vivid yellow, but it is a different color and flavor entirely. Imagine preparing such classics as paella or risotto with turmeric—the spice would overpower the dish. Better to omit the saffron entirely or, in the cases where it is necessary, make another dish. (As with all rules, I have my exceptions—sometimes I make *sa fregula* with turmeric).

½ cup dried white beans or 2 cups cooked, drained
white beans
Large pinch saffron threads
1 garlic clove
Salt to taste
1 tablespoon dry white wine
1 tablespoon white wine vinegar
2 tablespoons olive oil
Pinch *each:* paprika and cayenne pepper
1 shallot, minced
Garnish: ¼ cup chopped fresh basil leaves or a
pinch of dried herbs

If using dried beans: soak overnight or do a quick soak (boil for 2 minutes, then let sit for 30 minutes in hot water). Drain and add fresh water to cover. Bring to a boil, then reduce heat and simmer over low heat until tender, about 30 to 40 minutes, depending on the beans. Drain. Set beans aside and keep warm.

Make the dressing: crush the saffron (a mortar and pestle is great for this), then add garlic and a pinch of salt; crush together until it forms a golden paste, then add white wine, vinegar, olive oil, paprika, cayenne, and minced shallot. Pour this over the drained, warm beans. Taste for seasoning.

Serve garnished with a sprinkling of basil or dried herbs.

192 CALORIES PER SERVING
7 G FAT
1 G SATURATED FAT
0 MG CHOLESTEROL
24 G CARBOHYDRATES
9 G PROTEIN
7 MG SODIUM

Chickpea Salad in Tomato Vinaigrette from Santa Eulalia

Serves 4 as a *tapa*

I once stayed high in the mountains on the Balearic island of Ibiza. In between days of white-washing the 300-year-old farmhouse, feeding the chickens, and weeding the garden we searched the island for wild foods to eat. Arugula, purslane, lemons, capers, rosemary, wild asparagus—all made their way into our salad bowl. We even gathered salt from the rocks along the sea.

To take a break we slipped into the little town of Santa Eulalia for evenings spent sitting next to a cool fountain, nibbling *tapas* and sipping sherry while we watched the calm Mediterranean Sea.

Adding tomatoes to the vinaigrette in this recipe is delicious and very traditional in Andalucia (where the *tapas* bar owners were from). One of the nicest dishes you can eat on a limp, deflating day is a plate of tomatoes in tomato vinaigrette.

> 4 garlic cloves
> Large pinch of salt
> 1 or 2 ripe tomatoes, diced (canned tomatoes may be substituted)
> 2 tablespoons wine vinegar
> 2 tablespoons olive oil
> 1/2 onion, chopped
> 1/2 *each*: red and green bell pepper, coarsely chopped or diced
> 2 or 3 ripe fresh tomatoes, diced
> 1 1/2 cups cooked drained chickpeas
> Black and/or cayenne pepper to taste
> 1/2 teaspoon dried oregano or mixed herbs
> *Garnish:* 1 tablespoon chopped fresh parsley or green onions

Crush the garlic together with several large pinches of salt in a mortar and pestle until it forms a paste. Work in the tomato, then the vinegar and oil, until it forms an emulsion.

Mix this dressing with the onion, red and green pepper, ripe diced tomatoes, chickpeas, pepper, and oregano and place in a bowl. Serve sprinkled with parsley or green onions.

175 Calories per serving
8 g Fat
1 g Saturated Fat
0 mg Cholesterol
22 g Carbohydrates
6 g Protein
53 mg Sodium

Meze, Antipasti, and Tapas

Dolmathes (Dolmathakia)

BROWN RICE-FILLED VINE LEAVES

Serves 6 as a *meze*. Double or triple the recipe as desired: not only are these great for parties, the leftovers are delicious.

Brown rice may not be the traditional filling, but I find that its nutty whole grain flavor adds great character to this classic dish. It even makes meat redundant, even for dedicated carnivores.

Steam these little gems with large pieces of garlic tucked in between leaf parcels; it perfumes the *dolmathes* and by the time they are cooked through, the little garlic slivers are sweet and tender.

Once prepared, *dolmathes* last about 5 days in the refrigerator.

> 40 or so vine leaves, either fresh or brined
> 2¹/₂ to 3 cups cooked brown rice (long or short grain)
> ¹/₄ cup raisins
> 3 green onions, thinly sliced
> ¹/₄ to ¹/₂ teaspoon cumin
> ¹/₈ to ¹/₄ teaspoon cinnamon
> 1 egg, lightly beaten
> 3 tablespoons plain yogurt
> Juice of ¹/₂ lemon
> 1 head garlic, cloves separated and peeled, cut coarsely or into slivers (if you get tired of this task, leave some whole)
> 2 tablespoons olive oil

If using fresh vine leaves, blanch them; if using brined vine leaves from a jar or vacuum pack, rinse them well. Set aside.

Mix the cooked rice with raisins, green onions, cumin, cinnamon, beaten egg, yogurt, and lemon juice.

Stuff the vine leaves: place one in your left hand, shiny side down, spoon in about 1 to 2 tablespoons of the rice mixture (depending on the size of the leaf), then fold the leaf into a cigar shape—bottom first, then the sides, then the top—and roll it up.

Arrange the stuffed vine leaves in a steamer, layering and studding with the cut-up garlic cloves. Drizzle with olive oil.

Steam for about 40 minutes or long enough for the garlic to grow soft and the leaf wrappings to become tender. Remove them from the heat and let them cool.

Serving Suggestion
Serve the dolmathes *with lemon wedges for squeezing, or with a bowl of yogurt for dipping.*

194 CALORIES PER SERVING
6 G FAT
1 G SATURATED FAT
37 MG CHOLESTEROL
30 G CARBOHYDRATES
6 G PROTEIN
31 MG SODIUM

Salata bi Adas

LENTIL SALAD WITH SPINACH AND TOMATOES

Serves 4 as a *tapa* or side dish

This is an eastern Mediterranean salad, although its Moorish flavorings make it perfect for *tapas* as well.

Crusty bread is good alongside, as you can scoop up little bits of lentils without bothering to pick up a fork or spoon.

1/2 cup dried lentils (brown or green)
2 bay leaves
1 onion, chopped
5 garlic cloves, chopped
1 to 2 tablespoons olive oil, or as needed
1/4 teaspoon cumin, or as desired
Large pinch of ground coriander
4 medium-size ripe tomatoes, chopped, or 4 canned tomatoes, chopped, plus their juice
1/2 cup spinach, cooked and chopped
Salt and hot pepper seasoning (such as Tabasco), to taste

Soak the lentils in cold water for an hour or longer. Drain and add fresh water to cover, along with the bay leaves. Bring to a boil, then reduce heat and simmer, covered, for about 20 minutes or until the lentils are just tender.

Remove the lentils from the heat and leave, covered, to cool in the liquid until the lentils are quite tender but not mushy. Drain the lentils.

Lightly sauté the onion and half the garlic in the olive oil; when softened, add the cumin, coriander, tomatoes, and spinach, then add the lentils and cook together for a few minutes to meld flavors.

Season the mixture with salt and hot pepper seasoning, sprinkle with the remaining garlic, and serve either warm or cool.

Serving Suggestion

If served cool, drizzle with olive oil and include lemon slices to squeeze over the lentils. If served warm, accompany with a big dollop of yogurt.

159 CALORIES PER SERVING
4 G FAT
1 G SATURATED FAT
0 MG CHOLESTEROL
24 G CARBOHYDRATES
9 G PROTEIN
29 MG SODIUM

Pane con Ammogghio

BREAD WITH SICILIAN TOMATO SALSA

Serves 4 to 6

Ammogghio is a fresh tomato sauce eaten in Sicily with a variety of foods such as bread and grilled vegetables; I like it with olive oil-basted grilled artichokes.

1 pound diced ripe tomatoes

3 garlic cloves, finely chopped

4 to 5 tablespoons olive oil

1 tablespoon balsamic vinegar, or to taste
  Pinch *each:* Coarse salt and sugar to taste
  Pinch hot pepper flakes

1 teaspoon dried oregano, rubbed through the hands, or 2 teaspoons chopped fresh marjoram or oregano leaves

1 loaf country bread (very fresh), sliced and lightly toasted, then rubbed with garlic

Combine the tomatoes with the garlic, olive oil, and balsamic vinegar. Season them with the coarse salt, sugar, hot pepper flakes, and dried oregano or chopped fresh herbs. Let the tomatoes sit to blend flavors; I like to chill them lightly at this point.

Arrange the garlic-rubbed toast on plates and serve with the tomato salsa spooned over it.

299 CALORIES PER SERVING
11 G FAT
2 G SATURATED FAT
0 MG CHOLESTEROL
44 G CARBOHYDRATES
7 G PROTEIN
404 MG SODIUM

Piadine con Rucola

FLATBREAD TOPPED WITH CHEESE AND ARUGULA

Serves 4 as an *antipasto* or *primo piatto* (first course)

Piadine, a specialty of Emilia-Romagna, are flat breads much like flour tortillas—like flour tortillas, they are sold in shops to take home and top with whatever your appetite fancies. In fact, I use flour tortillas in their place rather than make either from scratch.

Piadine are typically served as an *antipasto*, the bland flat cakes topped with hot savory mixtures, cheese, and/or salads.

4 *piadine* or flour tortillas
8 ounces Italian fontina or medium Asiago cheese,
    coarsely shredded
1 bunch young arugula
    Olive oil
    Balsamic or red wine vinegar to taste
2 garlic cloves, chopped
    Salt and pepper to taste

Top the *piadine* or tortillas with the cheese and arrange them on a baking sheet. Heat the broiler. In the meantime, dress the arugula with olive oil, vinegar, garlic, and salt and pepper. Broil the cheese-topped *piadine* or tortillas until the cheese melts and lightly browns.

Top the *piadine* or tortillas with some of the dressed arugula and serve right away.

422 CALORIES PER SERVING
22 G FAT
11 G SATURATED FAT
66 MG CHOLESTEROL
32 G CARBOHYDRATES
21 G PROTEIN
559 MG SODIUM

Focaccia al'Uovi

Two-Grape Focaccia

Makes one focaccia; serves 4 to 6

Focaccia, chewy in the center but crisp around the edges, is prepared with a variety of toppings that are pressed into the dough before baking. While most toppings are savory, fruit toppings make a sweet change: one of my favorites is raisins soaked in *grappa* (the distilled Italian firewater), but during grape season the fresh, juicy fruit are my choice.

With the variety of grapes available these days, I find that using a combination of grapes not only looks charming, but provides a more complex flavor for the focaccia. Choose muscat grapes, seedless Thompson or flame, tiny champagne grapes, or your choice from the marketplace or garden. If your grapes have seeds, cut into halves and seed before using.

1   batch yeast-risen dough for pizza (page 308);
for 2 tablespoons of the water, substitute an anise-scented liqueur or drink (such as anisette or *pastis*)

1   bunch *each:* muscat grapes (cut into halves and seeded) and small purple grapes (whole if unseeded, halved and seeded if they have seeds)

1/2   to 1 teaspoon aniseed

5   to 6 tablespoons sugar
Pinch of salt

Let the dough rise a first time, then punch down and press out thinly onto an olive-oiled baking sheet. Press the grapes (cut side down and close together) into the dough, then sprinkle the top with aniseed, sugar, and salt.

Leave the focaccia to rise a second time, about 35 minutes or until the dough has puffed up between the grapes.

Heat the oven to 400°F. Bake the focaccia until the grapes are softened and the dough is golden around the edges and cooked through, about 25 minutes. *Focaccia al'Uovi* is good either warm or at room temperature.

Serving Suggestion

Store-bought bread dough, such as that sold frozen, may be used, or prepare a double batch of yeast dough next time you bake bread and freeze half to make this focaccia.

402 CALORIES PER SERVING
6 G FAT
1 G SATURATED FAT
0 MG CHOLESTEROL
76 G CARBOHYDRATES
10 G PROTEIN
382 MG SODIUM

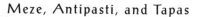

Crostini are little Italian toast canapés: crisp and ready to be topped with all sorts of savory toppings. *Crostini* are eaten as snacks, *meze*, nibbles with an afternoon aperitif, or a midmorning cappuccino.

Sometimes *crostini* are served as is, surrounding a bowl filled with a savory spread; at other times they are topped with grated cheese, then popped under the broiler to melt.

 # Crostini alla Pomodori e Caperi

TOMATO AND CAPER CROSTINI

Serves 4 to 6 as an *antipasto*

These little tidbits give an instant hit of southern Italian flavor. Enjoy with a glass of rustic red wine or cooling mineral water on a sunny afternoon.

3 to 4 ripe tomatoes, finely chopped
1 to 2 tablespoons tomato paste
3 garlic cloves, chopped
  Small pinch of sugar
2 tablespoons capers, drained
  Generous pinch dried oregano
1/2 red onion, chopped
1/2 to 3/4 cup shredded white cheese such as mozzarella
1/2 to 1 baguette, cut into thin slices

156 CALORIES PER SERVING
3 G FAT
1 G SATURATED FAT
5 MG CHOLESTEROL
25 G CARBOHYDRATES
6 G PROTEIN
341 MG SODIUM

Combine the tomatoes with the tomato paste, garlic, sugar, capers, oregano, onion, and cheese.

Arrange the baguette slices on a baking sheet and toast one side only. Turn each baguette slice over and spread the untoasted side thickly with cheese mixture.

Broil the baguette slices until the cheese melts and the edges are lightly browned.

Serve right away.

Crostini alla Fagioli e Rucola

CRISP GARLIC TOAST WITH WHITE BEANS AND ARUGULA

Serves 6 to 8 as an *antipasto* or 4 to 6 as a *primo piatto* (first course)

A rich spread of puréed white beans and sautéed onions heaped onto garlic-rubbed toast and topped with leaves of pungent arugula—besides being a traditional Tuscan *antipasto*, it was our family friend Rachel Goldberger's favorite dish at her recent twenty-first birthday bash.

          1 baguette, cut into slices
          2 onions, chopped
          3 tablespoons olive oil, or as needed
    1 1/2 cups drained cooked white cannellini beans
      4 to 6 garlic cloves
          Pinch thyme
    1/2 to 1 teaspoon vinegar, or to taste
          Salt and pepper to taste
          2 bunches young arugula or about 2 cups mixed
          spring greens

Toast the baguette slices on both sides in a 375 to 400°F oven until golden. Remove from heat and let cool.

Sauté the onion in about a tablespoon of olive oil until quite soft and golden. Add to the drained beans and purée, along with 2 cloves of chopped garlic; season with thyme, vinegar, and salt and pepper and set aside.

Cut the remaining garlic cloves into halves, then rub the toasted baguette slices on both sides with garlic.

Dress the arugula or mixed spring greens with a tablespoon or two of olive oil.

Drizzle the baguette slices with olive oil, then arrange them on plates. Spread them with a thick layer of puréed beans, then with a handful of arugula or mixed spring greens. Serve right away.

270 CALORIES PER SERVING
7 G FAT
1 G SATURATED FAT
0 MG CHOLESTEROL
41 G CARBOHYDRATES
9 G PROTEIN
309 MG SODIUM

Crostini alla Formaggio e Romarino

ROSEMARY AND MELTED CHEESE CROSTINI

Serves 4 as an *antipasto* or *stuzzichino*

Ah, I love these—it might be the herbal scent of rosemary or the milky tang of cheese; whatever else it might be, I know for sure that it is the abundance of garlic.

3 to 5 garlic cloves, chopped

2 to 3 tablespoons chopped fresh rosemary

1 cup shredded white cheese such as mozzarella or Monterey Jack

1/4 cup crumbled feta cheese or a lower-salt fresh cheese

1/4 cup grated pungent cheese such as Asiago, Parmesan, aged goat cheese, or pecorino

1/2 baguette, cut into thin slices

Combine the garlic, rosemary, and cheese. In the meantime, heat the broiler.

Arrange the baguette slices on a baking sheet and toast on one side. Turn them over and spoon cheese mixture onto the untoasted sides, then pop back under the broiler and broil until the cheese melts and the edges turn golden brown.

Serve right away.

284 CALORIES PER SERVING
10 G FAT
6 G SATURATED FAT
30 MG CHOLESTEROL
31 G CARBOHYDRATES
15 G PROTEIN
612 MG SODIUM

Meze, Antipasti, and Tapas

Crostini de Carciofi

ARTICHOKE CROSTINI

Serves 4 to 6 as an *antipasto* or *stuzzichino*

Artichoke *crostini*, a glass of wine, and a crowded piazza—a marvelous way to enjoy watching the late afternoon slip into evening. These *crostini* also make a good appetizer for a barbecued meal, as you can toast the whole thing on the grill while the rest of your meal cooks.

Homemade artichoke *pesto*—no more than highly seasoned, puréed cooked artichokes—is delicious; bottled artichoke *pesto* is quite good, too. Either is delicious in this dish.

½ to 1 baguette, sliced thinly
1 recipe Artichoke Pesto (page 163, Spaghetti with Artichoke Pesto)
4 ounces feta cheese, thinly sliced or crumbled, or a lower-salt fresh cheese
4 to 6 ounces melting cheese such as mozzarella or Monterey Jack
A drizzle of olive oil

Heat the broiler. Lightly toast the baguette slices on both sides until they just turn golden.

Spread the tops with Artichoke Pesto, then sprinkle with a layer of feta cheese followed by a layer of mild white cheese.

Drizzle with olive oil and broil until the cheese melts. Serve hot.

400 CALORIES PER SERVING
20 G FAT
7 G SATURATED FAT
30 MG CHOLESTEROL
41 G CARBOHYDRATES
20 G PROTEIN
737 MG SODIUM

Tartines au Chèvre et Tapenade

BLACK OLIVE CANAPÉS WITH BASIL AND GOAT CHEESE

Serves 4 as an hors d'oeuvre

A *tartine* in France, or *tartina* in Italy, is a slice of bread spread with butter or soft cheese, usually topped with either a sweet or savory spread.

2 to 3 ounces black olive paste
2 garlic cloves, finely chopped
½ baguette, sliced thinly
4 ounces (approximately) goat cheese
  Garnish: Handful fresh basil leaves, thinly sliced

Combine the black olive paste with the garlic and set aside.

Spread the baguette slices with goat cheese, then top each with a layer of olive-garlic paste.

Garnish with the basil and serve.

274 CALORIES PER SERVING
12 G FAT
5 G SATURATED FAT
13 MG CHOLESTEROL
30 G CARBOHYDRATES
10 G PROTEIN
736 MG SODIUM

Meze, Antipasti, and Tapas

Crostini alla Formaggio di Caprina e Pomodori Secchi

TARTINA OR CROSTINI OF GOAT CHEESE, SUN-DRIED TOMATO, AND BASIL

Serves about 6

Use either fresh or lightly toasted baguette slices: the first will be tender and soft, the second crisp and crunchy. Both are good.

1/2 to 1 baguette, sliced

6 ounces soft goat cheese such as Montrachet or California chèvre, preferably garlic or herb scented

20 or so marinated sun-dried tomatoes (page 276; or from a jar), cut into shreds or pieces
   Garnish: 20 or so fresh basil leaves, whole or shredded

If toasting baguette slices, toast both sides under the broiler.

Arrange the toasted or fresh sliced baguette on a plate or platter and spread generously with goat cheese, then top each with a few pieces of sun-dried tomato.

Garnish with a whole basil leaf, or a few shreds, and serve right away.

196 CALORIES PER SERVING
8 G FAT
5 G SATURATED FAT
13 MG CHOLESTEROL
21 G CARBOHYDRATES
9 G PROTEIN
334 MG SODIUM

DISHES OF YOGURT AND CHEESES

❧ Tzadziki

YOGURT AND CUCUMBERS WITH GARLIC AND MINT

Serves 6 to 8 as a *meze* dip or 4 for lunch when thinned with a little ice water and served as a cold soup

Cooling yogurt reeking deliciously of garlic and made even more refreshing by the addition of lots of cucumber is a dish that you find throughout much of the Mediterranean. Known as *cajig, jajik,* and *cacik,* among other names, it's a favorite in Greece, Turkey, and Israel, through the Balkans, Middle East, then on to Iran and India.

Usually served as a dip or salad as part of a *meze,* it can be thick enough to spread or thin enough to dip into; sometimes it's thinned with cold water and spooned up as soup.

Really good yogurt makes the best *tzadziki:* sheep's milk yogurt is best of all, although difficult to find in the United States.

Besides yogurt, cucumber, mint, and garlic, anything goes: some add raisins, crushed walnuts, or a handful of other herbs such as dill, green onions, tarragon, or cilantro. In addition, the cucumber may either be diced or shredded coarsely. Some salt the cucumber first to remove excess liquid; this slightly pickles the cucumber if it is left on for longer than 30 minutes and, while sometimes it's rather nice, I usually forgo this process.

I find that there are only three things necessary for a good *tzadziki:* enough salt, enough garlic, and enough time for it all to chill and meld its flavors.

Tzadziki lasts for up to a week and often longer, in the refrigerator, conveniently ready to be spooned up as desired.

> 1 European or English cucumber or 2 American cucumbers peeled and seeded
> 1 quart yogurt
> 5 or more garlic cloves, crushed or finely chopped
> ½ to 1 teaspoon dried mint, crushed between the hands
> Salt to taste
> Handful (about ¼ cup) of chopped fresh mint leaves
> *Optional:* 2 tablespoons fresh chopped dill, 1 tablespoon fresh chopped tarragon, or 3 to 4 tablespoons chopped green onions

Finely dice or coarsely shred the cucumber and mix with yogurt, garlic, dried mint, and salt. If desired, add dill, tarragon, or green onions.

Chill for at least 1 hour, preferably 2 hours or overnight.

Serve sprinkled with fresh mint leaves.

85 CALORIES PER SERVING
2 G FAT
1 G SATURATED FAT
7 MG CHOLESTEROL
11 G CARBOHYDRATES
7 G PROTEIN
83 MG SODIUM

Labaneh bil Dukkah

YOGURT CHEESE WITH OLIVE OIL AND MIXED SPICE TOPPING

Serves 4 as a *meze* or for breakfast

From the eastern Mediterranean comes this light zesty cheese based on draining the excess liquid from yogurt so that it is spreadable. In the Middle East this would be made with sheep's milk yogurt; I've used whole cow's milk yogurt and it's been very good.

It is served for breakfast, snacks, or *meze* in Egypt, Israel, Lebanon, and neighboring lands with a drizzle of olive oil and a sprinkling of *dukkah* (spices, herbs, and ground nuts), with warm pita or other flat bread to scoop it up with.

Labaneh can also be rolled into balls, then layered in a jar with olive oil and spices, and kept for several weeks.

Labaneh
2 cups whole milk yogurt

1 teaspoon salt

1 piece of cheesecloth, large enough to fit in a strainer with edges to fold over and lightly cover the cheese

Dukkah
$^1/_2$ to 1 teaspoon ground coriander

$^1/_2$ to 1 teaspoon ground cumin

$^1/_2$ teaspoon dried marjoram or thyme

1 to 2 teaspoons sumac*

2 to 3 tablespoons blanched and peeled almonds or hazelnuts, lightly toasted and coarsely ground

1 tablespoon sesame seeds

Olive oil as desired

For the labaneh: Stir the yogurt and salt together, then place in the cheesecloth and set in a strainer over a bowl. Let it sit for 1$^1/_2$ to 2 days, exuding its excess liq-

*Sumac is a tart red seasoning powder made from a dried berry, most often sprinkled over rice. It is distantly related to poison sumac but is completely harmless.

46

uid. Drain the bowl every so often so that the yogurt thickens to the consistency of a light soft cream cheese.

For the dukkah: Combine the coriander, cumin, marjoram or thyme, sumac, almonds or hazelnuts, and sesame seeds.

Serve the chilled, prepared *labaneh* drizzled with olive oil and sprinkled with the *dukkah,* or roll into balls and keep, chilled, in spiced olive oil.

FIVE WAYS TO EAT LABANEH BALLS IN OLIVE OIL

For breakfast Mixed with sliced cucumber, crushed garlic, shredded mint leaves, and a sprinkling of salt.

Middle Eastern pizza (*lahmahjoon*) Make small savory tomato-garlic-spinach pizzas by spreading very thin flat bread such as *lavash* or flour tortillas with tomato paste, crushed garlic, oregano, and a handful of cooked, squeezed chopped spinach; sprinkle with pecorino, Parmesan, or Asiago; and broil until heated through. Serve hot, dotted with bits of *labaneh,* a sprinkling of cilantro, and a few shakes of hot pepper seasoning.

With spicy spaghetti A friend from Turkey and Israel served this to me: *al dente* spaghetti dressed with a simple, garlicky tomato sauce, served with a dollop of *zhug* or other chili seasoning and a ball of *labaneh* for each person to toss into his/her pasta as desired.

Grilled eggplant Spread with *labaneh,* then serve with *zhug* or other hot sauce, and a sprinkling of cilantro.

Sandwich roll Spread a crusty roll with *labaneh* moistened with olive oil, then fill with sliced vegetables: shredded rocket, diced cucumber, chopped onion, green pepper, a handful of herbs such as fresh dill or tarragon, and a few black olives. Close up and press together.

105 CALORIES PER SERVING
7 G FAT
3 G SATURATED FAT
15 MG CHOLESTEROL
7 G CARBOHYDRATES
5 G PROTEIN
320 MG SODIUM

Meze, Antipasti, and Tapas

Salata Filfil be Laban

ROASTED RED PEPPERS AND BROWNED EGGPLANT WITH YOGURT AND MINT

Serves 6 to 8 as part of a *meze*

Eaten throughout the Balkans and Middle East in a variety of guises, peppers, eggplant, and yogurt are especially delicious with a chunk of bread for dipping, a plate of glistening black olives for a rich contrast, and tiny glasses of fire water such as arak, raki, or ouzo (although a cooling glass of fruit juice mixed with mineral water is nice, too).

As always, using a nonstick pan can seriously reduce the amount of oil you need for the eggplant; but for maximum flavor, you will need to use some.

2 medium-size or 1 large eggplant, cut into thin slices
Salt as needed
4 tablespoons olive oil, or as desired
2 red bell peppers, roasted, peeled, and diced
4 garlic cloves, finely chopped
1 to 1½ cups rich yogurt (or yogurt mixed with sour cream—nonfat sour cream is fine)
Garnish: 2 tablespoons chopped fresh mint leaves

Sprinkle the eggplant with salt and let it sit for 20 minutes or so, to draw out the bitter juices. Rinse the eggplant and dry it well on a clean towel. Sauté the eggplant in olive oil until it is lightly browned. Combine the eggplant with roasted peppers, garlic, and yogurt.

Let it cool, taste for seasoning, then serve sprinkled with mint.

106 CALORIES PER SERVING
8 G FAT
1 G SATURATED FAT
3 MG CHOLESTEROL
7 G CARBOHYDRATES
3 G PROTEIN
34 MG SODIUM

VARIATION
Biber Yogurtlu
(Turkish Pepper and Yogurt Salad)
Omit the eggplant and prepare only with peppers: use both red and green roasted peppers for more complex flavor.

 Labaneh Salateen

EGYPTIAN FETA SPREAD WITH MINT AND CUCUMBER

Serves 4 as a *meze* or side dish

This dish is of quintessential Mediterranean charm—is there a country in the eastern Mediterranean and shores of North Africa that doesn't prepare a version of this salady *meze*? Each mouthful is rich with bites of juicy cucumber, salty feta, and fresh tangy yogurt, with its hit of garlic and mint, its fragrant whiff of olive oil.

Serve garnished with ripe tomatoes or heaped onto a plate and sprinkled with paprika, then strewn with chopped green onions and black olives.

6 ounces feta cheese, diced, or choose a less salty
   fresh cheese
2 tablespoons plain yogurt
2 tablespoons olive oil
2 garlic cloves, chopped
2 tablespoons fresh mint, thinly sliced
½ European or English cucumber, unpeeled (unless
   peel is bitter), diced

Combine the feta or other fresh cheese with the yogurt, olive oil, garlic, mint, and cucumber.

Eat right away, or chill until ready to serve.

189 CALORIES PER SERVING
16 G FAT
7 G SATURATED FAT
38 MG CHOLESTEROL
5 G CARBOHYDRATES
7 G PROTEIN
482 MG SODIUM

Barley Grit Salad with Yogurt and Garlic

Serves 4 as a *meze* or 2 for lunch

I once lived in a semi-abandoned village in the Galilee and worked at a dude ranch on the road to Tiberias—although the truth is that I worked in the kitchen of the dude ranch, as I nurse an irrational fear of horses. Many of the staff were North African and prepared various dishes from their former homes. This appetizer-dip was one of my favorites, the uneven grits of barley adding delightful texture to the tart yogurt. Like all of my favorite dishes, the garlic taste comes through loud and clear.

Purchase the barley grits in a natural foods store, or grind pearl barely in a coffee grinder. If you don't have a grinder for the barley grits, simply prepare the barley whole.

$\frac{1}{3}$ cup barley grits or $\frac{1}{2}$ cup pearl barley
$\frac{1}{2}$ cup yogurt or more, as desired
2 garlic cloves, finely chopped
Juice of $\frac{1}{2}$ lemon, or to taste
Salt and pepper to taste
Garnish: Thinly sliced green onions or several pinches of fresh herbs such as marjoram or finely chopped mint

If using a coffee grinder, whirl the barley around until it forms uneven grits, with some grains crushed and others nearly whole.

Place the barley grits in a bowl with water to cover and leave it in the refrigerator for 2 hours or overnight. Drain and place the barley in a saucepan or steamer with enough water for cooking.

Cook the barley until it is tender in just enough water as needed to cook the grain but not so much as to drown it. Drain when tender (this will depend on the grain and how long it has soaked—it might be 5 minutes or 15 minutes).

Combine the cooked, drained barley with the yogurt, garlic, lemon, and salt and pepper. Let cool. Serve cool or at room temperature, sprinkled with green onions or perhaps fresh herbs or mint.

85 Calories per serving
1 G Fat
0 G Saturated Fat
2 MG Cholesterol
17 G Carbohydrates
4 G Protein
27 MG Sodium

Fromage Frais au Chermoula

PRESSED TOFU OR FRESH CHEESE IN CHERMOULA

Serves 4 to 6 as a *meze, antipasto,* or snack

Although fresh cheese is the traditional choice for this simple North African countryside dish, I have become fond of using a very untraditional tofu in its place: the soybean curd blandness contrasts deliciously with the pungent herbs and spices.

Whether using cheese or tofu, this nibble is delicious as part of a selection of little salads such as *Salata Carotta* (page 10), *Aubergine Marocaine* (page 58), and sliced cucumber sprinkled with garlic and salt; for a *meze* serve along with crusty bread, olives, green onions, and other fresh herbs.

8 to 12 ounces firm tofu or fresh cheese such as a not-too-salty feta, fresh mozzarella, or minouri
Salt to taste (unless using feta cheese, which will not need extra salt)

3 to 5 garlic cloves, chopped

3 to 4 tablespoons chopped fresh cilantro

1/4 to 1/2 fresh chili, such as serrano or jalapeño, finely chopped

1/4 to 1/2 teaspoon cumin
Juice of 1/2 lemon, or to taste
Accompaniment: 10 or so wrinkled black oil-cured olives and 1 roasted, peeled green pepper cut into strips

If using tofu, press out the excess water by placing the whole block of tofu on top of a clean dishcloth, then cover with another clean dishcloth and press lightly, firmly, and evenly. Remove the cloth and leave the tofu uncovered on a plate for about 2 hours before using, to dry out even more. If using cheese, omit this step.

Slice the tofu or cheese into thick slices. If using tofu or mozzarella, sprinkle with salt; if using feta, do not.

Sprinkle the tofu or cheese with the garlic, cilantro, chili, cumin, and lemon juice.

Eat right away, or let it marinate until ready to serve. Accompany with olives and green pepper strips.

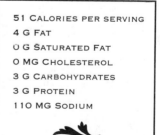

51 CALORIES PER SERVING
4 G FAT
0 G SATURATED FAT
0 MG CHOLESTEROL
3 G CARBOHYDRATES
3 G PROTEIN
110 MG SODIUM

❧ Spiedini di Peperoni

ROLLS OF ROASTED PEPPERS STUFFED WITH CHEESE AND AROMATICS

Serves 4 as a *meze* or first course

I first ate these rolls of roasted red peppers stuffed with cheese, diced tomatoes, garlic, and basil, then baked until melty in a garden in a Sicilian vineyard, sitting at a big cloth-covered wooden table. We nibbled on them as we awaited the rest of the meal—the pasta, salads, and crusty bread with tomato–olive oil dipping sauce—and downed swallows of deliciously rough red wine in between bites.

The *spiedini* are skewered to hold them together, then baked in a big pan to catch all the juices, which are then spooned over the savory peppers. Don't discard any of the crispy browned bits of cheese that escape from the peppers—they are a treat either to spoon over the peppers or to nibble on clandestinely in the kitchen.

Red and yellow peppers are best but green may be used, too. A selection not only looks pretty but also gives a good variety of flavors.

8 peppers: preferably 2 *each* yellow and green and 4 red
1 to 2 teaspoons olive oil
2 to 4 garlic cloves, chopped
2 to 3 tablespoons thinly sliced basil or 1 tablespoon finely chopped fresh rosemary
2 or 3 diced tomatoes (canned is fine)
4 to 6 ounces shredded mozzarella or Asiago cheese
2 to 3 tablespoons Parmesan cheese

Roast the peppers until they are charred. Peel and cut off each end, saving the bits for other purposes such as sauce, pasta, or salad. You will be left with roasted pepper cylinders; slice each to form a rectangle.

Lightly coat each pepper rectangle with olive oil. Then, working one at a time, sprinkle with garlic, basil or rosemary, tomato, and cheese. Roll up tightly to enclose the mixture.

Meze, Antipasti, and Tapas

Skewer with a heavy metal skewer or a bamboo skewer that you have soaked in water. The skewering helps keep the peppers closed as they bake.

Arrange the rolled, stuffed, and skewered peppers in a baking pan and bake at 400°F for about 15 minutes, or long enough to see the cheese melt and ooze out deliciously. If using bamboo skewers, you can serve the *spiedini* as they are; metal skewers will be very hot and dangerous, so you should remove the skewers for your guests, taking care not to burn your hands.

Serve right away, sprinkled with more herbs if desired.

> 151 CALORIES PER SERVING
> 7 G FAT
> 4 G SATURATED FAT
> 18 MG CHOLESTEROL
> 14 G CARBOHYDRATES
> 10 G PROTEIN
> 187 MG SODIUM

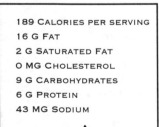 Parsley Salata

TAHINA, PARSLEY, MINT, AND CILANTRO DIP

Serves 6 to 8 as a *meze* or dip

This *tahina* sauce is green with parsley, but its herbal flavors include more than parsley: fresh mint and cilantro add their sweet and pungent flavors, too.

I used to love this as a *meze* in a little café in the old part of Jerusalem, sitting at a table set in a cobbled courtyard on warm evenings, with one or two wild cats nuzzling my legs in hopes of a treat.

The seasonings should be adjusted to taste—sometimes I like this dip reeking of garlic and spices, other times I like the green herbal flavors to shine through. It makes a marvelous dip for parties or spread on crusty bread for grilled eggplant and pepper sandwiches.

1   cup *tahina* (page 279)
    Juice of 2 lemons, or more to taste
3   garlic cloves, chopped
1   bunch parsley, chopped
1/2 cup or so *each*: chopped cilantro and fresh mint
    Salt and hot pepper seasoning such as Tabasco
    to taste
1/8 teaspoon turmeric
1/8 teaspoon curry powder, or to taste
    Seeds from 3 or 4 cardamom pods
1/8 teaspoon cumin seeds
    Garnish: Drizzle of olive oil, several black olives,
    several pickled hot peppers

189 CALORIES PER SERVING
16 G FAT
2 G SATURATED FAT
0 MG CHOLESTEROL
9 G CARBOHYDRATES
6 G PROTEIN
43 MG SODIUM

Stir the *tahina* until it is smooth, then mix in lemon juice, garlic, parsley, cilantro, and mint. Season with salt, hot pepper seasoning, turmeric, curry, cardamom, and cumin.

To serve, spread the dip onto plates or spoon into a bowl and drizzle with olive oil. Garnish with olives and pickled hot peppers.

 Spanish Pâté of Toasted Almonds, Black Olives, and Cilantro

Serves 3 or 4 as a *tapa*

Spread onto little slices of tender baguette, this makes a sprightly *tapa*, its salty-savory quality particularly good with a glass of icy chilled *fino* sherry.

I was introduced to *tapas* in what has to be the epicenter of tapas tasting: Seville's Santa Cruz Barrio. We bounced, hopped, and crawled from *tapas* bar to *tapas* bar until I thought—since it was an hour or so after midnight—it was surely time to go home. My Andalucian buddies were horrified: "Don't you want to see the famous Flamenco? It begins in several hours." So much for my stamina.

At some time in the evening we ate this olive and nut pâté spread onto small slices of bread.

3 tablespoons slivered almonds
1 garlic clove, chopped
2 tablespoons black olive paste
2 tablespoons olive oil
2 tablespoons chopped cilantro
2 green onions, thinly sliced

Lightly toast the nuts in a heavy ungreased frying pan until lightly golden. Let cool.

Crush the nuts in a mortar and pestle or food processor until they form a chunky meal, then add the garlic and work together. Stir in the remaining ingredients and taste for seasoning.

116 CALORIES PER SERVING
12 G FAT
1 G SATURATED FAT
0 MG CHOLESTEROL
2 G CARBOHYDRATES
1 G PROTEIN
197 MG SODIUM

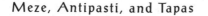

Aubergine Marocaine

EGGPLANT WITH THE FLAVORS OF A MOROCCAN SOUK

Serves 4 to 6 as a *meze*

The important thing to remember about preparing Aubergine Moroccaine is to cook it down and evaporate enough of the liquid so that the eggplant mixture forms a pastelike spread, with its flavors rich and intense. The last-minute addition of yogurt lightens it but could be omitted if desired, with the hit of lemon increased to taste.

1 medium to large-size eggplant, cut into $^3/_4$-inch cubes
Salt as desired
2 tablespoons olive oil, or more as desired
1 large onion, coarsely chopped
3 to 5 garlic cloves, chopped
$^1/_2$ fresh chili, such as jalapeño or serrano, chopped
$^1/_2$ teaspoon cumin
$^1/_4$ teaspoon *each*: turmeric and ground coriander
$^1/_8$ teaspoon ground ginger
$1^1/_2$ to 2 tablespoons paprika
1 cup diced tomatoes (canned is fine)
Sugar to taste (to balance any acidity in the tomatoes)
2 to 3 tablespoons yogurt
Juice of $^1/_2$ lemon
2 tablespoons chopped cilantro

Generously sprinkle the eggplant with salt and let it sit for 20 minutes or so to draw out the bitter juices. Eggplant that is salted absorbs less oil; however, the salt leaves behind its sodium, so you'll need to choose between the two. You can omit salting if desired.

Rinse the eggplant and dry it well on a clean towel. Brush the eggplant with 1 tablespoon of the olive oil or lightly sauté it in a nonstick frying pan. Remove from heat and let it cool.

Lightly sauté the onion, half the garlic, and the chili pepper for a moment or two in the remaining tablespoon of olive oil until softened, then sprinkle in the spices and continue to cook a few moments.

Add the tomatoes and cook until the mixture is saucelike. Add the browned eggplant, lower the heat to a simmer, and cook over low heat for 10 to 15 minutes, mashing the eggplant coarsely with a fork as it cooks. The mixture will take on a pastelike consistency, with oil exuding from the solids around the edge of the pan.

Remove the eggplant-tomato mixture from the heat and stir in the remaining garlic, lemon juice, yogurt, and cilantro. If you've not salted the eggplant, it will need salt now. Taste for seasoning (including a dash of sugar if needed) and enjoy at room temperature.

79 Calories per serving
5 g Fat
1 g Saturated Fat
0 mg Cholesterol
9 g Carbohydrates
2 g Protein
8 mg Sodium

Patlican Tavasi

TURKISH GRILLED EGGPLANT WITH GARLIC-TAHINA YOGURT SAUCE

Serves 4 as a *meze* or side dish

Grilled eggplant, imbued with the scent of smoke from cooking over a fire, is paired with a variety of sauces and marinades throughout the Mediterranean. There are hundreds, thousands, uncountable variations of grilled eggplant dishes from Spain to France, Italy, Albania, Greece, Turkey, the eastern Mediterranean, and across North Africa.

This Turkish version is my current favorite: the eggplant is scored and grilled, then cut into pieces and mixed with a yogurt-*tahina* sauce. It is garlicky, tangy, and perfect for a summer evening *meze*.

For convenience, prepare the eggplant on the grill when you're grilling another meal; the next day, the eggplant is cooked, smoky, and cool, ready to make into *Patlican Tavasi*.

> 1 eggplant, cut into halves, cut sides scored
> Salt as needed
> 2 to 3 tablespoons olive oil
> 1 teaspoon cumin seeds, or more to taste
> 1 cup *tahina*
> 1½ cups plain yogurt
> 3 garlic cloves, finely chopped
> Lemon juice to taste
> Salt and black or cayenne pepper to taste
> 2 to 3 tablespoons chopped cilantro
> *Garnish:* Black oil-cured olives

Sprinkle the eggplant with salt and olive oil, then grill it over hot coals on both sides until lightly browned in spots and tender-fleshed. Remove the eggplant from the grill, drizzle it with the remaining olive oil, and leave it to cool.

When the eggplant has cooled, cut it into bite-size pieces; remove the skin only if it is tough.

Combine the cumin, *tahina,* yogurt, garlic, and lemon juice. Season with salt and black or cayenne pepper to taste. Gently mix the eggplant into the yogurt-*tahina* mixture, taste for seasoning, and chill until ready to serve.

Serve sprinkled with cilantro and garnished with black olives.

488 CALORIES PER SERVING
41 G FAT
6 G SATURATED FAT
5 MG CHOLESTEROL
23 G CARBOHYDRATES
16 G PROTEIN
133 MG SODIUM

Pâté Forestier

WILD MUSHROOM AND GREENS PÂTÉ

Serves 6 to 8

This pâté tastes quintessentially south-of-France, although it is not based on the authentic but very rich and fatty duck, pork, and goose livers, but surprisingly, on that master of disguises, puréed soy beans.

Serve this pâté in appealing slabs or scooped out of its own earthenware baking dish and offer a few tart *cornichons* (tarragon-scented tiny pickles).

4½ ounces raw soybeans or 12 ounces cooked (canned is fine)

3 garlic cloves, chopped

1 to 2 tablespoons olive or vegetable oil

1 cup vegetable broth
Water as needed (up to ⅔ cup)

1 onion, chopped

2 tablespoons butter

1 pound mushrooms, coarsely chopped

2 tablespoons brandy

8 ounces raw spinach leaves

½ cup texturized vegetable protein in ground beef form

½ cup dry whole-wheat or rustic white bread crumbs

2 eggs, lightly beaten

2 bouillon cubes, crumbled
Black pepper to taste

½ teaspoon *each*: fresh thyme, marjoram, and rosemary or large pinch each, dried

6 bay leaves

If using dried beans, cook the beans according to the basic package directions. Drain the cooked beans; if using canned beans, rinse well and then drain. Purée the beans as smoothly as possible. Set aside.

Lightly sauté 1 garlic clove in a tablespoon of the oil, then add the bean purée and cook with the garlic for a few minutes. Add the stock and cook until the beans have absorbed most of it, then return to the food processor and purée a second time. Set the mixture aside.

Sauté the onion and remaining garlic in the butter until they have lightly browned, then add the mushrooms and sauté over medium-high heat, letting the mushrooms brown. Add the brandy and continue to cook for a few minutes, until the liquid has evaporated. The mushroom mixture should now be highly flavored, very brown, and quite dry.

Combine the sautéed mushroom mixture with the puréed bean mixture in a food processor, allowing chunks of the mushrooms to remain to give the pâté texture. Set aside.

Cook the spinach in a tiny amount of water until the spinach is bright green and just cooked through. Remove from heat and drain off the excess liquid (reserve for other uses, such as soup, sauces, etc.). Mix the spinach with the reserved puréed bean and mushroom mixture, then add the texturized vegetable protein, bread crumbs, eggs, crumbled bouillon cubes, pepper, and herbs, except the bay leaves, mixing well so that the bouillon cubes dissolve.

(CONTINUED)

Pour this mixture into a lightly oiled or buttered terrine, loaf tin, or glazed round casserole dish and smooth the top. Press the bay leaves into the surface of the mixture and drizzle the remaining oil over the top.

Heat the oven to 325 to 350°F. Bake the pâté, covered, for about an hour, or until the top has browned, is sizzling, and the pâté has puffed up a bit.

Remove the pâté from the oven, leave to cool slightly, then remove the cover or lid. Place a piece of foil or a plate on top of the pâté and put a heavy weight (such as large tin of beans) on top. This gives the terrine the characteristic dense texture of a pâté.

When it has cooled, cover or wrap the pâté in plastic and chill until ready to serve. The pâté should keep for about 4 or 5 days, well covered or wrapped, in the refrigerator. Serve with crusty bread and *cornichons*.

VARIATION

Pâté aux Champignons et les Herbes

Omit the spinach and add 1 pound of exotic mushrooms: chanterelles, shiitakes, oysters, cepe/porcini, portobello, morels, etc. Dried mushrooms, rehydrated and combined with milder fresh mushrooms, may be used instead. Season with 2 tablespoons chopped herbs such as parsley, sage, rosemary, and so forth, then proceed as with the basic recipe.

214 CALORIES PER SERVING
11 G FAT
3 G SATURATED FAT
62 MG CHOLESTEROL
16 G CARBOHYDRATES
15 G PROTEIN
475 MG SODIUM

Tortilla de Andaluz

ANDALUCIAN OLIVE PRESSERS' TORTILLA OF POTATOES, RED AND GREEN PEPPERS, TOMATOES, AND HERBS

Serves 8 to 10 as a *tapa*, about 4 as a main course

Flat, firm, thick omelets—called *tortillas*—are one of Spain's most beloved dishes. To illustrate the importance of tortillas in the national psyche, once when I visited Spain I found a television station devoted, 24 hours a day, to tortilla making. Whenever I flipped on the screen the chef was whipping up yet another version of this ever-present omelet. In between there were various snippets of international news, but little to interfere with the importance of the tortillas.

Usually served at room temperature, they may be cut into little pieces and served as a *tapa* or left whole and stuffed into a loaf of crusty bread for a sandwich that serves a whole family. In the summer, a tortilla might be eaten along with a bowl of cool gazpacho for a late-night supper.

The most commonly found tortilla throughout Spain is made with potatoes and onions only, but the following tortilla is my favorite: the bottom layer is the traditional mixture of potatoes and onions, while the top layer is rich with scarlet peppers and tomatoes. It is an Andalucian classic, fed to me chunk after delicious chunk by a 94-year-old olive grower in Seville with what I suspect were less than noble intentions. (But he was charming! And this tortilla is marvelous!)

Although the ingredients are simple and not terribly different from those of other flat omelets, there is a secret to making a tortilla: after cooking the various batches of vegetables, remove them from the pan and let cool slightly, then add to the beaten eggs and let it all sit together for about 30 minutes. This lets the flavors of the potatoes, onions, and other vegetables permeate the eggs.

A tortilla may be made in a frying pan on top of the stove and cut into wedges, or baked in the oven in a flat pan and cut into squares.

4 medium-large potatoes, peeled and diced
1 or 2 onions, diced
8 garlic cloves, coarsely chopped
3 to 5 tablespoons olive oil
    Salt and pepper to taste
    Large pinch or two dried or fresh thyme or marjoram
1 *each*: red and green pepper, diced
4 ripe tomatoes, diced (canned is fine)
4 to 6 eggs, lightly beaten

(CONTINUED)

Sweat the potatoes and onion with half the garlic in several tablespoons of olive oil by cooking in a heavy frying pan over low heat, covered. Cook 10 to 15 minutes, turning once or twice to ensure even cooking. The potatoes are ready when they are cooked through but firm and lightly browned in places.

Season generously with salt and pepper and thyme or marjoram and place in a bowl; leave to cool slightly.

In the same pan that you have used to cook the potatoes, sauté the peppers and tomatoes with the remaining garlic until just softened, about 5 minutes. Remove from heat and season generously with salt and pepper, thyme or marjoram.

Combine the potatoes with two-thirds of the beaten egg and, in a separate bowl, combine the peppers and tomatoes with the remaining egg. If possible, leave to sit for at least 10 minutes, although 30 minutes is traditional. If not possible, do not worry; proceed to make the tortilla.

Heat the remaining olive oil in a heavy frying pan, then pour in first the potato mixture and cook a minute or two over a low to medium heat, picking up the edges and letting the liquid flow underneath.

Pour the pepper-tomato mixture on top of the potatoes and continue to cook a few minutes longer or until the tortilla is firm about halfway through to the middle.

Place under the broiler and cook until the top is lightly golden and flecked with brown color, and the center is no longer liquid. (To bake, pour the olive oil into a shallow rectangular baking pan. Add the potato layer first, then pour the pepper-tomato layer over the top. Bake in a 350°F oven for about 30 minutes or until firm and lightly golden on top. It will puff as it bakes but flatten out again as it cools.)

Remove the tortilla from the broiler or oven and let it cool.

Serve at room temperature in squares or wedges.

125 CALORIES PER SERVING
6 G FAT
1 G SATURATED FAT
85 MG CHOLESTEROL
14 G CARBOHYDRATES
4 G PROTEIN
33 MG SODIUM

Muckver

TURKISH FRITTERS OF ZUCCHINI AND FETA CHEESE

Serves 4 as a *meze*

These traditional Turkish fritter-like pancakes combine the freshness of zucchini with the salty tang of cheese, crispy-edged from frying and melting with cheese and tender vegetables inside.

Since they are rich, several are plenty; and since they are tender to the point of softness, they must be eaten with a fork rather than with the fingers as they might fall apart.

I like to serve them with a dab of *zhug* and/or a sprinkling of cumin, but they are equally good served plain or with a squeeze of lemon.

2 zucchini, coarsely grated and placed in a colander
2 eggs, lightly beaten
3 ounces feta cheese, crumbled
3 ounces mozzarella or other white cheese, grated
About 3 tablespoons flour, or enough to bind the zucchini mixture
Pinch of baking soda
Pinch *each:* dried mint and marjoram or oregano
Black pepper to taste
A very small amount of olive oil for frying in a non-stick pan

Combine the zucchini with the eggs, feta, and mozzarella. Stir in the flour, baking soda, mint and marjoram or oregano, and black pepper. If the mixture seems too thin, add a little more flour.

Heat a heavy nonstick frying pan, then add a tiny bit of oil and make fritters by placing a tablespoon or two of the mixture into the hot pan, slightly flattening each cake as you go.

Cook the fritters over medium-high heat, letting the edges cook to a nutty brown hue. The fritter-pancakes should be slightly firm; if too runny they will fall apart when you turn them.

Meze, Antipasti, and Tapas

Turn the fritter-pancakes and cook the other side. They are ready when nutty brown in color and firm enough to hold together, although they will be fairly soft inside.

Remove the *muckver* from the hot pan and serve with either a dusting of cumin, a dab of *zhug*, or wedges of lemon.

297 CALORIES PER SERVING
24 G FAT
8 G SATURATED FAT
137 MG CHOLESTEROL
8 G CARBOHYDRATES
13 G PROTEIN
392 MG SODIUM

Polpetes me Domates

DILL-SCENTED POTATO, ONION, AND CHEESE PATTIES WITH TOMATO

Serves 6 as a *meze,* 4 as a main course

Polpetes are particularly revered in Crete, where I once spent a winter living in a whitewashed house at the edge of the waterfront in Aghios Nikolaos.

The chic boutiques closed for the season, gray rains subdued summer's vivid landscape, and the village settled down to the quiet of winter—except, thankfully, for the lively little café-restaurant next door, which made these delicious little potato croquettes (the *imam bayildi* is courtesy of many dinners there, as well).

3 large-size baking (Idaho) potatoes

5 green onions, thinly sliced

3 ripe tomatoes, diced (canned is fine)

1 onion, finely chopped

1 tablespoon lemon juice

2 to 3 tablespoons chopped fresh dill weed; or 1/2 to 1 teaspoon dried dillweed

1/2 to 3/4 cup grated cheese such as Asiago, sharp cheddar, or a combination of young and aged Jack or Jack and Parmesan

2 eggs, lightly beaten

Salt and pepper to taste

3 to 5 tablespoons flour, plus extra for dredging

1 tablespoon olive oil

Wash the potatoes and cut them into halves. Cook the potatoes in rapidly boiling salted water until they are tender, then drain. (I leave the peel on; you can, too, or remove it as you desire.) Mash the potatoes and let them cool.

Mix in the green onions, tomatoes, chopped onion, lemon juice, dill, cheese, and eggs; add salt and pepper as desired, then add flour a little bit at a time until the potato mixture reaches the desired consistency. It should be firm enough to hold together but soft enough so that it doesn't have a bread dough consistency, which could be tough when cooked.

Chill the potato mixture for at least 2 hours.

Flour the palms of your hands and form the mixture into small (about 1 to 1½ inches), slightly flattened balls or larger ovals (about 4 or 5 inches by 2 inches). Keep in the refrigerator while the oven heats.

Preheat the oven to 375°F. Place one or two baking sheets in the oven for 5 to 10 minutes to heat. Remove one baking sheet, brush it with olive oil, then quickly arrange the potato patties on it, about an inch apart. Brush the patties with more olive oil, then bake for 15 to 20 minutes, turning once or twice so that they are browned on all sides. (Alternatively, you can brown them in a heavy nonstick frying pan in a tablespoon or less of olive oil.)

Serve hot.

Advance Preparation
Pan brown the patties until they are lightly golden, then arrange them on a cookie sheet. When ready to serve, bake them in a 375°F oven until sizzling hot and golden brown.

208 CALORIES PER SERVING
9 G FAT
3 G SATURATED FAT
80 MG CHOLESTEROL
24 G CARBOHYDRATES
8 G PROTEIN
132 MG SODIUM

TWO

SALADS

Ensalada Estilo Moro, *Frisée with Green Olives, Blue Cheese, and Tomato-Cumin Vinaigrette*

Salade aux Herbes Marocaines, *Moroccan Salad of Herbs, Cucumbers, Tomatoes, and Olives*

Salade de Tomates du Vieux Nice, *Tomato Salad with Feta or Goat Cheese and Sweet Basil from the Old Town of Nice*

Panzanella, *Tuscan Salad of Bread, Tomatoes, Olives, and Herbs*

Horta Vuno Salata, *Greek Mountain Herb Salad*

Salata Carnabit, *Lebanese Chopped Cauliflower Salad with Ripe Tomatoes*

Salade Tiède d'Asperges Sauvages et Champignons, *Warm Salad of Asparagus, Field Mushrooms, and Mesclun*

Salade Marocaine, *Moroccan Salad of Chopped Vegetables*

Salade Tiède de Frisée, *Warm Salad of Smoked Tofu, Two Colors of Grapes, Walnuts, and Frisée*

Xato, *Catalan Salad of Frisée with Almond-Garlic-Chili Sauce*

Salade Panachée, *Mixed Greens Salad with Herbs, Beets, and Blue Cheese Toast*

Tabbouleh, *Lebanese Cracked Wheat, Parsley, and Mint Salad with Lemon Dressing*

Pomodori e Avocati in Salsa di Limoni, *Tomatoes and Avocados in Cumin-Lime Vinaigrette*

Ajotomate, *Spanish Tomato Salad with a Dressing of Pounded Garlic and Tomato*

Emincé de Tomates au Chèvre, *Salad from the Hills behind the Côte d'Azur*

THREE UTTERLY REFRESHING SALADS FROM THE MAGHREB

TOMATES ET CITRONS PRESERVÉS, *Tomato, Onion, and Preserved Lemon Salad*

SALAT MESCHOUI, *Roasted, Chopped Vegetable Salad*

MAGHREB SALAD OF CHOPPED RAW VEGETABLES WITH LEMON AND HOT PEPPERS

MEDITERRANEAN salads: endless combinations, exquisitely refreshing, the essence of Mediterranean eating. At their best when so simple and fresh they take your breath away and refresh you with each bite.

Whatever is freshest in market or garden is in the salad bowl. In summer it might be shreds of pungent rocket, bitter *treviso,* or refreshing Romaine.

That quintessential taste of the Mediterranean, *mesclun*, is a specialty of Nice: a mixture of greens ranging from baby lettuces to herbs and wild shoots and leaves. At any given time you might find, for example, wild rocket, succulent purslane, wispy chervil, wild garlic, baby *frisée*, lambs' lettuce (*mache*), and young spinach. In Spain, Greece, and in Israel's Galilean hills I've also foraged for salads, eating greens and herbs one could never buy in a market.

Tomatoes, cucumbers, and peppers, ripe from the sunshine, appear on your plate for lunch, dinner, and often for breakfast, too.

In winter, salads change with the season. Drizzling rainy days grow cold crops: cabbage is cut into shreds and dressed with olive oil, lemon, oregano; potatoes are doused with mint, green onions, lemon juice; and carrots might be tossed with a spicy *chermoula*.

Fresh white cheeses such as feta, goat, and mozzarella, or a pungent blue cheese make a bright counterpoint to these salads, as do handfuls of whatever herb is sweetest, most fragrant at the moment. And always present are the gentle emollient of olive oil, the caress of tart lemon.

Ensalada Estilo Moro

FRISÉE WITH GREEN OLIVES, BLUE CHEESE, AND TOMATO-CUMIN VINAIGRETTE

Serves 4

I sampled this salad of young, *frisée*-leafed lettuce dressed with cumin-tomato vinaigrette and studded with stuffed green olives and crumbled cheese (such as *manchego* or the pungent blue *cabrales*) not long ago on a drive from Andalucia to Madrid.

For our main course we ate wild asparagus scrambled with eggs, and White Beans (or Chickpeas) Simmered with Pumpkin and Sweet and Spicy Red Peppers (page 206).

$^1/_4$ teaspoon cumin seeds
1 or 2 garlic cloves, finely chopped or crushed in mortar and pestle
1 large or 2 smallish ripe tomatoes, chopped
3 tablespoons olive oil
2 tablespoons sherry vinegar
 Pinch sugar if needed
 Salt and cayenne pepper to taste
1 to 2 head(s) young *frisée*, torn or cut into bite-size fronds (about 4 to 6 cups in volume)
4 to 6 ounces pungent but rich blue cheese
$^1/_4$ cup pimiento-stuffed green olives, drained

In a food processor, crush the cumin, garlic, and chopped tomatoes, then work in the olive oil. When it has formed a smooth emulsion, work in the sherry vinegar. Season the dressing with sugar, salt, and cayenne pepper to taste.

Arrange the *frisée* leaves on a platter and garnish with the blue cheese and olives. Chill until ready to serve.

When ready to serve, give the dressing a final spin in the processor and pour over the salad as desired.

215 CALORIES PER SERVING
19 G FAT
7 G SATURATED FAT
21 MG CHOLESTEROL
6 G CARBOHYDRATES
7 G PROTEIN
559 MG SODIUM

Salade aux Herbes Marocaines

MOROCCAN SALAD OF HERBS, CUCUMBERS, TOMATOES, AND OLIVES

Serves 4 to 6

Anything green and fragrant can be added to this most Mediterranean of salads: herbs such as watercress, basil, arugula, fennel, cilantro, to name a few. Preserved lemons and a bit of their liquid makes a particularly good addition.

Be sure to chop the parsley and mint by hand because in a food processor it becomes too fine—the parsley sticks unpleasantly in your throat and the mint is brutalized. Cutting it with a big sharp chef's knife will give you a fluffy, light mound of herbs.

1 cup *each:* coarsely chopped parsley and fresh mint leaves
¼ cup oil-cured black Mediterranean-style olives
1 European cucumber, diced, or 2 American cucumbers, peeled, seeded, and diced
2 or 3 tomatoes, diced
3 cloves garlic, finely chopped
1 onion, finely chopped
3 tablespoons olive oil, or to taste
1 tablespoon vinegar, or to taste
Salt and pepper as desired

Combine the parsley and mint, then toss with the olives, cucumber, tomatoes, garlic, and onion. Chill until ready to serve.

Dress with olive oil, vinegar, and salt and pepper.

108 CALORIES PER SERVING
8 G FAT
1 G SATURATED FAT
0 MG CHOLESTEROL
9 G CARBOHYDRATES
2 G PROTEIN
94 MG SODIUM

Salade de Tomates du Vieux Nice

TOMATO SALAD WITH FETA OR GOAT CHEESE AND SWEET BASIL FROM THE OLD TOWN OF NICE

Serves 4 as a first course, 2 or 3 as a main course

We were flying out of Nice in the afternoon when a fierce, terrifying storm of near-biblical proportions whirled in from the sea, turning blue skies into a dark, foreboding maelstrom in what seemed like seconds.

The Mediterranean, until that moment azure blue and tranquil, turned inky and wild. It rose with sudden, terrifying force, smashing onto the tarmac. The airport was closed and all flights either canceled or diverted to Marseilles.

Being a nervous flier, I did what I do best: I worry. The French did what they do best: they arranged dinner.

Our meal began with the following salad, which lifted our spirits so effectively we didn't notice that the sky had cleared and the sea was once again glass-smooth blue. Our plane was waiting patiently, but no one was hurried. It was France after all; we stayed for the full three courses.

One of the delightful things about the salad—in addition to the juicy, ripe tomatoes—was the sheer abundance of sweet, fragrant leaves of basil. It looked like a grassy knoll on the plate and smelled like heaven. You can adjust the amount more judiciously if you like.

8 to 10 large ripe tomatoes or enough to cover a big platter (if available, use a variety of different colors/types of tomatoes; each has its own flavor as well as color and shape)

3 or 4 garlic cloves, finely chopped

3 tablespoons olive oil, or as desired

1 tablespoon red wine vinegar, or as desired
Salt to taste

4 ounces goat cheese or feta (preferably sheep's milk), cut into bite-size pieces

1 bunch sweet basil leaves, about 1/2 cup
Garnish: Handful of black Niçoise olives

Arrange the tomatoes on a platter, then sprinkle them with garlic, olive oil, vinegar, and salt.

Just before serving, garnish with goat cheese or feta, then with the sweet basil leaves—crush them slightly with your fingers as you scatter them over the dish (this will release even more of their sweet-spicy aroma). Sprinkle with the olives.

Serve right away.

VARIATION

I have served this tomato salad in a very inauthentic but delicious and healthful way: by substituting tofu for the cheese. Olive oil, garlic, and tomatoes cloak the mild tofu deliciously; use 4 to 6 ounces of plain tofu, cut into bite-size pieces.

241 CALORIES PER SERVING
18 G FAT
6 G SATURATED FAT
13 MG CHOLESTEROL
16 G CARBOHYDRATES
8 G PROTEIN
155 MG SODIUM

Panzanella

TUSCAN SALAD OF BREAD, TOMATOES, OLIVES, AND HERBS

Serves 4 to 6

The first time I ate *panzanella* was as part of an *antipasto* served in Tuscany, the array of savory little courses set out on a rustic wood table. It tasted like the essence of summer and was exquisitely refreshing on a sultry August night.

But making salads of bread is not peculiar to Tuscany. Throughout the Mediterranean are mixtures of crisp, olive oil and vinegar-dressed vegetables tossed with dry bread. In the eastern Mediterranean it is *fattoush*—pita bread tossed with salad. In other regions it is a crusty country loaf. Sometimes the pita breads are filled with salad, layered, and left to marinate in the vegetable juices and dressing; in Rome, salads are heaped onto slices of dried bread and left to soak until the bread is deliciously wet and tastes of olive oil, vinegar, garlic, and vegetables.

Such salads are delicious and healthy; they are also exquisitely frugal, using up the bits of bread that dry and go stale in the brutal heat. (If you're making it in a more temperate climate you may dry the bread in the oven.) The following recipe is a result of eating many plates of *panzanella:* in a trattoria in the hills of Tuscany, a recipe from the train conductor's mother on the Rome-Paris route, a *panzanella* served for a summer's beachside lunch on the Ligurian coast.

Many recipes instruct that the bread be soaked and squeezed dry. Although traditional, I find that even with a good squeeze there is often simply too much water left and the resulting dish can be a bit insipid. Instead, I like the moisture that lots of diced vegetables, especially juicy tomatoes, provide. Sometimes, too, I add tomato juice to the vegetables and dressing, to be soaked up by the bread.

²/₃ pound French or Italian bread, cut into cubes or slices

3 cups diced ripe tomatoes, plus their juices

1 *each:* red and yellow pepper, diced

8 to 10 garlic cloves, chopped

2 to 3 tablespoons fresh herbs such as marjoram, rosemary, oregano, or thyme
Optional: ¹/₄ cup chopped fresh basil

¹/₂ cup pitted and halved black Mediterranean-style olives

¹/₂ stalk celery, diced
¹/₂ cup olive oil
 4 tablespoons red wine vinegar

    Combine everything and chill until ready to serve.

    Adjust the seasonings, adding more olive oil and vinegar to taste, as well as a bit of tomato juice if the bread remains too dry.

SAGE

359 CALORIES PER SERVING
22 G FAT
3 G SATURATED FAT
0 MG CHOLESTEROL
36 G CARBOHYDRATES
6 G PROTEIN
368 MG SODIUM

Horta Vuno Salata

GREEK MOUNTAIN HERB SALAD

Serves 4 to 6

Gathering herbs and wild greens is a national pastime in Greece. Each region and island has those that grow best in its soil, and each season has its specialties. Sometimes you will find yourself in a countryside taverna, sitting at a little table, the scent of thyme all around you. At other times it will be rosemary that lures you for a walk through the countryside.

Hearty, pungent greens such as dandelion, beet greens, and so forth are picked and cooked, dressed with olive oil and lemon, and eaten as the doted-on dish called *horta*.

Here I've used a base of arugula and baby *frisée*, their tangy, bitter tonic flavor adored in Greece; you can use any greens that have a good, strong flavor—a *mesclun* mixture would be fine. Include in the salad whichever herbs are available, and you are free to grow them or buy them—you do not need to pick them wild.

3 to 4 cups mixed arugula, baby *frisée,* and whichever other young full-of-character greens are available

2 tablespoons *each:* coarsely chopped fresh mint leaves, fresh fennel or dill, and cilantro or parsley

1 tablespoon chopped borage, including the lovely blue flowers (leave the flowers whole)

1 to 2 teaspoons fresh marjoram leaves, pulled from the stems

1 red onion, very thinly sliced

4 to 6 ounces feta cheese, cut into bite-size cubes

1/4 to 1/2 cup black olives of choice, preferably Greek ones

3 to 6 tablespoons olive oil, or as desired

2 to 4 tablespoons lemon juice or white wine vinegar

Toss the greens with the herbs, then arrange them on a platter and decorate the top with onion, feta cheese, and black olives. Chill until ready to serve.

Just before serving, dress the salad with olive oil and lemon or vinegar.

135 CALORIES PER SERVING
12 G FAT
4 G SATURATED FAT
17 MG CHOLESTEROL
4 G CARBOHYDRATES
3 G PROTEIN
323 MG SODIUM

Salads

Salata Carnabit

LEBANESE CHOPPED CAULIFLOWER SALAD WITH RIPE TOMATOES

Serves 4 as a first course or *meze,* 2 or 3 as part of a main course

This eastern Mediterranean salad of chopped, lightly cooked cauliflower, redolent of garlic and dressed with olive oil and lemon, makes an utterly refreshing lunch or picnic dish, or a predinner *meze* along with tiny glasses of fiery arak or ouzo.

1 head cauliflower, broken into small florets
2 garlic cloves, chopped
1 to 2 tablespoons lemon juice
1 to 2 tablespoons olive oil, or to taste
  Salt and pepper to taste
  Optional: 3 ripe tomatoes, cut into wedges

Boil or steam the cauliflower until it is tender, then drain or remove from steamer. Let it cool.

Cut up the cauliflower coarsely, then mash it with a potato masher so that the cauliflower forms small bits; if it is very tender it can be mashed, but I think the flavor is fresher when the cauliflower is lightly cooked and slightly crispy.

Combine the cauliflower with the garlic, lemon juice, olive oil, and salt and pepper to taste. You could serve with ripe tomato wedges sprinkled with salt.

VARIATION

I've been served this dish as a *meze* salad enriched with a generous amount of spiced *tahina* and a dollop of tangy yogurt.

57 CALORIES PER SERVING
4 G FAT
0 G SATURATED FAT
0 MG CHOLESTEROL
6 G CARBOHYDRATES
2 G PROTEIN
15 MG SODIUM

Salade Tiède d'Asperges Sauvages et Champignons

WARM SALAD OF ASPARAGUS, FIELD MUSHROOMS, AND MESCLUN

Serves 4

Warm salads are quintessential bistro food; this one comes from Gascony, where I tasted it dressed with a prune-steeped vinegar.

If either wild arugula or wild asparagus is available, use it instead of their tamer, cultivated siblings; it adds a strong, wild *frisson* to the salad.

Serve with good crusty bread, preferably a sourdough or levain, to scoop up the tangy greens and vegetables.

1/4 cup pine nuts

2 to 3 cups *mesclun* (mixed baby greens)

Handful of arugula, preferably wild

2 tablespoons chervil

1 tablespoon chopped fresh tarragon

1 tablespoon chopped chives

2 garlic cloves, finely chopped

5 shallots, chopped

2 tablespoons olive oil

1 1/2 tablespoons raspberry or other fruit vinegar or mild wine vinegar

1/2 bunch very thin spindly asparagus spears or several handfuls of wild asparagus

Several handfuls of fresh field or exotic mushrooms such as shiitake, chanterelle, oyster, morel, porcini, portobello, and so forth, cut into bite-size pieces

Salt and pepper to taste

Lightly toast the pine nuts in an ungreased heavy frying pan or in a 350°F oven, turning every so often, until they are flecked with golden brown color, about 10 minutes. Set aside.

Toss the *mesclun,* arugula, chervil, tarragon, chives, half the garlic, and half the shallots in a salad bowl, then dress the greens mixture with 1 tablespoon of the olive oil and ½ to 1 teaspoon of the vinegar.

Blanch the asparagus briefly, then rinse with cold water. It should be bright green and crisp-tender.

Heat the remaining olive oil and lightly sauté the remaining shallots, then add the mushrooms and cook for a few minutes. Add the asparagus. Cook a few moments, then pour in the remaining vinegar. Cook over high heat until the vinegar reduces in volume and concentrates, about 5 minutes. Do not let the asparagus overcook. Season with the remaining garlic, and salt and pepper to taste.

Pour the hot mushrooms and asparagus onto the dressed greens, then sprinkle with the reserved pine nuts and serve right away.

99 CALORIES PER SERVING
8 G FAT
1 G SATURATED FAT
0 MG CHOLESTEROL
7 G CARBOHYDRATES
4 G PROTEIN
11 MG SODIUM

Salade Marocaine

MOROCCAN SALAD OF CHOPPED VEGETABLES

Serves 4

Tomatoes, cucumber, peppers, onion, olives, cumin, and paprika: this salad is eaten nearly every day in summertime Morocco.

Red peppers, fresh mint, radishes, even diced orange might be added. The important thing is that the salad be impeccably fresh, chilled, and the flavors given a chance to get to know each other—and that the day be hot enough to truly appreciate it.

8 to 10 ripe tomatoes, sliced
Salt as desired
1 teaspoon *each:* cumin and paprika
1 large European cucumber or 2 or 3 American cucumbers, peeled, seeded, and sliced thinly
2 green peppers, seeded and cut into thin rings
1 small to medium-size red onion, peeled and cut into rings
2 garlic cloves, peeled and chopped
Optional: 1/2 to 1 fresh hot pepper of choice, such as jalapeño or serrano, thinly sliced
10 to 15 black Mediterranean olives
2 to 3 tablespoons olive oil, or as desired
2 to 3 teaspoons vinegar, or to taste
2 tablespoons *each:* chopped parsley and cilantro

175 CALORIES PER SERVING
9 G FAT
1 G SATURATED FAT
0 MG CHOLESTEROL
23 G CARBOHYDRATES
4 G PROTEIN
74 MG SODIUM

Arrange the tomatoes on a plate and sprinkle with a little of the salt, cumin, and paprika, then arrange cucumber(s), green peppers, and onion, sprinkling with a bit more of the salt, spices, chopped garlic, and hot pepper as you go along.

Garnish with the olives, dress with olive oil and vinegar, and sprinkle parsley and cilantro over the top.

Chill the salad until ready to serve.

Salads

Salade Tiède de Frisée

WARM SALAD OF SMOKED TOFU, TWO COLORS OF GRAPES, WALNUTS, AND FRISÉE

Serves 4

This is a vegetarian version of a bistro classic from France's southwest. The smoky flavor of tofu adds its savor to the tangy warm vinaigrette. If you like, you could use a thick, lean bacon or smoked turkey, duck, or chicken in place of the tofu.

1/4 cup shelled walnuts, halved
4 cups frisée lettuce, torn into pieces
1 1/2 tablespoons walnut oil
1 1/2 tablespoons olive oil
3 garlic cloves, chopped
2 to 3 tablespoons chopped chives
2/3 to 1 cup grapes, preferably seedless; a combination of green and flame is appealing
Salt and pepper to taste
8 ounces smoked tofu, diced
5 shallots, chopped
1/4 cup red wine vinegar

Lightly toast the walnuts in a heavy ungreased pan until fragrant and slightly darkened in color. Remove from the pan and set aside.

Combine the *frisée* with the walnut oil and half the olive oil, garlic, chives, and grapes; season with salt and pepper. Arrange in a salad bowl and set aside.

Sauté the tofu and shallots in a heavy frying pan in the remaining olive oil until the shallots are softened, 2 to 3 minutes. Pour in the vinegar and boil down until reduced to about half.

Pour the hot tofu and vinegar dressing over the olive oil-tossed *frisée* and grapes, and sprinkle with walnuts. Serve right away.

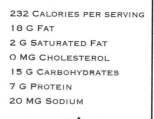

232 CALORIES PER SERVING
18 G FAT
2 G SATURATED FAT
0 MG CHOLESTEROL
15 G CARBOHYDRATES
7 G PROTEIN
20 MG SODIUM

 # Xato

CATALAN SALAD OF FRISÉE WITH
ALMOND-GARLIC-CHILI SAUCE

Serves 4

Xato—pronounced *schato*—is a salad of slightly bitter young *frisée* paired with a pungent sauce/dressing of pounded almonds, garlic, olive oil, and chili. *Xato* is robust and sometimes rough: often a splash of sherry smoothes out its harsh edges.

It is the pairing of slightly bitter and fresh greens with the rich and strongly flavored sauce that is so pleasing. I like to serve a plate of ripe summer tomatoes cut into wedges alongside.

3 garlic cloves, peeled and coarsely cut up
Pinch salt
3 tablespoons toasted ground almonds*
$\frac{1}{2}$ teaspoon hot pepper flakes or $\frac{1}{4}$ fresh red chili, such as jalapeño or serrano, or to taste
3 tablespoons olive oil
1 tablespoon wine vinegar
Optional: 1 tablespoon sherry
1 or 2 tender small to medium-size heads of *frisée* (enough for 4 portions)
3 medium-size ripe tomatoes, cut in wedges

*Toasted ground almonds: Either grind dry roasted low-salt or unsalted almonds in a coffee grinder/food processor to a mealy consistency or buy almond meal (in a natural food shop) and lightly toast in an ungreased pan until it smells fragrant and turns just slightly golden brown. Do not let burn.

Pound the garlic with the salt in a mortar and pestle; this releases more of the garlicky flavor and aroma than a food processor does, although you can use the latter.

Add the almonds and hot pepper flakes/chili and combine well, then add the olive oil 1 tablespoon at a time, mixing well between additions until it forms a thick, saucelike mixture.

Mix in the vinegar, and sherry if using, and adjust the seasoning.

Serve in a bowl, with the *frisée* to dip in, accompanied by the tomatoes.

154 CALORIES PER SERVING

13 G FAT

2 G SATURATED FAT

0 MG CHOLESTEROL

9 G CARBOHYDRATES

3 G PROTEIN

58 MG SODIUM

Salade Panachée

Mixed Greens Salad with Herbs, Beets, and Blue Cheese Toast

Serves 4

Crisp greens studded with nuggets of red beets and toast spread with pungent blue cheese. The greens themselves were exciting: a handful of purslane, a few strands of wild arugula and wild asparagus added to the mix. The best way to eat this salad, we discovered, is by alternating little bites of greens and cheese toast.

Beets are quintessential bistro food in nearly every corner of France. Sold in the marketplace already cooked, they are tossed into salads, sliced and paired with potatoes, and shredded into vinaigrettes.

3 or 4 medium to large beets or 2 pounds of mixed golden and red beets
4 ounces baguette (about 8 slices)
Olive oil for brushing
1 quart or so mixed greens
2 tablespoons *each*: chopped chives, shallots, parsley, and chervil
2 tablespoons soft unsalted butter
2 garlic cloves, chopped
6 ounces sharp blue cheese such as Roquefort or Maytag blue
Dash *each*: lemon juice and cayenne or Tabasco sauce
2 to 3 tablespoons olive oil, or as desired
2 teaspoons sherry vinegar, balsamic vinegar, or lemon juice
1 teaspoon white wine vinegar

Cook the beets until tender: either steam for 40 minutes or bake in a 375°F oven for about an hour. When tender, remove from heat and let cool. The skins should rub right off. Slice and set aside (if using both golden and red beets, keep them separate so that their colors don't run into each other).

Brush the baguette slices with olive oil, then arrange on a baking sheet. Bake at 375 to 400°F for about 20 minutes, turning once or twice, until the toast is lightly golden brown. Remove from the oven and let cool slightly on a rack.

Meanwhile, toss together the salad greens with the chives, shallots, parsley, and chervil. Set aside.

Mix the butter, garlic, and blue cheese; when smooth, season with lemon juice and cayenne or Tabasco. Set aside.

Dress the greens and herbs with olive oil, vinegar or lemon juice, and white wine vinegar then arrange on a plate and top with sliced beets. Pour any excess dressing over the beets.

Spread the toast thickly with the cheese mixture, piling it up enticingly, then serve 2 toasts per person, along with the greens and beets.

409 CALORIES PER SERVING
27 G FAT
13 G SATURATED FAT
56 MG CHOLESTEROL
27 G CARBOHYDRATES
14 G PROTEIN
1,015 MG SODIUM

❧ Tabbouleh

LEBANESE CRACKED WHEAT, PARSLEY, AND MINT SALAD WITH LEMON DRESSING

Serves 4 to 6

This classic Lebanese grain and vegetable salad has become a favorite throughout the Mediterranean, especially in the south of France.

A good *tabbouleh* can vary widely: sometimes it consists mostly of parsley, with just enough bulgur to give it heft; other times it becomes a decidedly cracked wheat salad flavored with the herbs and vegetables. It's important that the salad taste utterly fresh and that it be fragrant with onion and fresh mint.

Serving it mounded on a bed of small, young Romaine leaves or vine leaves not only looks very appealing but makes the eating participatory: instead of individual portions, each diner can take a leaf and wrap up a spoonful of the salad, top it with a dollop of yogurt, and pop it into the mouth!

  1 cup bulgur wheat
  1 bunch green onions, thinly sliced
 1 1/2 cups chopped fresh parsley
  2/3 cup fresh mint leaves
  1/4 cup olive oil, or as desired
   Juice of 1 1/2 to 2 lemons
   Salt and pepper to taste
  1 cucumber, peeled, seeded, and diced (or half a European cucumber)
  2 tomatoes, seeded and diced
   Romaine lettuce leaves or vine leaves (if fresh, parboil; if jarred, rinse first with cold water before lining the plate with them)
   Yogurt as desired

Soak the bulgur wheat in cold water to cover for $1/2$ hour, then drain and spread out in a shallow baking dish to lightly dry, about 10 minutes.

Add the green onions to the bulgur and squeeze together, repeating until the bulgur has combined well with the green onion flavor. You can, of course, simply combine the two without the squeezing step, but this step makes the subtle difference between an okay *tabbouleh* and an exceedingly good one.

Lightly toss in the parsley and mint, then dress with olive oil, lemon juice, and salt and pepper to taste (*tabbouleh* takes quite a bit of salt and lemon).

Tabbouleh may be prepared in advance to this point. Just before serving, toss with cucumber and tomato, and add more olive oil, lemon, and salt and pepper to taste.

Serve on a bed of Romaine lettuce leaves or vine leaves, with a bowl of cooling yogurt on the side.

VARIATION

Prepare *tabbouleh* with cooked wheatberries instead of bulgur. The rich chewy grains are delicious dressed with the tangy dressing and fresh herbs.

---

192 CALORIES PER SERVING
10 G FAT
1 G SATURATED FAT
0 MG CHOLESTEROL
25 G CARBOHYDRATES
4 G PROTEIN
22 MG SODIUM

Pomodori e Avocati in Salsa di Limoni

TOMATOES AND AVOCADOS IN CUMIN-LIME VINAIGRETTE

Serves 6

This zesty little tomato and avocado salad—spiced with the provocative scent of cumin and a splash of sour lime—was my lunch one afternoon on a visit to a Sicilian vineyard. No doubt the exotic flavoring was a result of the proximity of North Africa, less than a hundred miles away over the Mediterranean Sea.

8 to 10 or so ripe tomatoes, sliced (enough to fill a platter or serving plate)
2 or 3 ripe avocados, peeled and sliced thickly
2 or 3 green onions, thinly sliced
2 tablespoons olive oil
2 teaspoons lime juice
Finely grated zest of 1 lime
1/2 teaspoon toasted cumin seed or 1/4 teaspoon ground cumin
Salt and pepper if desired

Arrange the tomatoes and avocados on a platter or serving plate, then sprinkle with green onions. Drizzle with olive oil and lime juice. Sprinkle with lime zest and cumin seed (or ground cumin), adding salt and pepper if desired.

Serve right away at room temperature, or chill up to 2 hours until ready to serve.

177 CALORIES PER SERVING
15 G FAT
2 G SATURATED FAT
0 MG CHOLESTEROL
12 G CARBOHYDRATES
3 G PROTEIN
22 MG SODIUM

Salads

Ajotomate

SPANISH TOMATO SALAD WITH A DRESSING OF POUNDED GARLIC AND TOMATO

Serves 4

Wrinkly black olives, wedges of hard-cooked egg, handfuls of fresh herbs—any or all of these make fine garnishes for this simple, vigorous salad. Pounding tomato into the vinaigrette is typically, deliciously Andalucian; use the dressing on steamed or grilled prawns, warm cooked beans, or roasted peppers.

3 or 4 garlic cloves, chopped
    Generous pinch of salt
10 ripe small to medium-size tomatoes (2 diced and 8 sliced)
2 tablespoons (or to taste) red wine vinegar, sherry vinegar, or lemon juice
2 tablespoons olive oil
    Pinch sugar if needed
    To serve: 2 hard-cooked eggs, peeled and cut into quarters, and 8 to 10 wrinkly black olives

Purée the garlic with the salt, preferably using a mortar and pestle. Add 2 tomatoes (the diced ones) and purée to make a smooth mixture, then work in the vinegar or lemon juice and olive oil until the mixture emulsifies.

Arrange the sliced tomatoes in a bowl. Sprinkle them with salt (and sugar if needed), then pour over them the garlic-tomato dressing.

Chill until ready to serve, then garnish with eggs and olives.

163 CALORIES PER SERVING
11 G FAT
2 G SATURATED FAT
107 MG CHOLESTEROL
13 G CARBOHYDRATES
5 G PROTEIN
131 MG SODIUM

Emincé de Tomates au Chèvre

SALAD FROM THE HILLS BEHIND THE CÔTE D'AZUR

Serves 4 as a first course

We ate this one afternoon in the last of the sultry summer, when tomatoes were sweet and juicy. Salty green olives, tangy goat cheese, crisp pungent onion, and slightly bitter arugula balanced it beautifully.

Any interesting greens such as purslane, pea greens, *mizuna,* wild arugula, or blanched wild asparagus is delicious added to the pile of greens.

6 ripe tomatoes, thinly sliced; reserve juice
  Salt to taste
3 to 5 garlic cloves, chopped
1 red onion, thinly sliced
8 to 15 pimiento-stuffed green olives, halved or sliced
1 bunch rocket leaves
4 ounces mild soft goat cheese
  Several large pinches of dried *herbes de Provence*
3 tablespoons olive oil, or as desired
1 tablespoon wine vinegar, or as desired

Arrange the tomatoes on a plate along with their accumulated juices. Sprinkle them with salt and garlic, and scatter the top with red onion and olives.

Top the tomato salad with the rocket or other greens, then dot with bite-size lumps of the goat cheese. Sprinkle with *herbes de Provence,* drizzle with olive oil and vinegar, and eat right away.

251 CALORIES PER SERVING
20 G FAT
6 G SATURATED FAT
13 MG CHOLESTEROL
14 G CARBOHYDRATES
8 G PROTEIN
740 MG SODIUM

Salads

THREE UTTERLY REFRESHING SALADS FROM THE MAGHREB

Each of these salads uses sweetly perfumed, tart, and silken preserved lemons. Purchase from a shop, or make your own (see Salted Lemons, page 278). In a pinch, use a bit of ordinary fresh lemon flesh, juice, and zest.

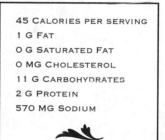 ## Tomates et Citrons Preservés

TOMATO, ONION, AND PRESERVED LEMON SALAD

Serves 4 as a side dish or *meze*

I ate this salad in a café in the old port of Essaouira: the combination of thinly sliced onion and ripe tomato with nuggets of preserved lemon and a splash of their tangy juices is one of the most deliciously refreshing salads I've tasted. It's unusual enough to stimulate with each bite, with no fat in the dressing as a little bonus.

4 ripe tomatoes, thinly sliced
1 sweet (or not too strong) onion, peeled and thinly
   sliced lengthwise
1 preserved lemon, diced; reserve the liquid
   Optional: salt and a squeeze of fresh lemon to taste

Arrange the tomatoes and onions on a plate, then dot with the preserved lemon.

Drizzle the tomatoes with the juice of the preserved lemon, and season with salt and fresh lemon juice if needed. Serve chilled.

45 CALORIES PER SERVING
1 G FAT
0 G SATURATED FAT
0 MG CHOLESTEROL
11 G CARBOHYDRATES
2 G PROTEIN
570 MG SODIUM

Salat Meschoui

ROASTED, CHOPPED VEGETABLE SALAD

Serves 4 to 6 as a side dish

This Tunisian salad can be eaten as a side dish or *meze*. Like its cousin, the Spanish *escalivada*, selected vegetables are grilled and, when cool, peeled and diced, then eaten as a salad. Like *escalivada, salat meschoui* is best started right after a barbecue—you can toss the vegetables onto the dying embers, and the next day's *salat meschoui* is practically finished. The vegetables can also be easily cooked over the kitchen stove.

Fresh raw vegetables can be added to this salad: celery, cucumber, or herbs; and pungent seasonings like capers, diced oil-cured olives, hot peppers. But it is also very nice in its roasted vegetable purity.

2 onions, cut into halves

1 head garlic, cut in half

1 *each*: red and green bell pepper

6 to 8 medium-size flavorful tomatoes

1 preserved lemon, diced; reserve 1 tablespoon preserved lemon juice

1 tablespoon olive oil (2 tablespoons if roasting in the oven)

1 tablespoon fresh lemon juice

Cook the onions, garlic, peppers, and tomatoes either over an open grill or in your kitchen. If using a grill, lightly char each vegetable, then place in a pan, covered, to cool and let the skins loosen and the juices gather. If using your kitchen, cook the peppers over the open fire of a gas flame, letting them char as in roasting any sort of pepper. Char the onion and garlic in a small ungreased frying pan over medium-low heat, covered, until the vegetables are charred and soft. Leave covered to cool. Roast the tomatoes in a casserole dish in a 400°F oven for about 40 minutes or until charred and softened. Let cool until the next day.

Peel the peppers and slice them thin. Set them aside.

Remove the skins from the onions and garlic. Coarsely chop them and add them to the peppers.

Peel the tomatoes, squeezing the skin to extract the juices and let the concentrated small amount of tomato mixture drip into the onions and peppers. Dice the tomatoes and add, along with any juices from the roasting pan, to the onion-garlic-pepper mixture.

Add the preserved lemon and a little of the juice, olive oil, and fresh lemon juice. Taste for seasoning.

79 Calories per serving
3 G Fat
0 G Saturated Fat
0 MG Cholesterol
14 G Carbohydrates
2 G Protein
477 MG Sodium

Maghreb Salad of Chopped Raw Vegetables with Lemon and Hot Peppers

Serves 4

This salad should be brash, spicy, and lemony, and a little salty as well.

Serve with other salads on a blisteringly hot day, with soft pita or other flat breads alongside, or with crusty French bread for dipping. Delicious as a *meze* to precede a couscous.

1   European cucumber
1   onion, peeled
3   ripe tomatoes
2   green peppers
1/2 hot green chili, finely chopped
    Pinch cumin
1   tablespoon chopped cilantro
1   preserved lemon, diced, plus a tablespoon or two of the juice
    Juice of 1/2 fresh lemon
    Salt as needed

Dice the cucumber, onion, tomatoes, and green peppers.

Toss them with the chili, cumin, cilantro, preserved lemon and its juices, fresh lemon juice, and salt as needed. Taste for seasoning and add more hot green chili if desired.

73 CALORIES PER SERVING
1 G FAT
0 G SATURATED FAT
0 MG CHOLESTEROL
17 G CARBOHYDRATES
3 G PROTEIN
711 MG SODIUM

THREE

SOUPS

Two Little Recipes for Portuguese Chicken Soup

Canja de Galinha, *Lemon-Mint Chicken Broth*

Sopa a Alentejara, *Chicken Soup with a Paste of Garlic and Cilantro*

Hot Soups

Shepherds' Soup from the Island of Djerba

Khoriatiki Soupa, *Greek Tomato Soup with Bulgur Wheat and Mountain Sage*

Minestra alla Estate, *Corn and Tomato Soup with Brown Beans, Basil, and Cheese Ravioli*

Minestra alla Pomodori e Patate, *Tomato-Vegetable Broth with al Dente Diced Potato*

Ciorba, *Turkish Turnip Soup with Rice, Red Beans, Cilantro, and Mint*

Minestra alla Pomodori, *Mint-Scented Tomato Broth with Diced Cheese*

Minestra alla Zucchini, *Italian Zucchini Soup with Pasta and Fresh Herbs*

Minestra di Fave e Pasta, *Fresh Fava Bean Broth with Ditalini Pasta and Aged Goat Cheese*

Minestra alla Giardino, *Yellow and Green Beans in Broth with Tubetti*

Sopa Roja, *Purée of Red Bell Pepper and Tomato*

Sopa de Tomate con Higos or Oliaigua amb Tomatics, *Tomato and Fig Soup with Orange Juice and Grapes*

Soupe à l'Ail, *Garlic Soup with Couscous from the South of France*

Aromatiki Soupa, *Greek Island Yellow Split Pea Soup*

Sopa de Ajo Castellana, *Castilian Garlic Soup Thickened with Rye Flatbread*

Tomato, Barley, and Red Lentil Soup with Preserved Lemon and Mint from Al-Maghreb

Cold Soups

Zoque, *Red Gazpacho Made from Tomato and Pepper*

Schlada, *Chilled Roasted Green Pepper and Tomato Soup*

Gazpacho Blanco de Malagueño, *White Almond and Fruit Gazpacho*

La Soupe Froide aux Courgettes, *Chilled Zucchini-Leek Bisque with Basil and Lemon*

Throughout the Mediterranean soups may be eaten at nearly every meal and in every season. Soups are a necessity in an area that has traditionally known poverty and scarcity, as it can stretch small quantities of ingredients to fill both the soup pot and the hungry belly.

In the summer, hot soup replenishes the body when the weather is hot and depleting; some say the perspiration it raises on the forehead is nature's own air-conditioning system. Cool soups such as gazpacho are like any cooling drink: they, too, refresh when the temperature climbs.

And soups make such delicious use of the vegetables of summer: lightly cooked bits of light and lithe zucchini, peas, peppers, fragrant herbs, and ripe tomatoes, among others.

As winter approaches, warming soups of hardy vegetables and dried legumes, such as beans and lentils, simmer in cauldrons throughout the area to warm the body and comfort the soul as rains and icy weather descend on the Mediterranean.

Country to country, region to region, most Mediterranean people probably eat soup for one of their daily meals every day.

Canja de Galinha

LEMON-MINT CHICKEN BROTH

Serves 4

Serve bowls of this hot chicken soup with a squeeze of lemon and a crumbling of dried mint or a spoon of chopped fresh mint.

6 cups hot chicken broth
1 lemon, cut into wedges
2 teaspoons dried mint or 2 tablespoons chopped
   fresh mint

Serve hot broth in bowls with a squeeze of lemon and a sprinkling of mint.

31 CALORIES PER SERVING
0 G FAT
0 G SATURATED FAT
0 MG CHOLESTEROL
5 G CARBOHYDRATES
4 G PROTEIN
134 MG SODIUM

Sopa a Alentejara

CHICKEN SOUP WITH A PASTE OF GARLIC AND CILANTRO

Serves 4

This soup is traditionally served with a poached egg and croutons of toasted bread.

1 garlic clove
  Pinch salt
2 tablespoons chopped fresh cilantro
1 to 2 tablespoons olive oil
4 to 6 cups hot chicken broth

Purée garlic, salt, chopped cilantro, and olive oil.

Stir this into the hot chicken broth, then ladle the soup into bowls.

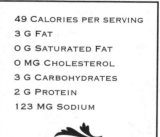

49 CALORIES PER SERVING
3 G FAT
0 G SATURATED FAT
0 MG CHOLESTEROL
3 G CARBOHYDRATES
2 G PROTEIN
123 MG SODIUM

Shepherds' Soup from the Island of Djerba

Serves 4

The island of Djerba, lying off the coast of Tunisia, has many fascinating tales to tell, although I'm just beginning to learn them. It is one of the world's top growers of saffron, with fields upon fields of pale blue-violet awaiting the long and tedious task of extracting the golden pistils.

A Chassidic rabbi told me that according to Jewish folklore, if a member of the priest caste steps foot on the island, he or she will die immediately and mysteriously. Curiously, however, there has long been a Jewish presence on Djerba.

The hillsides are dotted with flocks of sheep tended in the traditional manner by shepherds. This soup is adapted from a recipe described to me by one of those shepherds. Although he was adamant that the yogurt must be made from sheep's milk, I have tried it with ordinary cow's milk yogurt and it was very good, too.

1 leek, diced
6 garlic cloves, chopped
1 1/2 cups diced tomatoes and their juices (canned is fine)
1/2 cup pearl barley
1 quart low-sodium chicken or vegetable stock
2 pinches saffron
2 cups yogurt
2 tablespoons chopped fresh mint
2 teaspoons chopped fresh dill or 1/4 teaspoon dried dillweed
1 teaspoon cilantro or fresh tarragon
3 green onions, chopped
Salt and cayenne pepper to taste
1 lemon, cut into wedges

Sauté the leek with half the garlic until softened, then add the tomatoes and cook a few minutes to soften.

Add the barley and stock, then cover and cook until the barley is tender, about 40 minutes.

When ready to serve, bring the soup just to boiling, then add the saffron and remove from heat.

Combine the yogurt with reserved garlic, mint, dill, cilantro or tarragon, and green onions. Ladle in some of the hot soup and stir well, then ladle in a bit more, and continue to smooth.

Stir the yogurt mixture into the hot soup and season with salt and cayenne pepper. Serve hot, each portion garnished with a lemon wedge.

SAFFRON

Saffron, harvested from the stigmas of the saffron crocus, needs to be picked by hand. It takes 75,000 to 100,000 stigmas to reach the weight of a pound, making saffron the most expensive spice on earth. Cherished throughout the eastern Mediterranean, saffron was introduced to Spain by the Arabs during the time of Moorish rule; today it scents and seasons much of the cuisine, including perhaps Spain's most famous dish, *paella*. Saffron is eaten in a variety of savory dishes along the northern Mediterranean shores: pounded into sauces such as Provence's *rouille,* vegetable soups, rice dishes (including the classic *risotto alla Milanese*), and pastas, both in the sauce and in the pasta itself.

221 CALORIES PER SERVING
2 G FAT
1 G SATURATED FAT
7 MG CHOLESTEROL
40 G CARBOHYDRATES
12 G PROTEIN
191 MG SODIUM

Khoriatiki Soupa

GREEK TOMATO SOUP WITH BULGUR WHEAT AND MOUNTAIN SAGE

Serves 4

The hillsides of many Mediterranean islands are blanketed with rough, weedlike herbs. Each step you take is scented with thyme, rosemary, or the almost medicinal aroma of mountain sage, their perfume released when crushed underfoot.

Often the herbs are brewed into a bracing tea, strong enough to ward off Mediterranean winter colds, or simmered into soups such as this one I spooned up on the island of Crete in a little taverna-café I came across on an afternoon hike.

- 1 onion, chopped
- 1 carrot, diced
- 3 garlic cloves, coarsely chopped
- 2 tablespoons olive oil
- 1 1/4 pounds diced tomatoes (either fresh or canned); reserve the juice
- 3 cups vegetable broth/stock
- 1/4 cup bulgur wheat
- 5 to 8 sprigs or *bouquet garni* of Greek mountain sage or other aromatic Mediterranean dried herb

Lightly sauté the onion, carrot, and garlic in olive oil until softened, then add the tomatoes and cook a few minutes until somewhat saucelike. Add the broth/stock, bulgur wheat, and sage, bring to boil, reduce the heat, and cover and simmer until the bulgur is tender, about 10 minutes.

Remove the sprigs of sage before serving, as they will have given all of their flavor and aroma by the end of cooking, leaving behind only unpleasant bits of tough leaves to chew on.

Serve hot.

VARIATION

Me Bamies (with Okra)

Okra, silky textured and slightly viscous, makes a delicious addition to Khoriatiki Soupa. Add a handful of okra, sliced about $^1/_8$ to $^1/_4$ inch thick, to the simmering soup when you add the bulgur wheat. When the bulgur is done, the okra should be tender as well. For a less stringy soup, use small, tender okra and add them whole.

SAGE

181 CALORIES PER SERVING
8 G FAT
1 G SATURATED FAT
0 MG CHOLESTEROL
27 G CARBOHYDRATES
4 G PROTEIN
765 MG SODIUM

Minestra alla Estate

CORN AND TOMATO SOUP WITH BROWN BEANS, BASIL, AND CHEESE RAVIOLI

Serves 4

Summer soup: thin savory broth filled with kernels of sweet corn, the garden flavor of ripe tomatoes, earthy brown beans, and the scent of sweet basil. Add to this some cheese ravioli and you have the makings of a rambunctious and lively soup reminiscent of an Italian summer.

Although corn is still not eaten in Italy as often as it is in America, you do find it served—often with tomatoes, such as in a salad or pizza, or teamed with tomato broth, as in this recipe. The cobs give a subtle flavor to the broth, so don't be tempted to leave out the step of cooking them first.

2	ears of corn
2	cups water
1	medium onion, chopped
2	tablespoons olive oil
4	garlic cloves, chopped
2	cups low-sodium chicken or vegetable broth
2	cups diced tomatoes (either fresh or canned)
8	large cheese ravioli
1/2	cup cooked brown beans, such as cranberry, Borlotti, pinto, or Anasazi
	Salt and pepper to taste
1/4	cup thinly sliced fresh basil
	Grated cheese for sprinkling, such as Romano or Asiago

Cook the ears of corn in water for only about 5 minutes. Remove them from the water and set aside to cool. Reserve the cooking water.

Sauté the onion in olive oil until softened, then add the garlic, stir a moment, and pour in the broth, tomatoes, and corn cooking water. Let simmer.

112

Meanwhile, cut the corn kernels off of the cobs and set aside.

Cook the ravioli until *al dente,* then drain. Place one or two in each bowl.

Add the reserved corn to the simmering soup along with the beans, then taste for salt and pepper.

Ladle the hot soup over the ravioli, and top each bowl with a sprinkling of basil and grated cheese.

313 CALORIES PER SERVING
9 G FAT
1 G SATURATED FAT
0 MG CHOLESTEROL
48 G CARBOHYDRATES
14 G PROTEIN
239 MG SODIUM

Minestra alla Pomodori e Patate

TOMATO-VEGETABLE BROTH WITH AL DENTE DICED POTATO

Serves 4

This garlic-scented tomato broth floats tiny bits of chopped parsley and *al dente* potatoes. It makes a marvelous summer supper, although I admit to having eaten it for breakfast.

- 1/2 medium-size onion, chopped
- 1 medium-large baking potato, peeled and diced
- 2 garlic cloves, chopped
- 1 to 2 tablespoons olive oil, or as needed
- 1 medium-large tomato, diced
- 1 cup mixed vegetable juice such as V-8
- 3 cups low-sodium chicken or vegetable broth/stock
  Salt and pepper to taste
- 2 teaspoons chopped fresh parsley

Sauté the onion, potato, and garlic in olive oil over medium-high heat, letting the onion and potato lightly brown in places, about 5 minutes. Add diced tomato and continue to cook over high heat for a minute or two.

Add the vegetable juice and boil for 2 to 3 minutes, then pour in the broth/stock and cook another 6 to 8 minutes or until the potatoes are just cooked.

Taste for salt and pepper, sprinkle with parsley, and serve.

131 CALORIES PER SERVING
4 G FAT
1 G SATURATED FAT
0 MG CHOLESTEROL
22 G CARBOHYDRATES
4 G PROTEIN
296 MG SODIUM

Soups

❧ Ciorba

TURKISH TURNIP SOUP WITH RICE, RED BEANS, CILANTRO, AND MINT

Serves 4

This tangy, herb-scented soup is simple to make, very economical, and low in fat. Enough for the practicality: it tastes delicious.

2 small to medium-size turnips, peeled and cut into bite-size pieces
1 quart low-sodium chicken or vegetable broth/stock
2 garlic cloves, chopped
2 tablespoons chopped fresh cilantro
2 tablespoons chopped fresh mint
1/2 cup drained cooked red kidney beans
1/8 teaspoon cinnamon
    Salt and hot pepper seasoning to taste
    Juice of 1/2 lemon, or as desired
1/2 to 3/4 cup cooked rice
    Pinch of turmeric to taste

Combine the turnips, broth/stock, garlic, cilantro, mint, kidney beans, and cinnamon. Bring to a boil, then reduce heat and cook for about 10 minutes or until the turnips are just tender. Season with salt and hot pepper seasoning, then squeeze in the lemon juice.

Spoon cooked rice into 4 bowls; ladle hot soup over the rice. Sprinkle with a tiny bit of turmeric, then serve right away, with extra lemon and hot pepper seasoning as desired.

100 CALORIES PER SERVING
0 G FAT
0 G SATURATED FAT
0 MG CHOLESTEROL
20 G CARBOHYDRATES
6 G PROTEIN
131 MG SODIUM

Minestra alla Pomodori

MINT-SCENTED TOMATO BROTH WITH DICED CHEESE

Serves 4

From the Italian island of Lipari comes this soup of summer.

Halloumi is the cheese I use in this clear, savory soup, as it keeps its shape and softens but doesn't melt into the soup the way other cheeses might. Unfortunately, it's quite salty. Monterey Jack is a good substitute, although slightly characterless and tending to melt into a soft puddle at the bottom of the bowl. Fresh mozzarella is good, although it can string mercilessly.

2 garlic cloves, chopped

2 tablespoons olive oil

1 cup diced tomatoes (either fresh or canned)

3 cups low-sodium chicken or vegetable broth/stock

1/4 to 1/2 teaspoon dried mint or 2 to 3 teaspoons chopped fresh mint
Salt (if needed) and pepper to taste

2 to 3 ounces *halloumi* or other firm but fresh white cheese, diced

Warm the garlic in olive oil until it begins to turn golden, then add the tomatoes and cook a few minutes.

Pour in the broth/stock and bring to boil. Cook over medium heat for 5 to 10 minutes or until the soup becomes flavorful, then season with mint and taste for salt and pepper.

Place a spoonful or two of diced cheese into each bowl, then ladle in the hot soup. Serve right away.

141 CALORIES PER SERVING
11 G FAT
4 G SATURATED FAT
13 MG CHOLESTEROL
5 G CARBOHYDRATES
6 G PROTEIN
149 MG SODIUM

116

Minestra alla Zucchini

ITALIAN ZUCCHINI SOUP WITH PASTA AND FRESH HERBS

Serves 4

A small splash of dry white wine added to this simple little soup gives a subtle smoothness and added complexity.

- 4 cups low-sodium chicken or vegetable broth/stock
- $^1/_2$ cup dry white wine
- 1 teaspoon chopped fresh marjoram or rosemary
- 1 pound zucchini, sliced
- 3 ounces pasta such as penne or other macaroni shapes
- 3 garlic cloves, chopped
- 1 to 2 tablespoons olive oil
   Hot pepper flakes to taste
- 2 to 3 tablespoons thinly sliced fresh basil
   Grated cheese, such as Asiago or Romano, for sprinkling

Heat the broth/stock with white wine, marjoram or rosemary, and zucchini. Cook until the zucchini is tender, about 10 minutes.

Meanwhile, cook the pasta until it is *al dente,* then drain and set aside.

Warm the garlic in olive oil until fragrant and lightly golden, then sprinkle in the hot pepper flakes.

Just before serving pour the garlic–hot pepper oil into the soup and serve ladled over drained pasta, topped with a sprinkling of basil and grated cheese.

---

151 CALORIES PER SERVING
4 G FAT
1 G SATURATED FAT
0 MG CHOLESTEROL
22 G CARBOHYDRATES
6 G PROTEIN
95 MG SODIUM

Minestra di Fave e Pasta

FRESH FAVA BEAN BROTH WITH DITALINI PASTA AND AGED GOAT CHEESE

Serves 4

Fava beans are quintessential Mediterranean fare: when very young they are eaten raw as a *tapa* or *meze;* when a bit more mature, they are stirred into risotti, pastas, soups, and stews.

Many people lack the enzyme to digest fava beans, and some may even be allergic to the little legumes; so first-time tasters should have only a small portion.

For the most delicious, digestible fava beans, they should be double-peeled. This means that not only must they be removed from their pods, but the tough skin enclosing each bean must be stripped away. How long this soup takes to make, therefore, depends on how quickly you can peel the little favas. Allow extra time (possibly a great deal of time) if you are a neophyte.

Young tender lima beans, either fresh or frozen, may be used in place of fava beans, as can young peas or diced asparagus.

2 cups raw fresh young favas, shelled
4 to 6 ounces ditalini or other small macaroni pasta
1 small onion or 5 to 7 shallots, chopped
5 garlic cloves, chopped
3 to 5 tablespoons olive oil
2 tablespoons chopped fresh parsley
6 cups low-sodium chicken or vegetable broth/stock
Salt and pepper to taste
Grated cheese, preferably a dry goat cheese such as a Sardinian pecorino or an aged California goat cheese

Blanch the fava beans for 1 to 2 minutes, then drain. When they are still warm but cool enough to handle, peel.

Meanwhile, cook the pasta. Drain and set aside.

Sauté the onion or shallots with half the garlic in olive oil until the onion is softened, then sprinkle in the parsley and peeled favas and cook a few moments together.

118

Add the broth/stock and bring to boil, then simmer for 5 minutes or so until the favas are tender and the soup is flavorful. Add the remaining garlic and season with salt and pepper.

Add the pasta to the soup and heat it through, then ladle it into bowls and sprinkle with grated goat cheese.

263 CALORIES PER SERVING
11 G FAT
1 G SATURATED FAT
0 MG CHOLESTEROL
32 G CARBOHYDRATES
10 G PROTEIN
156 MG SODIUM

Minestra alla Giardino

YELLOW AND GREEN BEANS IN BROTH WITH TUBETTI

Serves 4

Tender yellow and green beans simmer with little pastas, cooked *al dente,* in a rosemary-scented broth with lots of diced vegetables. The last-minute flavoring of garlic warmed in olive oil adds another layer of flavor to what otherwise is a simple little soup.

4 cups low-sodium chicken or vegetable broth/stock
6 garlic cloves (5 sliced and 1 chopped)
1 small carrot, diced
1 celery stalk, chopped
3 medium-size tomatoes, diced
3 to 5 ounces tubetti pasta or small seashells
1/4 pound tender young green beans, trimmed and cut into bite-size pieces
1/4 pound yellow beans, trimmed and cut into bite-size pieces
1 teaspoon chopped fresh rosemary
2 to 3 tablespoons olive oil
Salt and pepper

Combine the broth/stock with the 5 cloves of sliced garlic, carrot, celery, and tomatoes and bring to a boil. Cook over medium heat for about 10 minutes or until the carrot is tender and the soup is fragrant.

Meanwhile, cook the pasta. Drain and set aside.

Add the green beans, yellow beans, and rosemary to the soup and cook for about 5 minutes or until the beans are just tender.

Add the 1 chopped garlic clove and olive oil and mix well, then add the drained pasta to the soup and serve.

191 CALORIES PER SERVING
8 G FAT
1 G SATURATED FAT
0 MG CHOLESTEROL
26 G CARBOHYDRATES
6 G PROTEIN
114 MG SODIUM

Sopa Roja

PURÉE OF RED BELL PEPPER AND TOMATO

Serves 4

This Spanish soup is the essence of red pepper and tomatoes, a brilliant orange-colored purée full of bright clear flavor.

Prepare on a day of melting heat, since this delicious soup is not very demanding to make. Bread thickens the soup, in the ancient tradition that the Moors brought to Spain.

- ½ onion, chopped
- 2 red peppers, seeded and diced
- 4 or 5 tomatoes (either ripe or canned), diced; reserve the juice
- 1 to 2 tablespoons olive oil
- 5 garlic cloves, chopped
- 2 slices country or rustic bread (2 to 3 ounces), cut or broken into 1½-inch cubes
- 1 cup dry white wine
- 2 cups low-sodium chicken or vegetable broth/stock
  Salt and pepper to taste
- 4 ounces sour cream (lowfat or nonfat is fine) or Greek yogurt
- 1 to 2 teaspoons fresh chopped marjoram or oregano

Lightly sauté the onion and red peppers (and tomatoes, if using fresh) in the olive oil with half the garlic, cooking until softened, then add the bread and continue cooking about 5 minutes longer.

Add the wine and broth/stock (and tomatoes, if using canned), bring to a boil, then simmer for 10 to 15 minutes or until the vegetables and bread are quite soft and the alcohol in the wine has evaporated and lost its harshness.

Purée, season with salt and pepper, then serve in bowls, each serving garnished with a dollop of sour cream or Greek yogurt and marjoram or oregano.

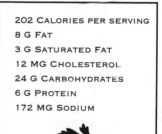

202 CALORIES PER SERVING
8 G FAT
3 G SATURATED FAT
12 MG CHOLESTEROL
24 G CARBOHYDRATES
6 G PROTEIN
172 MG SODIUM

Sopa de Tomate con Higos or Oliaigua amb Tomatics

TOMATO AND FIG SOUP WITH ORANGE JUICE AND GRAPES

Serves 6

To appreciate this luscious Minorcan soup, you must prepare it with ripe, sweet-tart tomatoes, preferably freshly picked organic ones. The figs must be sweet and soft enough to nearly melt on your tongue, and the grapes should be crisp and juicy. And you must eat it sitting in a garden at the end of summer when the days are still very hot, letting its refreshment cool you as you spoon it up. Traditionally in Minorca a chunk of salty cheese is eaten alongside.

We ate this the first evening we arrived on the Balearic island of Ibiza. Our friend Paul prepared it from his garden tomatoes, oranges, and grapes—we contributed the figs, which we'd picked on the drive from the airport, stopping the car and jumping out for a quick raid of the roadside trees. It was winter already in London; we had turned on our heating and donned double layers of sweaters and socks. Now here we were sitting in a vineyard, surrounded by luscious growing fruit.

I've since made it in California during an Indian Summer heat wave, and it was equally good.

1/2	stale baguette or other country French bread, thickly sliced
1	medium or 1/2 large onion, chopped
5	garlic cloves, chopped
3	to 4 tablespoons olive oil
2	bay leaves
1	to 1 1/2 teaspoons paprika
	Generous pinch of cayenne or other hot seasoning such as hot paprika or red pepper flakes
3	pounds ripe tomatoes, diced
1	tablespoon or more sugar
1	cup orange juice, or to taste
3	cups low-sodium chicken or vegetable stock
	Salt, pepper, and sugar to taste
12	to 16 ripe sweet figs, sliced
20	to 30 seedless grapes, sliced into halves

Prepare the toast: place the sliced stale bread on a baking sheet and bake at 350°F or until just lightly golden. If the bread is very stale, do not bother toasting; use as is.

Lightly sauté the onions and half the garlic in 2 tablespoons of the olive oil; when the onions are softened, add the bay leaves, paprika, cayenne or other hot seasoning, tomatoes, and sugar. Cook over medium heat until the tomatoes grow saucelike and reduce in volume to about 2 to 3 cups, 15 to 20 minutes.

Add half the orange juice and the stock, and cook over medium heat until a flavorful soup forms, another 10 to 15 minutes.

Add the remaining garlic and orange juice to the soup; season with salt, pepper, and sugar.

Ladle the hot soup into bowls and place a piece of stale bread on top of each. Drizzle with olive oil, then scatter several slices of figs and grapes around the soup. Eat at once.

321 CALORIES PER SERVING
9 G FAT
1 G SATURATED FAT
0 MG CHOLESTEROL
56 G CARBOHYDRATES
7 G PROTEIN
268 MG SODIUM

Soupe à l'Ail

GARLIC SOUP WITH COUSCOUS FROM THE SOUTH OF FRANCE

Serves 4 to 6

Garlic soup is beloved along the Mediterranean coastline of Spain and France, at times no more than a bowl of water simmered with a head of garlic, at other times an elegant concoction of garlic, cream, stock, and herbs. It occupies the position of all-purpose tonic that chicken soup holds in eastern European Jewish culture: it cures everything. In fact, there is a saying in Provence, "Aigo bouido sauva la vido," or "Garlic soup will save your life."

The double dose of garlic in this soup is a combination of simmered mild garlic and the fragrant hot flash of fresh raw garlic pounded to a paste and added at the last minute. If you have a rind left over from grating Parmesan cheese, now is a good time to use it: toss it into the stock when you cook the garlic—it adds a gentle, rich, soft edge to the soup.

12 garlic cloves, peeled and coarsely cut up
6 cups vegetable broth (thinned with water, or bouillon cube mixed with water)
Pinch dried *herbes de Provence* or several leaves of fresh sage, a sprig of rosemary, and a few sprigs of thyme
1 teaspoon salt
2 to 3 tablespoons olive oil
1/4 cup dried instant couscous
1/4 to 1/2 cup freshly grated Parmesan cheese
Salt and black or red pepper to taste

Combine 8 garlic cloves with broth and herbs in a saucepan and bring to a boil. Cook over medium-high heat until the garlic is softened, about 10 minutes.

Meanwhile, crush the remaining garlic with salt, using a mortar and pestle or food processor (a mortar and pestle will release more of the garlic's fragrant oils). When the garlic becomes pastelike, stir in 1 tablespoon

124

When the garlic becomes pastelike, stir in 1 tablespoon of olive oil. Set aside.

Stir the couscous into the hot soup, stirring a few minutes until it is tender and the liquid thickens slightly, then stir in the Parmesan cheese and a small amount of the garlic–olive oil paste, to taste, adding more or less as you desire. Season with salt and black or red pepper, as desired. Stir in remaining olive oil and serve right away.

108 CALORIES PER SERVING
6 G FAT
1 G SATURATED FAT
3 MG CHOLESTEROL
10 G CARBOHYDRATES
5 G PROTEIN
508 MG SODIUM

Aromatiki Soupa

GREEK ISLAND YELLOW SPLIT PEA SOUP

Serves 6 or more

My first winter in Europe was spent on the Greek Mediterranean island of Crete. When summer's warmth and colorful vegetables disappeared from the market—where had the eggplants, zucchini, and tomatoes gone?—cold weather vegetables such as celery root, carrots, and potatoes and dried legumes such as lentils, split peas, and beans took their place. Often they were simmered into hearty soups, such as this one, seasoned with Mediterranean herbs and spices.

A trick for a stronger, fuller cumin flavor was shown to me by the village spice seller: start with cumin seeds rather than ground cumin; lightly toast the seeds in an ungreased heavy skillet until they turn slightly darker and smell very strong and delicious. Remove from the pan and crush; these days I use a mortar and pestle, although the spice-shop man used an empty wine bottle turned onto its side. Freshly ground and toasted cumin seeds smell and taste gorgeous.

> 1 onion, chopped
> 1 carrot, chopped
> ½ celery root, peeled and diced, plus several tablespoons of celery leaves, chopped
> 2 tablespoons olive oil
> 2 bay leaves
> 1 teaspoon cumin
> ¼ to ½ teaspoon dried sage
> 1 to 1½ cups split peas (yellow, green, or a combination of both)
> 1½ quarts vegetable stock
> 6 garlic cloves, coarsely cut up
> Large pinch of cayenne pepper
> *To serve:* Crisp homemade garlic croutons

Lightly sauté the onion, carrot, and celery root in the olive oil until the onion is soft, then add the bay leaves, cumin, sage, and split peas. Stir a moment to two, then add the stock, garlic, and cayenne.

Simmer for 1 to 2 hours; taste for seasoning and serve with crisp croutons, if desired.

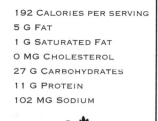

192 Calories per serving
5 g Fat
1 g Saturated Fat
0 mg Cholesterol
27 g Carbohydrates
11 g Protein
102 mg Sodium

Sopa de Ajo Castellana

CASTILIAN GARLIC SOUP THICKENED WITH RYE FLATBREAD

Serves 4 to 6

Garlic soup is eaten by nearly everyone in Spain, in a myriad of guises; for many it is the soup that grandmothers make to comfort and nourish or the soup a harried mother makes when little else is on the shelf. Garlic soup often incorporates small amounts of seasonal vegetables; it may be chunky or smooth, a thin savory broth, or a thick soup rich with beaten egg and/or cheese, crushed bread, or pounded nuts.

This soup is a russet-hued bowlful: it's soft yet spicy, with a velvety consistency that comes from frying garlic and bread together and using that to thicken the soup.

But when I prepared this I had only a small amount of bread and added several crisp rye cracker-like flatbreads instead. Their grainy-dark goodness gave added depth to the soup; if you don't have any on hand, a similar result could be achieved by using whole wheat peasant bread or by adding a slice of wheatberry bread to the country bread in its place.

10 garlic cloves, peeled and lightly crushed, then sliced
2 to 3 tablespoons olive oil
2 to 3 ounces country bread, cut into croutons or small pieces
3 crisp rye flatbread crackers, such as Rye Crisp, preferably made only with coarse rye flour and water; or wheatberry, seven-grain, or whole wheat country bread
1 quart low-sodium chicken or vegetable broth
Salt and pepper
1/2 to 1 teaspoon paprika
1/2 to 3/4 cup dry to medium dry sherry
1/2 to 1 teaspoon vinegar (red wine or sherry)
Hot pepper seasoning such as Tabasco or Cuaca
Garnish: Several pinches of cumin

Lightly cook the garlic in olive oil until the garlic is just golden, then remove the garlic from the oil.

Cook the bread and rye crackers in the oil, until the bread is golden and lightly crisped.

Add the broth, salt and pepper, paprika, half the sherry, vinegar, and the reserved garlic. Bring to a boil, then reduce the heat and simmer for 10 minutes or until the bread is somewhat dissolved and the crackers are very soft and in small pieces.

Purée with the remaining sherry, then adjust the seasoning and add hot pepper seasoning to taste.

Reheat and serve hot, each portion sprinkled with cumin.

153 CALORIES PER SERVING
5 G FAT
1 G SATURATED FAT
0 MG CHOLESTEROL
17 G CARBOHYDRATES
4 G PROTEIN
182 MG SODIUM

Tomato, Barley, and Red Lentil Soup with Preserved Lemon and Mint from Al-Maghreb

Serves 4

This North African soup is amazingly easy to prepare, but the sweetly scented lemon adds an unusual and marvelous twist to the simple grain and legume soup.

Cooking the barley and lentils apart from the rest of the ingredients keeps the soup from becoming murky, and lets you add as much of the barley-lentil mixture as you like (save the rest for stews, casseroles, and other soups, or freeze it).

Diced summer vegetables, such as zucchini or yellow crookneck squash, make a delicious addition to this soup, too. If you've no preserved lemon, substitute the grated zest and de-seeded diced flesh of half a lemon.

$^1/_2$ cup barley
$^1/_2$ cup red lentils
 4 garlic cloves, chopped
 2 stalks celery, chopped
 1 to 2 tablespoons olive oil
$1^1/_2$ cups diced tomatoes (fresh or canned); reserve the juice
$1^1/_2$ quarts low-sodium chicken or vegetable stock
$^1/_4$ teaspoon or several large pinches dried mint, crumbled
$^1/_2$ preserved lemon, diced; reserve 2 to 3 tablespoons of the liquid
 Optional: Juice of 1 lemon
 Salt and a small dash cayenne pepper or Tabasco sauce to taste

Combine the barley and red lentils in a saucepan with water to cover by about an inch. Bring it to a boil, then reduce the heat and simmer, covered, until the barley is just tender and the red lentils have softened or melted into the broth. Add a little extra water if needed during cooking to keep the barley and lentils from burning. The barley should cook in about 40 minutes; check the package instructions to confirm this or to see if they need soaking. Different types of barley will need different treatments.

Lightly sauté the garlic and celery in the olive oil for a few moments, then add the tomatoes and cook about 5 minutes. Add the reserved barley-lentil mixture, the stock, mint, and preserved lemon.

Cook over medium-low heat for 15 to 20 minutes or until the flavors have melded together. Season with the liquid from the preserved lemon (or fresh lemon juice) and a dash of salt and cayenne pepper or Tabasco sauce to taste and extra mint, if desired. Serve right away.

VARIATION

North African Soup with Squash
Add 1 or 2 diced summer squash such as zucchini or yellow crookneck during the last 15 minutes of cooking.

191 CALORIES PER SERVING
4 G FAT
1 G SATURATED FAT
0 MG CHOLESTEROL
32 G CARBOHYDRATES
10 G PROTEIN
715 MG SODIUM

COLD SOUPS

During the sultry summer season in the Mediterranean, when the idea of eating steamy hot food is singularly unappealing, the refreshment of cool, chilled soups is deliciously welcoming.

Throughout the lands that touch the sea there are a variety of cold soups, some rough and simple (more like liquidy salads), others smooth and sophisticated.

Gazpacho, of course, is the dish that first comes to mind when we think of Mediterranean cold soups, or indeed any cold soup at all. On hot days, one sees Spanish farmworkers in the fields, sheltered under the shade of a cooling tree, drinking great bowls of gazpacho to replenish their vitality.

But gazpacho is not just one definitive soup—it is a whole genre of cold salady soups, embracing a wide variety of flavors, textures, and ingredients, depending on regions and tastes. Gazpacho can be creamy or sharp, slightly sweet with grapes and almonds, or mysteriously Arabian with the Moorish souvenir of cumin. And while gazpachos are traditionally made with tomatoes, peppers, and cucumbers, there are gazpachos, like the Andalucian *salmorejo,* that are thick with diced hard-cooked egg and lots of bread, and gazpachos that are light and brothy. Gazpachos might be based on dried beans, avocado, or zucchini, or be bright red from peppers, like the Andalucian gazpacho known as *zoque.*

Usually, however, gazpachos don't have much in the way of fresh herbs since in the heat of summer most fresh herbs cease to thrive. The exceptions are cilantro, parsley, mint, as well as shoots of green garlic, which are all occasionally pounded into the cooling soups of summer.

Although we chill gazpacho in our modern refrigerators, its big chill traditionally came from standing all night in the cellar (*bodega*) on a cold stone floor or by diluting the soup with cool, cool water hauled up from a deep well.

⚘ Zoque

RED GAZPACHO MADE FROM TOMATO AND PEPPER

Serves 4 to 6

This Andalusian cold soup revitalizes, with its taste of robust garlic, peppers, and tomatoes awash in spicy broth. Although not traditional, I like to add a few small ice cubes to melt in. Cold ice water may be added instead.

5 garlic cloves, chopped
  Pinch salt
1 red bell pepper
2 ripe tomatoes
2 slices (2 ounces) French bread, crusts removed
2 to 3 tablespoons sherry vinegar
  Small pinch cumin
  Generous seasoning of salt to taste
  Dash cayenne pepper or Tabasco
2 tablespoons olive oil
1 quart low-sodium chicken or vegetable broth/stock
  Garnish: 2 tablespoons chopped fresh cilantro

Purée the garlic with a pinch of salt, then add the pepper, tomatoes, and bread, puréeing or pounding until the mixture takes on a coarse, uneven texture. You do not want a smooth purée, rather bits and chunks in a smooth broth.

Mix in the vinegar, cumin, salt, and cayenne or Tabasco, then stir in the olive oil and add to the stock/broth. Chill the soup until you are ready to serve.

Before serving, adjust the seasoning—gazpacho takes quite a bit of salt—and serve with ice cubes or icy water added and cilantro sprinkled on top.

92 CALORIES PER SERVING
5 G FAT
1 G SATURATED FAT
0 MG CHOLESTEROL
10 G CARBOHYDRATES
3 G PROTEIN
137 MG SODIUM

~~ Schlada

CHILLED ROASTED GREEN PEPPER AND TOMATO SOUP

Serves 4

This cold, salad-like Moroccan soup, some say the precursor to gazpacho, is cooling on a summer's day. Like a true gazpacho, there are no herbs in it, just pounded vegetables. I find it more flavorful to pound the garlic and peppers in a mortar and pestle—although more work, the pounding brings out garlic's strong flavor and presses out the juices from the peppers in a more aesthetic way than does the even chopping of a food processor.

If you don't feel like making soup, omit the stock and you can serve this as a sort of soupy, salady dip with crusty bread to soak up the juices.

2 or 3 garlic cloves, peeled and coarsely chopped
  Several pinches salt
2 roasted green peppers, stems, seeds, and peels removed
1 cup diced tomatoes
$^1/_2$ cup tomato juice (or substitute 1$^1/_4$ cup diced canned tomatoes plus their juice for the diced tomatoes and tomato juice)
3 cups low-sodium chicken or vegetable stock
  Pinch to $^1/_4$ teaspoon cumin
  Juice of $^1/_2$ lemon, or to taste
1 tablespoon olive oil
  Several shakes hot pepper seasoning
$^1/_2$ cucumber, preferably a European cucumber, diced (if using an American cucumber, peel and seed before dicing)
8 small ice cubes or break several large ice cubes into pieces

Purée the garlic with the salt, then unevenly chop and pound the peppers with the garlic. You'll want to extract quite a bit of the juice, leaving small to medium-size pepper bits with a salad-like consistency.

Pound the tomato to an equally rough texture, then combine the peppers, tomatoes, tomato juice, stock, cumin, lemon juice, olive oil, and hot pepper seasoning and mix well. Next, stir in the cucumber. Adjust the seasoning with salt and hot pepper.

Serve each bowl with an ice cube or two floating in it.

76 CALORIES PER SERVING
4 G FAT
0 G SATURATED FAT
0 MG CHOLESTEROL
10 G CARBOHYDRATES
3 G PROTEIN
181 MG SODIUM

Gazpacho Blanco de Malagueño

WHITE ALMOND AND FRUIT GAZPACHO

Serves 4 to 6

Perfumed with garlic and the sweetness of almond, an echo of fruitiness from apples, grapes, and cucumber—this cold soup may sound unlikely, but spoon after cooling spoon it is utter refreshment.

While apples are not often thought of as Mediterranean fruit, they do grow in the area. I especially like the Golden Delicious variety in this soup, as I think its flavor enhances that of the almonds.

$1/4$ cup untoasted almonds, slivered, blanched, peeled
3 garlic cloves
4 tablespoons olive oil
A few drops almond extract or essence
Juice of $1 1/2$ lemons, plus extra to taste
1 slice white bread (preferably Spanish, French, or Italian country bread), crusts removed
2 cups cold vegetable stock (water mixed with a bouillon cube, heated and cooled is fine)
1 cup apple or white grape juice
2 sweet flavorful apples, cored and diced (peeled if desired)
$1/2$ European cucumber, diced
Salt and pepper as needed
Several large pinches dried mint

186 CALORIES PER SERVING
12 G FAT
2 G SATURATED FAT
0 MG CHOLESTEROL
19 G CARBOHYDRATES
3 G PROTEIN
60 MG SODIUM

Crush the almonds in a mortar and pestle or food processor, then add the garlic and crush them together; add the olive oil, almond extract, and lemon juice and mix until it forms a paste.

Pour cold water to cover over the bread, let it sit a few minutes, then squeeze and add to the almond mixture and purée together. Add the stock, juice, half the apples, and half the cucumber and whirl to combine.

Chill until ready to serve. Enjoy sprinkled with the remaining apples and cucumbers.

La Soupe Froide aux Courgettes

CHILLED ZUCCHINI-LEEK BISQUE WITH BASIL AND LEMON

Serves 6

In France's sultry south, along its long Mediterranean coast, chic little cold soups are whipped up with summer's vegetables; I sampled this one in Cannes. The soup is subtle and creamy, but enriched only with a bit of milk and much lighter than it tastes. The lemon gives it added refreshment, and the basil imparts its distinctive sweet perfume.

What made this soup even more delicious was something you won't find in any California restaurant regardless of how chic or how good the food: a poodle sat next to me. I couldn't ask for more.

3 leeks, cleaned and thinly sliced
2 tablespoons butter or olive oil
2 zucchini, diced
3 cups low-sodium chicken or vegetable stock
3 garlic cloves, coarsely chopped
1 cup milk
1½ lemons, one for squeezing, half sliced thin for garnish
2 teaspoons (approximately) thinly sliced basil, preferably small-leaf basil

Lightly sauté the leeks in butter or olive oil unti softened, then add the zucchini and stock. Bring to a boil, then reduce the heat and cook until the vegetables are tender. Remove from the heat and add the garlic.

Blend in the milk, then chill until ready to serve.

When the soup is very cold, squeeze in the lemon, and serve each bowl with a slice or two of lemon, a sprinkling of basil, and an ice cube or two.

93 CALORIES PER SERVING
5 G FAT
3 G SATURATED FAT
14 MG CHOLESTEROL
10 G CARBOHYDRATES
4 G PROTEIN
112 MG SODIUM

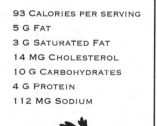

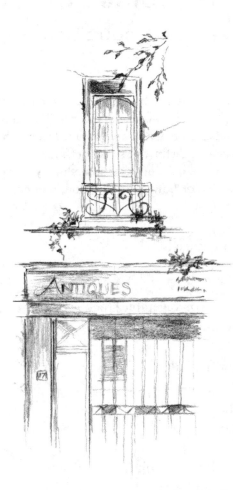

FOUR

PASTA, RICE, POLENTA, AND COUSCOUS

PENNE ALLA PASTORA, *Pasta Quills with Ricotta and Feta, Scattered with Young Arugula*

MEZZALUNA, *Cheese-Filled Pasta with Tomato Sauce and Fresh Basil*

FETTUCINE AL LIMON CON ZUCCHINI, PISELLI, ASPARAGI, E SPINACI, *Lemon-Scented Ribbons of Pasta with Zucchini, Peas, Asparagus, and Spinach*

CONCHIGLIE E ZUCCHINI, *Seashell Pasta with Thinly Sliced Browned Zucchini and Basil-Tomato Sauce*

MACARONIA ME ELIES KE SALTSA DOMATAS, *Pasta with Green Olive Paste and Tomato Sauce*

SPAGHETTI ALLA POMODORI, FAGIOLINI, E FORMAGGIO DI CAPRA, *Spaghetti with Double Tomato Sauce and Romano Beans, Garlic Oil, and Goat Cheese*

PANZEROTTI CON ZUCCHINI E NOCI, *Mushroom Ravioli with Zucchini, Ricotta, and Walnuts*

FREGULA CON ZUCCHINI E AGLIO, *Sardinian Couscous with Zucchini and Garlic Butter*

PASTA AL'AGLIO CON LENTICCHE, *Spicy Lentil Pasta with Garlic and Parsley*

CAPPELLINI CON BROCOLI E RUCOLA, *Angel Hair Pasta with Broccoli, Arugula, and Hot Pepper–Garlic Oil*

MACARONI À LA MAROCAINE

ORZO ME SPANAKI KE SALTSA DOMATAS, *Greek Orzo with Cinnamon-Scented Tomatoes, Spinach, and Feta*

SPAGHETTI ACCIURATA, *Spaghetti with Black Olives, Rosemary, Goat Cheese, and Hot Pepper*

SPAGHETTI ALLA CARCIOFI, *Spaghetti with Artichoke Pesto*

ORZO ME TYRA, *Greek Island Orzo with Lemon-Garlic Butter and Feta Cheese*

WHEAT for making bread, pasta, and couscous has been a staple of the Mediterranean diet for centuries. Combined with fresh things from the garden, the always present olive oil, fragrant garlic and herbs, preserved condiments, and bits of rich or strong-flavored cheeses, wheat is the mainstay of cuisine in the Mediterranean today as well.

There is, of course, not enough room to share all of the marvelous pasta, rice, and couscous dishes so beloved in the Mediterranean. The following are only a handful. See Chapter 3 for soup recipes that feature pasta and couscous, and for delectable brown rice-stuffed vine leaves refer to Chapter 1.

Penne alla Pastora

PASTA QUILLS WITH RICOTTA AND FETA, SCATTERED WITH YOUNG ARUGULA

Serves 4 to 6

The phrase *alla pastora* refers to the countryside and to dishes of simple countryside foods, such as this one of hot pasta tossed with milky fresh cheese and a handful of greens.

The combination of ricotta and feta approximates the fresh cheese that you might find in Sicily. Serve with a plate of black olives and a salad of ripe tomatoes and sweet basil.

12 ounces ricotta cheese
 3 garlic cloves, finely chopped
 6 to 8 ounces feta cheese, crumbled
 1 teaspoon or a generous sprinkling of dried mixed
    herbs such as *herbes de Provence*
 3 tablespoons olive oil, more if needed
 1 pound penne pasta
20 to 25 oil-cured black olives, pitted and diced
    Salt and pepper to taste
 2 tablespoons chopped parsley, preferably Italian
    flat leaf

Mix the ricotta, garlic, feta, herbs, and about half the olive oil. Set it aside while you cook the pasta.

Cook the penne until *al dente,* then drain.

Toss the hot drained pasta with the cheese mixture, then add the remaining olive oil, black olives, and salt and pepper to taste.

Serve right away, sprinkled with parsley.

481 CALORIES PER SERVING
18 G FAT
7 G SATURATED FAT
33 MG CHOLESTEROL
59 G CARBOHYDRATES
19 G PROTEIN
787 MG SODIUM

❧ Mezzaluna

CHEESE-FILLED PASTA WITH TOMATO SAUCE AND FRESH BASIL

Serves 4

Mezzaluna means half-moons, for the half-moon shapes of these pasta. Preparing *messaluna* using fresh Asian pasta may not seem very Mediterranean, but it results in a very tender and delicate dish—and it's so easy to make.

I ate these seductive little morsels in Naples and was reminded of the myth of the sirens, those beautiful mermaids who used music to lure sailors to their deaths. One of the sirens was Parthenope—who, poor soul, had a taste of her own tunes and drowned. It is told that her body washed up on the most beautiful place on the Italian coast; on that site Naples was later built. It is said that this tale explains why Naples is at once so beautiful, so seductive, and so very dangerous.

But it explains nothing about these delicious pastas: filled with ricotta cheese and sauced with tomatoes, they are food from the soul of the *mezzorgiorno,* Italy's sun-drenched south.

Note: *Gyoza* are Japanese pasta rounds. Along with wonton noodles, they make a delicious, extremely easy alternative to making your own pasta.

> 12 ounces ricotta cheese
> ³/4 cup grated cheese such as Parmesan or Romano
> 1 egg, lightly beaten
> Pinch nutmeg
> Salt and pepper to taste
> 12 ounces *gyoza* wrappers, wonton wrappers, or fresh pasta rounds, about 4 to 6 inches in diameter
> 2 cups diced tomatoes (fresh or canned); reserve the juice
> ¹/2 cup tomato juice
> 3 garlic cloves, chopped
> Handful of basil leaves, torn or lightly crushed
> 2 to 3 tablespoons olive oil

Heat the oven to 375°F.

Combine the ricotta cheese with half the Parmesan or Romano; mix well with the egg and season with nutmeg, salt, and pepper.

Place a tablespoon or so in the center of each pasta round; brush the edges with water, then fold over and press together to seal. Place in a single layer in a large flat gratin dish.

Combine the tomatoes with the tomato juice, garlic, and half the basil, then spoon over the pasta. Sprinkle with reserved Parmesan or Romano, drizzle with olive oil, and cover with foil.

Bake for 35 minutes or long enough for the pasta to cook through. About halfway through, test to see if the pasta is succulent enough; if not, add a little water or tomato juice.

Serve hot, sprinkled with remaining basil.

317 CALORIES PER SERVING
14 G FAT
5 G SATURATED FAT
71 MG CHOLESTEROL
33 G CARBOHYDRATES
18 G PROTEIN
608 MG SODIUM

Fettucine al Limon con Zucchini, Piselli, Asparagi, e Spinaci

LEMON-SCENTED RIBBONS OF PASTA WITH ZUCCHINI, PEAS, ASPARAGUS, AND SPINACH

Serves 4 to 6

This pasta is consummately refreshing, the tart squirt of lemon and array of fresh vegetables balancing the richness of a dab of butter.

Inspired by a pasta dish I ate in Amalfi, a stretch of the Italian coast that is known for its superb lemons, it makes a delightful first course on a warm summer's evening with a plate of grilled vegetables to follow. Any green spring vegetable is delicious in this instead of or in addition to the ones in the recipe—artichokes are particularly nice.

Spaghetti may be used in place of fettucine, and I think that cappellini (angel hair pasta) would be very nice, too.

8 garlic cloves, finely chopped or crushed
3 tablespoons butter
2 tablespoons olive oil
1/2 cup dry white wine or broth/stock
    The finely grated zest and squeezed juice of
    1 1/2 lemons
1 pound fettucine
8 to 10 asparagus stalks, cut into small, bite-size lengths
1/2 cup tiny peas, fresh or frozen and defrosted
2 small zucchini, thinly sliced
4 or 5 spinach leaves, cooked, squeezed, and chopped
1/4 cup chopped chives
1/4 cup grated Parmesan cheese, or to taste

Heat 6 cloves of garlic in half of the butter and 1 tablespoon of the oil; cook until fragrant but not browned, then add wine or stock and cook until it reduces by about half. Add the lemon zest and lemon juice and set aside while you cook the pasta.

144

Cook the fettucine in rapidly boiling salted water.

When the pasta is half cooked, add the asparagus, peas, zucchini, and spinach, and continue to cook the mixture until the pasta is *al dente* and the vegetables are just tender.

Drain the pasta and vegetables and toss with the sauce, remaining garlic, remaining butter, chives, and about ⅔ of the cheese. Serve right away, each portion drizzled with the remaining olive oil and sprinkled with the remaining cheese.

409 CALORIES PER SERVING
13 G FAT
5 G SATURATED FAT
19 MG CHOLESTEROL
60 G CARBOHYDRATES
13 G PROTEIN
134 MG SODIUM

Conchiglie e Zucchini

SEASHELL PASTA WITH THINLY SLICED BROWNED ZUCCHINI AND BASIL-TOMATO SAUCE

Serves 4 to 6

From the tip of Italy's boot to the northern reaches of the Ligurian coast, when it's zucchini season you can expect to find it in your pasta. Here the scent of basil perfuming the sauce reminds me of Liguria, where you can scarcely pass a windowsill in the summer without being engulfed in the scent of basil, growing from nearly every windowsill pot.

4 small to medium-size zucchini, thinly sliced
3 tablespoons olive oil, or as desired
3 garlic cloves, chopped
    Salt to taste
1 medium-size or 2 small to medium-size onions, chopped
2 cups diced tomatoes
1 tin tomato paste, about 2½ ounces
    Sugar to taste, if needed to balance the acidity of the tomatoes
    About ¼ cup fresh basil leaves, whole
    Optional: 3 tablespoons dry white wine
1 pound seashells or *gnochetti*
3 to 4 tablespoons freshly grated Parmesan (or similar) cheese

Sauté the zucchini quickly in 1 tablespoon olive oil until the zucchini is golden and lightly browned, but still fairly firm. Remove from the pan and add 1 garlic clove and salt to taste. Set this aside.

Lightly sauté the onion with the second clove of garlic in a tablespoon or so olive oil until the onion is softened, then add the tomatoes and cook over medium-high heat until saucelike but still fairly thin.

Add the tomato paste, sugar to taste if needed, and several sprigs of fresh basil, crushing it with a spoon to release its fragrance. Continue to simmer over low heat while you cook the pasta. If the mixture is too thick, add a few tablespoons of dry white wine and continue to cook.

Cook the pasta until it is *al dente,* then drain. Toss the hot drained pasta with the remaining olive oil.

Add the remaining garlic and sautéed zucchini to the sauce, then toss with the pasta and cheese. Tear the remaining basil leaves into small pieces and scatter them over the top of the pasta. Serve right away.

381 CALORIES PER SERVING
9 G FAT
2 G SATURATED FAT
2 MG CHOLESTEROL
63 G CARBOHYDRATES
12 G PROTEIN
163 MG SODIUM

Macaronia me Elies Ke Saltsa Domatas

PASTA WITH GREEN OLIVE PASTE AND TOMATO SAUCE

Serves 4 to 6

I'm always surprised at how much the Greeks like pasta, since I usually think of rice pilafs as "Greek." But so, too, is pasta: flat noodles, thick round bucatini-like pastas, and tiny orzo. The basil, however, in this dish is less than traditional—although most front porches and windowsills have a pot of basil growing, it is seldom eaten in food; instead, it is used to ward off flies (a failure in my opinion). But as untraditional as it is, its sweet herbal fragrance is delicious when added to pasta.

The traditional shape for pasta in this dish is a flat noodle, much like tagliatelle, but I've used seashells and gnocchi shapes happily, since the savory green olive paste gets caught up in the little nooks of the pasta.

1 onion, chopped
2 to 3 tablespoons olive oil
6 garlic cloves, chopped
1 pound fresh or canned tomatoes, diced; reserve the juice
1 tablespoon tomato paste
Salt and pepper to taste
Pinch sugar to taste
1 pound pasta of choice: ribbons such as tagliatelle, hollow indented pastas such as elbows or shells, etc.
4 tablespoons green olive paste or 5 to 6 tablespoons finely chopped green olives
1/4 cup (approximately) fresh basil leaves, whole
3 to 5 tablespoons grated cheese such as Kasseri, kefalotyri, or Parmesan
1 lemon, cut into wedges

Lightly sauté the onion in 1 tablespoon olive oil until it is softened, then add half of the garlic and cook a few moments. Add the tomatoes and cook until thickened, about 10 minutes. Stir in the tomato paste and taste for salt, pepper, and sugar.

Cook the pasta until *al dente,* then drain.

Warm the remaining garlic in the remaining olive oil until it becomes fragrant but does not change color. Toss in the pasta and mix well, then add the green olive paste.

Spoon the sauce over the pasta and toss lightly, then with your hands tear up the basil, crushing it lightly with your fingers as you do. Sprinkle the pasta generously with the cheese, then scatter the lightly crushed basil leaves over the pasta and serve right away.

Serve wedges of lemon on the side to squeeze over each plate if so desired.

372 CALORIES PER SERVING
10 G FAT
1 G SATURATED FAT
2 MG CHOLESTEROL
60 G CARBOHYDRATES
11 G PROTEIN
336 MG SODIUM

Spaghetti alla Pomodori, Fagiolini, e Formaggio di Capra

SPAGHETTI WITH DOUBLE TOMATO SAUCE AND ROMANO BEANS, GARLIC OIL, AND GOAT CHEESE

Serves 4 to 6

This makes a lusty dish, full of deliciously strong flavors and perfumes.

4 garlic cloves
  Pinch salt
1/4 cup olive oil
1 onion, diced
1/4 pound green Romano beans, trimmed and cut into bite-size lengths
3 cups diced tomatoes (canned is fine); reserve the juices
  Pinch sugar to taste
  Tiny pinch red chili flakes
1 tablespoon fresh marjoram leaves
4 to 5 tablespoons fresh basil, crushed and thinly sliced or torn
1 pound spaghetti or other pasta with holes and indentations, such as radiatore
4 ounces goat cheese, crumbled
3 tablespoons grated Parmesan or pecorino cheese

Make the garlic oil: place the garlic in a mortar and pestle and sprinkle with salt. Crush until it forms a paste, then slowly add 3 tablespoons of the olive oil. It will make a strongly scented sauce. Set aside.

In the remaining tablespoon of oil sauté the onion until softened, then add the green beans and half of the tomatoes and tomato juice and cook over medium heat until the tomatoes are well reduced and almost pastelike. The green beans should be tender. Season with sugar, chili flakes, and marjoram and set aside.

Cook the pasta until *al dente,* then drain. Toss the pasta with the still-warm tomato sauce, then add the remaining tomatoes and warm a few moments over low heat.

Sprinkle with the basil and mix gently, then serve right away, drizzled with the garlic oil, topped with nuggets of the goat cheese to melt in, and dusted with a blanket of Parmesan or pecorino.

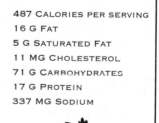

487 CALORIES PER SERVING
16 G FAT
5 G SATURATED FAT
11 MG CHOLESTEROL
71 G CARBOHYDRATES
17 G PROTEIN
337 MG SODIUM

Panzerotti con Zucchini e Noci

MUSHROOM RAVIOLI WITH ZUCCHINI, RICOTTA, AND WALNUTS

Serves 4 greedy eaters or 6 more restrained ones

This traditional ravioli dish, rich with mushrooms and walnuts, is lightened by the addition of zucchini. *Panzerotti* are triangle-shaped filled pastas; ravioli may be used instead.

A classic of the area around Genoa, you'll see the ingredients for it in the shops that line the twisting cobblestoned streets of the old city and smell the basil for it in flower pots that seem to thrive on each and every windowsill in town.

1½ cups walnuts
5 garlic cloves
Pinch salt
½ cup Parmesan cheese; more for passing at table
¼ cup chopped basil
¾ to 1 pound porcini ravioli
1 pound zucchini, thinly sliced
3 tablespoons olive oil
1 cup ricotta cheese
Few drops lemon juice
Salt and pepper to taste

Lightly toast the walnuts until they are fragrant and lightly golden. Remove them from the heat.

Crush the garlic with a pinch of salt; I like a mortar and pestle for this, although a food processor is acceptable. Add the walnuts, then continue to crush until a mealy consistency is achieved; the mixture should be studded with little chunks of walnut. Mix with the Parmesan cheese and basil, then set aside.

Cook the ravioli and zucchini in boiling salted water until both are *al dente,* 4 to 5 minutes.

Drain the pasta and vegetables, reserving a few tablespoons of the cooking water, then toss the hot pasta and zucchini with the olive oil, garlic-walnut-Parmesan-basil mixture, and ricotta, adding a little of the cooking water to keep the dish moist rather than dry and sticky. Add a drop or two of lemon juice, season with salt and pepper, then serve accompanied by extra Parmesan as desired.

513 CALORIES PER SERVING
34 G FAT
7 G SATURATED FAT
40 MG CHOLESTEROL
37 G CARBOHYDRATES
19 G PROTEIN
373 MG SODIUM

Fregula con Zucchini e Aglio

SARDINIAN COUSCOUS WITH ZUCCHINI AND GARLIC BUTTER

Serves 4 to 6

Fregula or *sa fregula* is a Sardinian pasta made of semolina grains rolled into tiny pellets much like couscous. The garlic butter is delicious on this, but you could mix the garlic with olive oil instead of butter.

Fregula is surprisingly easy to make and extremely satisfying to spoon up. The semolina flour is moistened with warm water and rubbed into grains with the fingers, then left to dry. The grains are then separated into large and small grains, a simpler task than it sounds, and each is cooked differently—the larger pellets with sauces and the tiniest grains in light soups. In this dish I've combined small and large grains.

Often the semolina is tinted by the addition of saffron, which adds more color than flavor; I've done the same with turmeric as well, but it is equally good without either.

Once dried, *fregula* lasts in hot dry weather for several weeks.

Optional: 3 pinches saffron threads or turmeric
3/4 to 1 cup boiling water, or more as needed
3 cups semolina flour
1/2 teaspoon salt
4 to 6 small tender young zucchini, sliced
5 garlic cloves, finely chopped
2 tablespoons butter, or as desired
Salt and pepper to taste

To make the fregula: dissolve the saffron or turmeric in boiling water and let it cool to warm room temperature.

Place about a quarter of the semolina in a flat shallow pan and sprinkle with several tablespoons of the warm water mixture. Rub the semolina flour into crumbs, then add 1/2 cup more of the semolina and a few tablespoons more of the water. Repeat, adding more semolina and water until all the semolina is used up and the mixture has formed uneven crumbs and pellets.

Spread out onto a baking sheet or clean cloth and let dry overnight, turning once or twice. The next day divide the mixture into large and small grains, using your fingers to brush the large ones to one side.

To serve: Place the zucchini in a saucepan filled with boiling water and cook until half tender. Add the large grains of pasta. Continue to cook a few minutes longer, or until the pasta is nearly tender, then add the small grains and continue to cook until both small and large grains are just tender. Drain.

Toss the cooked *fregula* and zucchini with garlic and butter, season with salt and pepper, and eat right away.

352 CALORIES PER SERVING
5 G FAT
3 G SATURATED FAT
11 MG CHOLESTEROL
64 G CARBOHYDRATES
12 G PROTEIN
223 MG SODIUM

Pasta al' Aglio con Lenticche

SPICY LENTIL PASTA WITH GARLIC AND PARSLEY

Serves 4 to 6

Use a really big pan for this so you can toss the pasta and lentils together well. The lentils will absorb the sauce and the pasta will absorb the richness of the lentils without becoming over-cooked in the process. Sometimes I add a spoonful or two of yogurt and a dusting of cumin to the hot pasta at the last minute.

8 garlic cloves, chopped or crushed
  Large pinch salt
3 tablespoons olive oil
$1/4$ small hot fresh red chili or several pinches hot pepper flakes
1 cup cooked lentils, drained (reserve 3 tablespoons of the cooking liquid for this recipe; save the rest for another use)
  Juice of $1/2$ lemon
  Large pinch *herbes de Provence*
1 pound spaghetti
  Salt and pepper to taste
$1/4$ to $1/2$ cup chopped parsley (or less, to taste)

Purée half of the garlic with a generous pinch of salt, then work in half the olive oil; set aside.

Heat the remaining garlic in the remaining olive oil until it is fragrant, then add the red chili/hot pepper flakes and stir together a moment or two. Keep your face well away from the fumes and take care not to inhale the fumes or let them irritate your eyes.

Add the drained lentils and cook a few minutes in the garlic–hot pepper oil, then add the lemon juice, 3 tablespoons of the lentil cooking liquid, and *herbes de Provence* and cook together until the liquid evaporates.

Cook the spaghetti until it is *al dente*; drain.

Toss the hot drained spaghetti with the lentils and cook together over medium heat for a moment or two to heat through. If the pasta seems dry, add a tablespoon or two of pasta cooking water or lentil cooking liquid.

Season with salt and pepper and toss with the reserved garlic oil and chopped parsley. Serve right away.

402 CALORIES PER SERVING
8 G FAT
1 G SATURATED FAT
0 MG CHOLESTEROL
68 G CARBOHYDRATES
13 G PROTEIN
5 MG SODIUM

Cappellini con Brocoli e Rucola

ANGEL HAIR PASTA WITH BROCCOLI, ARUGULA, AND HOT
PEPPER–GARLIC OIL

Serves 4

Utterly southern Italy, rustic and lusty. This makes a marvelous one-bowl supper in the hot summertime, especially with a salad of juice tomatoes alongside.

Use any pasta you like: rigatoni is nice, but so too is orzo.

1 pound angel hair pasta; reserve a small portion of the cooking water
1 bunch broccoli, cut into florets
1 bunch arugula, cut into bite-size pieces
8 garlic cloves, coarsely chopped
Large pinch hot pepper flakes or ½ fresh chili
3 tablespoons olive oil
Salt to taste
Parmesan or pecorino, if desired, to taste

Bring a large pot of salted water to a boil, then add the pasta and broccoli. Cook until the pasta is *al dente* and the broccoli is crisp-tender and bright green, about 5 minutes. Halfway through, add the arugula. Drain.

Heat the garlic, hot pepper, and olive oil gently in a large frying pan, then toss in the pasta and vegetables along with a tablespoon or two of the cooking water to keep it all moist. Salt to taste.

Serve right away, sprinkled with Parmesan or pecorino if desired.

575 CALORIES PER SERVING
13 G FAT
2 G SATURATED FAT
0 MG CHOLESTEROL
97 G CARBOHYDRATES
19 G PROTEIN
349 MG SODIUM

Macaroni à la Marocaine

Serves 4 to 6

A quickly tossed together pasta dish for when you have Spicy Moroccan Butter on hand or feel like whipping some up.

This was made for me by a friend whose family of Sephardic Jews came from North Africa. It was inspired by their tradition of adding the seasoned butter to couscous, she said, and was something her mother had made since she was a child. They use preserved lemon if they have any in the pantry and sometimes a sprinkling of grated cheese such as Parmesan, but since neither was on hand we used freshly squeezed lemon juice and it was marvelous.

To be perfectly honest, it is at its most delicious with more butter than required in the following recipe; but the cut-back version is very nice, too. To further whittle away animal fats, prepare the Spicy Moroccan Butter using half butter and half olive oil.

This makes a good side dish along with a bowl of steamed or grilled zucchini sprinkled with Parmesan or pecorino cheese.

12 to 16 ounces macaroni, preferably short tubes such
   as occhi di lupo, elbows, or small shells
 3 tablespoons Spicy Moroccan Butter (page 283), or
   as desired
   Juice of 1 lemon, or more to taste
   Salt and hot pepper to taste

Cook the macaroni until it is just tender, then drain.

Toss the cooked drained pasta with Spicy Moroccan Butter, lemon juice, salt, and hot pepper and serve right away.

230 CALORIES PER SERVING
4 G FAT
2 G SATURATED FAT
8 MG CHOLESTEROL
41 G CARBOHYDRATES
7 G PROTEIN
33 MG SODIUM

Orzo me Spanaki ke Saltsa Domatas

GREEK ORZO WITH CINNAMON-SCENTED TOMATOES, SPINACH, AND FETA

Serves 4

I first started making this dish when my neighbor in Greece wrote it down in the little note-book of recipes I was compiling. Most of the recipes became my first book, *Naturally Good* (Faber & Faber, Grove Press). For some reason this recipe stayed in my kitchen instead.

I have made it over and over for decades; sometimes with a little yogurt added, at other times with a little béchamel sauce for a creamier, comforting potful. Other pastas can be used in place of the orzo: in Corfu I have eaten it prepared with spaghetti-like pasta broken into short lengths, and I have made it in my own kitchen using little seashells (conchiglie).

12 ounces orzo or other pasta, such as broken up long pasta strands or little seashell shapes

1 onion, chopped

3 garlic cloves, chopped

2 tablespoons olive oil

1/4 teaspoon cinnamon

1/8 teaspoon *each:* allspice, oregano, and cumin

3 cups diced tomatoes (fresh or canned); reserve the juice
Sugar, salt, and pepper to taste

1/2 to 3/4 cup cooked spinach or chard, squeezed dry and cut into ribbons or coarsely chopped

6 to 8 ounces feta cheese, crumbled

4 ounces shredded white cheese, such as Monterey Jack
Sprinkling of Parmesan or pecorino Romano, as desired

Pasta, Rice, Polenta, and Couscous

Cook the orzo until half cooked, that is, *al dente* on the outside but still quite tough inside. Drain, rinse in cold water, then set them aside.

Lightly sauté the onion and garlic in the olive oil; when softened, sprinkle in the cinnamon, allspice, oregano, and cumin, cook a few moments, then add the tomatoes and simmer until saucelike and thickened. Season with sugar if the tomatoes are acidic, and salt and pepper to taste.

Heat the oven to 350°F. In the meantime, add the spinach or chard and orzo to the tomato mixture and warm it through. Spoon the mixture into a casserole or baking pan, toss with feta cheese, and sprinkle the top with shredded white cheese and Parmesan or pecorino.

Bake for 15 to 25 minutes or until the cheese topping melts and lightly browns in spots. Serve right away.

670 CALORIES PER SERVING
27 G FAT
13 G SATURATED FAT
63 MG CHOLESTEROL
80 G CARBOHYDRATES
28 G PROTEIN
960 MG SODIUM

❦ Spaghetti Acciurata

SPAGHETTI WITH BLACK OLIVES, ROSEMARY, GOAT CHEESE, AND HOT PEPPER

Serves 4 to 6

In Sicilian dialect, *acciurata* translates as "in bloom" but refers to oil-cured black olives, since they sometimes grow a thin white mold that looks as if they are in bloom. Any salty, flavorful black olive will do, but the oil-cured ones are the most pungent and I think best for this dish. Black olive paste, known as *olivada,* is fine.

3 to 4 tablespoons bread crumbs
3 to 4 tablespoons olive oil
1 pound spaghetti
6 to 8 garlic cloves, chopped
3 to 4 tablespoons black olive paste or $1/2$ cup oil-cured black olives, pitted and diced
1 to 2 tablespoons finely chopped fresh rosemary leaves
4 to 6 ounces goat cheese, crumbled or diced
Large pinch hot pepper flakes, or to taste

Toast the bread crumbs in a heavy nonstick frying pan with a tablespoon of the oil, letting the crumbs turn golden brown. Remove them from the heat and set them aside.

Cook the spaghetti until *al dente.* Meanwhile, combine the remaining olive oil with the garlic, olive paste or diced olives, rosemary, goat cheese, and hot pepper flakes. Do not mix well—leave the cheese in large chunky bits.

Drain the cooked pasta and toss it with the cheese mixture. Serve right away, sprinkled with the toasted bread crumbs.

437 CALORIES PER SERVING
15 G FAT
4 G SATURATED FAT
9 MG CHOLESTEROL
61 G CARBOHYDRATES
14 G PROTEIN
274 MG SODIUM

Spaghetti alla Carciofi

SPAGHETTI WITH ARTICHOKE PESTO

Serves 4

The first time I ate this it became an instant comfort food. The paste of artichoke, lemon, garlic, and basil is richly flavored without being heavy. I often vary the cheese—feta, goat cheese, sheep cheese, or any other light tangy cheese—and sometimes add an extra squeeze of lemon.

- 2 lemons, one cut in half and the other cut into wedges
- 6 artichokes, trimmed of their leaves and chokes, then cut into quarters or diced
- 3 to 5 tablespoons olive oil, or as desired
- 3 garlic cloves, chopped
- 1/4 cup pine nuts
- 1/4 cup basil, thinly cut or coarsely chopped
- 1/4 cup Parmesan cheese, plus extra for sprinkling at table
- 12 to 16 ounces spaghetti

Squeeze 1 lemon into a large pot of water, then bring it to the boil. Cook the artichokes in the lemon water until they are just tender, then drain and cool.

To make artichoke pesto: Purée the cooked artichokes with the olive oil, garlic, pine nuts, basil, and Parmesan cheese, whirling until it forms a pesto-like sauce.

Cook the spaghetti until *al dente,* then drain.

Toss the cooked, drained spaghetti with the artichoke pesto, then serve with a squeeze of lemon and a sprinkling of Parmesan.

594 CALORIES PER SERVING
19 G FAT
3 G SATURATED FAT
4 MG CHOLESTEROL
91 G CARBOHYDRATES
22 G PROTEIN
267 MG SODIUM

Orzo me Tyra

GREEK ISLAND ORZO WITH LEMON-GARLIC BUTTER AND FETA CHEESE

Serves 4

Crushing the garlic with a little salt gives a much stronger garlic flavor, but a smoother texture, without little bits of garlic scattered throughout.

A crumbling of feta cheese is delicious although optional—I usually have two helpings, the first without the cheese, the second with.

3 garlic cloves, peeled but whole
  Salt as desired
1 tablespoon olive oil
12 ounces orzo
3 tablespoons butter, or more as desired
  Freshly ground black pepper
  Juice of $1/2$ to 1 lemon, or to taste
  Optional: 4 ounces feta cheese, crumbled

Crush the garlic with a large pinch of salt in a mortar and pestle or food processor. Work in the olive oil and set aside.

Cook the orzo in rapidly boiling water until it is just tender, then drain. Toss the hot, drained orzo with butter, then season with salt, pepper, lemon juice, and the crushed garlic.

Serve right away, as is or sprinkled with feta cheese.

437 CALORIES PER SERVING
14 G FAT
6 G SATURATED FAT
25 MG CHOLESTEROL
65 G CARBOHYDRATES
11 G PROTEIN
93 MG SODIUM

Pasta, Rice, Polenta, and Couscous

❧ Kitchri

EGYPTIAN DISH OF RICE, PASTA, LENTILS, AND TOMATOES

Serves 4 to 6

This hearty, wholesome dish is much loved in Egypt, especially Cairo. You'll find stalls and restaurants specializing in the dish: order a bowl and you'll receive a scoop of mixed pasta, a scoop of plain rice, a ladleful of lentils, a tangle of crisp, brown fried onions, and a bowl of spicy hot tomato-garlic vinegar to sprinkle on.

It's one of the most satisfying dishes I can think of, a melange of textures and tastes from bland to spicy, soft to chewy.

Although red lentils are the ones used in Egypt, I like little brown or green lentils that keep their shape when you cook them and have an earthy, nutty flavor.

1½ cups cooked brown lentils
2 bay leaves
4 onions: 1 coarsely chopped, 3 thinly sliced
2 tablespoons vegetable oil
  Pinch sugar to encourage carmelization
  Pinch salt
1 cup raw rice
½ cup or so *each* (uncooked): macaroni such as penne, seashells, or elbows; flat shapes such as farfalle; and spaghetti, broken into several inch-long lengths
2 tablespoons olive oil
1½ cups diced ripe tomatoes (canned is fine); if using fresh, bring to a boil and cook until slightly thickened
5 garlic cloves
½ teaspoon salt, plus salt to taste
¼ teaspoon cinnamon
½ teaspoon sugar, or to taste
2 or 3 small hot chilies, or as desired
1 tablespoon vinegar
½ to 1 teaspoon *each:* cumin and ground coriander

(CONTINUED)

Combine the lentils in their cooking liquid with the bay leaves and the coarsely chopped onion. Place this over low heat, covered, to warm through.

Meanwhile, brown the remaining onions in the vegetable oil, cooking slowly until browned, sprinkling with a little sugar to encourage caramelization. Salt to taste and set aside.

Cook the rice in boiling water until *al dente;* drain if necessary, set it aside, and keep it warm.

Cook the pasta in rapidly boiling salted water, adding first the pasta that takes the longest to cook, then adding the remaining pasta, so that at the end of cooking they are all just tender, or *al dente.* Drain and toss lightly in 1 tablespoon of the olive oil. Set the pasta aside.

Heat the tomatoes. Keep them warm and set them aside.

Meanwhile, purée or crush the garlic with $1/2$ teaspoon salt until it forms a paste, then work in the remaining tablespoon olive oil. Stir half into the warm tomatoes, along with the cinnamon. Add up to $1/2$ teaspoon sugar or to taste to balance any acidity. Keep it warm.

Add the chilies, vinegar, cumin, coriander, and 3 tablespoons of the tomato mixture to the remaining garlic paste, and purée. Set it aside.

To serve: place several spoonfuls of both the rice and pasta in each bowl, then ladle over some of the cooked lentils and a spoonful or two of the tomato sauce. Scatter fried onions over the top and serve with the spicy garlic–hot pepper sauce for each person to add as desired.

567 CALORIES PER SERVING
11 G FAT
2 G SATURATED FAT
0 MG CHOLESTEROL
96 G CARBOHYDRATES
23 G PROTEIN
284 MG SODIUM

Pasta, Rice, Polenta, and Couscous

LEFTOVERS

Crostino alla Lenticche

Heat leftover bay leaf-scented lentils with a small amount of their liquid; season with salt and pepper. Cover and keep warm.

Prepare *crostini:* brush slices of baguette with olive oil and bake until crisp, then top with chopped garlic. Serve several *crostini* on each plate, each portion topped with a ladleful of hot lentils and a drizzle of olive oil. Top with shavings of Parmesan cheese; in Umbria, this is also served with shavings of truffles or truffle oil.

Eastern Mediterranean Pilaf of Two Rices and Browned Vermicelli

Serves 4

This is my favorite reliable old pilaf, one I have made in endless variations since my teen years. Sometimes I add dried fruit such as raisins, other times I use several types of rice as I have here. Whichever nuts you have on hand will probably be just fine; I have even prepared it with peanuts and while I'm not sure it was because I was hungry, it was quite tasty. Pine nuts are excellent and so are cashews.

This pilaf is great as an accompaniment to anything cooked on the grill or simply to a salad of leafy greens and herbs with a bowl of yogurt alongside.

$1/2$ cup raw brown rice
2 or 3 medium to large-size onions, thinly sliced
1 tablespoon olive oil
3 garlic cloves, thinly sliced
$1/4$ teaspoon cumin
  Several pinches of cinnamon
  Salt and pepper to taste
1 ounce spaghetti or vermicelli, broken up into
  2-inch lengths
2 tablespoons butter
1 cup raw white rice
2 cups stock or broth of choice
2 ounces dry roasted, preferably unsalted, almonds
  (if salted, rub them well with absorbent paper,
  perhaps just damp, to rid the nuts of their salt)

Parboil the brown rice for 15 to 20 minutes or until it is just short of *al dente,* that is, slightly firm but just a bit crunchy inside. Drain and rinse well in cold water, then drain again.

Brown the onion in the olive oil, cooking slowly until the onions are nicely browned, about 30 minutes. Add

Pasta, Rice, Polenta, and Couscous

the garlic during the last 10 minutes or so, then season the mixture with cumin and cinnamon, and salt and pepper, and set it aside.

Sauté the spaghetti or vermicelli in half of the butter, cooking it quickly until it browns, then remove it from the pan. Add the rest of the butter and sauté the white rice until it is lightly gilded, then add the drained brown rice and brown together for a minute or two. If you use a nonstick pan for these steps, you should be able to reduce the fat content significantly.

Return the browned pasta and rice to the pot, pour in the stock and stir together, then bring it to a boil. Reduce the heat, cover it tightly, and cook over very low heat until both the brown and white rice are just cooked through, 10 to 15 minutes, depending on your rice.

When the rice is *al dente,* remove the mixture from the heat and fluff it with a fork, then toss in the browned onions and garlic. Serve it heaped onto a platter, topped with a scattering of crisp roasted almonds.

VARIATION

Pilaf with Raisins, Cumin, Eggplant, and Garlic Yogurt
Prepare the pilaf as described above, but include $1/2$ cup or so raisins while the rice and pasta simmer. Meanwhile, slice 1 medium to large eggplant $1/4$ to $1/2$ inch thick and brush it with olive oil, then sprinkle it with salt, cumin, and cayenne. Broil the slices on both sides until light brown on the outside and tender inside.

Mix 1 chopped garlic clove with 1 cup yogurt and salt to taste.

Serve the pilaf mounded on a platter surrounded by the browned eggplant, with the yogurt sauce alongside to spoon on.

511 CALORIES PER SERVING
18 G FAT
5 G SATURATED FAT
17 MG CHOLESTEROL
76 G CARBOHYDRATES
11 G PROTEIN
112 MG SODIUM

⬲ Imjadara

EASTERN MEDITERRANEAN LENTIL AND BARLEY PILAF

Serves 4

Like the traditional Arabian combination of lentils and rice, lentils and barley make a rustic high-protein pilaf, filling and satisfying, delicious with a bowl of yogurt and a crisp vegetable salad.

Since lentils and barley take longer to cook than other substantial foods such as pasta or rice, I often cook a large batch and freeze them in $1/2$- to 1-cup portions, with a handful of ice cube-sized ones as well. Then when I wish to have lentils, they are waiting patiently, ready to be defrosted and cooked as I wish. Although they retain their shape better if they are first defrosted, the little lentil or barley cubes can be popped directly from the freezer into stews and soups and warmed with the rest of the pot. By the time the soup or stew is hot and ready to be eaten, so too are the barley or lentils.

1 or 2 medium-size onions, chopped
2 tablespoons olive oil or butter
3 to 5 garlic cloves, chopped
1 teaspoon cumin seeds
1 tablespoon paprika
  Large pinch *each:* curry powder and ground ginger
1 cup cooked barley
$1/2$ to 1 cup cooked lentils
2 bay leaves
1 cup low-sodium chicken or vegetable broth, or lentil cooking water flavored with powdered chicken or vegetable bouillon
  Salt and pepper to taste

Sauté the onion in the olive oil or butter until it is lightly browned, then add the garlic and cumin seeds and continue to cook a few minutes longer, until the garlic is fragrant and golden.

Sprinkle in the paprika, curry powder, and ginger, cook a few moments, then stir in the barley, lentils, and bay leaves.

Stir fry a few moments, then ladle in about half of the broth/lentil cooking water and continue to cook, stirring, until the liquid has cooked off. Repeat, until the mixture is mostly dry and the barley and lentils have absorbed the flavors of the spices and broth.

Season with salt and pepper and serve as desired.

176 Calories per serving
8 G Fat
1 G Saturated Fat
0 MG Cholesterol
24 G Carbohydrates
5 G Protein
27 MG Sodium

Pasta, Rice, Polenta, and Couscous

Risotto de Carciofi al'Limoni

ARTICHOKE RISOTTO WITH LEMON AND OLIVE OIL

Serves 4

This dish is from the Jewish Quarter in Rome, known for its splendid artichoke dishes. Artichokes *alla Judia* are perhaps the most famous: fried in olive oil until their leaves fan out like a crisp, brown, flower—people come from all over the world to sample these treats. But there are also stews of artichokes and legumes, artichoke omelets, artichokes added to pasta, and artichokes stirred into *risotti,* such as in the following recipe.

3 or 4 medium to large artichokes, trimmed to the hearts, then diced or sliced

1 medium-large onion, chopped

5 garlic cloves, crushed or chopped

2 to 3 tablespoons olive oil, or as desired

1½ cups Arborio rice

2 tablespoons chopped Italian flat leaf parsley

3½ to 4 cups hot broth or stock

¾ cup grated Parmesan, pecorino, or Asiago cheese, or as desired

2 lemons, 1 cut in half, the other cut into wedges

Salt and pepper to taste

Blanch the artichokes, rinse them with cold water, and set them aside.

Lightly sauté the onion and half the garlic in the olive oil until softened, then stir in the artichokes, rice, and half the parsley, and continue cooking until the rice has a golden tinge.

Slowly stir in the broth, beginning with ½ cup; when that is absorbed, add another half cup. Continue adding liquid about ¾ cup at a time, stirring and waiting until most of it has been absorbed before adding more.

When the rice is *al dente* and the liquid around it is souplike and savory, it is ready. Remove from the heat, stir in the remaining garlic, add the cheese, then squeeze in the lemon halves. Season with salt and pepper to taste.

Serve the *risotto* sprinkled with the remaining parsley and garnished with lemon wedges.

529 CALORIES PER SERVING

15 G FAT

4 G SATURATED FAT

12 MG CHOLESTEROL

82 G CARBOHYDRATES

17 G PROTEIN

445 MG SODIUM

Arroz con Garbanzos

RICE WITH CHICKPEAS AND TOMATO-PEPPER SAUCE, SPANISH STYLE

Serves 4

This Catalan rice dish is a culinary souvenir from a visit to the region of the Mediterranean coast that sits astride the French-Spanish border. It's a land of *paella* and rice dishes, and this dish of rice, chickpeas, and tomatoes won my heart—it's so robust and satisfying, and deliciously full of garlic.

Unfortunately, the separatists were having a resurgence of regional identity: to discourage visitors from outside the region they took down the local signs so that "foreigners," that is, anyone from outside the region, would get lost. We obliged them. A wrong turn at one of the now-unmarked roundabouts meant that our dinner guests ended up 200 miles away in Barcelona at just about the time dinner was ready.

$^1/_2$ onion, chopped
6 to 9 garlic cloves, chopped
1 red bell pepper, chopped
4 tablespoons olive oil
2 cups diced tomatoes
2 tablespoons tomato paste
Sugar, salt, and pepper to taste
1 cup risotto rice
$2^1/_2$ cups broth of choice
2 cups cooked and drained chickpeas
Garnish: 2 tablespoons chopped fresh marjoram or other herb as desired

Lightly sauté the onion, a third of the garlic, and the red pepper in half the olive oil until they are softened, then add the tomatoes and simmer for 20 to 30 minutes or until saucelike and thickened. Add the tomato paste and season with sugar, salt, and pepper to taste. Set aside.

Heat a third of the remaining garlic in 1 tablespoon of the remaining olive oil, then stir in the rice and cook until it is lightly gilded, about 3 minutes. Pour in half the broth, simmer for 10 to 15 minutes until it is absorbed, as if making *risotto,* then add the rest of the broth. Cook and stir until the rice is tender and the broth is absorbed.

Meanwhile, in a heavy nonstick frying pan heat the remaining tablespoon of olive oil and add the remaining garlic and the drained chickpeas. Cook them until lightly golden, then season with salt and pepper.

Toss the hot chickpeas into the hot rice and pour the tomato sauce over the top. Sprinkle with the herbs and serve right away.

498 CALORIES PER SERVING
16 G FAT
2 G SATURATED FAT
0 MG CHOLESTEROL
76 G CARBOHYDRATES
14 G PROTEIN
319 MG SODIUM

Polenta al Forno

ROSEMARY AND TOMATO-LAYERED POLENTA GRATIN

Serves 6

Polenta has long been eaten in many of Italy's regions, although the mixture has been made of corn only since the return of the New World explorers. Prior to that it was other grains that were made into polenta, usually millet and chestnuts, the latter still eaten as a rustic brown polenta in Corsica.

Freshly made polenta is soft, unctuous, like porridge; poured onto a board or into a pan, it firms up as it cools and can then be sliced and grilled or broiled, or layered into a casserole and baked.

Here it's layered with tomato sauce, seasoned with fresh rosemary, and sprinkled with grated cheese that melts in as it bakes.

1	cup cold water
1	cup polenta or coarse yellow cornmeal
2 1/2	cups boiling salted water
	Olive oil as needed—about 3 to 4 tablespoons in total
3 to 4	cups ripe diced tomatoes, plus juices
5	garlic cloves, chopped
	Salt and pepper to taste
	Pinch sugar if needed
2 to 3	tablespoons chopped fresh rosemary
1 1/2 to 2	cups shredded mozzarella or Monterey Jack cheese
1/2	cup grated Parmesan, Romano, or Asiago cheese

Stir the cold water into the polenta and set it aside to soften and swell for 10 minutes. Pour this soaked cornmeal mixture into the boiling salted water, stirring well to combine, then reduce the heat and simmer, stirring every so often, until the cornmeal is thickened and the grains are tender. This will take about 30 to 40 minutes, depending on the cornmeal; different kinds of meal will need different amounts of stirring, so this is a dish to keep your eye on.

Pasta, Rice, Polenta, and Couscous

If we were eating the polenta soft, we'd spoon it out of the pot and into warmed bowls, then ladle on a savory tomato sauce and grated cheese. For this dish, however, we're eating it firm. Pour the freshly cooked, soft hot polenta onto an oiled board or platter and leave it in a cool place to firm up, uncovered, for about 2 hours. It will then be ready for slicing for casseroles and grilling.

Heat the oven to 375°F. Cut the polenta into slices.

Drizzle a tiny amount of olive oil on the bottom of an earthenware casserole, scatter a little of the tomato, garlic, salt, pepper, sugar, and rosemary over the olive oil, then make a layer of polenta slices.

Repeat with the tomatoes, garlic, salt, pepper, and rosemary, adding a layer of cheeses, then begin again with the polenta and repeat with the layers of tomato, garlic, rosemary, and so forth until the polenta and sauce are all used up. End with a layer of sauce topped with cheese.

Bake for 35 to 40 minutes, until the cheeses are melted and lightly browned, the whole casserole bubbly and sizzling hot.

Serve right away.

264 CALORIES PER SERVING
15 G FAT
5 G SATURATED FAT
21 MG CHOLESTEROL
24 G CARBOHYDRATES
13 G PROTEIN
279 MG SODIUM

Polenta ai Funghi

POLENTA GRATINÉED WITH PORCINI AND CHEESE

Serves 4 to 6

This rich Venetian dish is seductive: redolent of porcini's woodsey scent, topped with melted cheeses, creamily soft polenta underneath.

I spooned into it one day as autumn was blending into winter. Chilled to the bone, surrounded by Venice's omnipresent water and lagoons, I got lost in the labyrinth of walkways and wandered hungrily into a little trattoria. This dish was on the blackboard (there was little else left) so I ordered it and hoped for the best, unprepared for just how good it would be.

You can use any mushrooms you like, but the woodsier scented mushrooms are the most delicious. You could also use ordinary domestic mushrooms combined with dried porcini mushrooms if you like.

1 recipe polenta (see Polenta al Forno, page 176)
  Optional: 3 to 4 tablespoons mascarpone cheese
4 tablespoons Parmesan or Asiago cheese
2 fresh porcini mushrooms, thinly sliced, or
  1/4 pound domestic mushrooms combined with
  about 1 ounce dried rehydrated porcini
1 onion, chopped
2 tablespoons butter
1/4 cup dry white wine
  Pinch *each:* nutmeg and rosemary or thyme
  Salt and pepper to taste
2 garlic cloves, chopped
1 to 1 1/2 cups shredded fontina or Monterey Jack
  cheese

Cook the basic polenta as in the preceding recipe for Polenta al Forno; stir in the mascarpone cheese if using, plus 2 tablespoons of Parmesan or Asiago cheese. Pour the polenta onto an oiled baking sheet and leave it to cool.

Cut the polenta into slices and arrange them on a baking sheet or in individual casserole dishes. Set it aside.

If using dried porcini, rehydrate: combine the porcini with water to cover and bring to a boil. Remove from the heat and let the mushrooms sit, covered, until they have rehydrated; this should take 15 to 30 minutes. Drain, saving the liquid for sauces or to drizzle over the polenta.

Sauté the onion in the butter until it is softened and golden, then add the fresh or rehydrated porcini and sauté together a few moments. Pour in the white wine and cook over high heat until it evaporates. If using rehydrated mushrooms, add the liquid from soaking the mushrooms and cook over high heat until the liquid reduces and has cooked down to a thin, flavorful sauce. Season with nutmeg, rosemary or thyme, and salt and pepper. Add the chopped garlic.

Turn on the broiler. Broil the sliced polenta on one side until it is hot and flecked with brown, then turn the slices over.

Spoon the mushrooms and their sauce onto the unbroiled side, then top with the shredded cheeses and remaining Pamesan or Asiago cheese. Broil until the cheeses melt and sauce sizzles around the polenta. Serve right away.

QUICKIE: POLENTA PIZZA

When making boiled polenta, pour leftover hot polenta onto a pizza pan or baking sheet. Let cool.

The next day top as for pizza: Sautéed mushrooms and/or green peppers, diced black oil-cured olives, lots of oregano, dabs of ricotta, a thick smear of tomato sauce, and a topping of mozzarella and Parmesan. Drizzle with olive oil and bake as for pizza, until the cheese topping is melted and lightly browned in places.

235 CALORIES PER SERVING
12 G FAT
7 G SATURATED FAT
36 MG CHOLESTEROL
25 G CARBOHYDRATES
9 G PROTEIN
282 MG SODIUM

❧ Couscous Végétarien

VEGETABLE COUSCOUS WITH THREE TYPES OF BEANS

Serves 6

Anyone who has eaten a superb couscous, tender-grained and moist, will realize that quick-cooked instant couscous is probably not going to give you those results. However, for a quick delicious dinner it is wonderful, especially if you moisten the grains beforehand and rub them between your fingers to lighten them.

Recently, in Nice, I was fed a delicious couscous that was served with vegetables along with a bowl of various beans and a selection of several sauces. The beans had absorbed the flavors of the stew they simmered in, and the sauces ranged from slightly spicy to hot enough to blister my tongue.

For hot sauces, try a bowlful of fragrant Zhug (page 277) and a little fiery *harissa* (recipe follows).

1 onion, chopped
4 garlic cloves, chopped
2 tablespoons olive oil
1 tablespoon paprika
$^1/_2$ teaspoon cumin
$^1/_4$ teaspoon *each*: ginger, coriander, and cinnamon
    Pinch *each*: turmeric and ground cloves
2 ripe tomatoes, diced
$1^1/_2$ quarts vegetable stock or water mixed with
    2 bouillon cubes
    The following vegetables: 1 carrot, 1 small sweet potato, 1 turnip, $^1/_2$ head cabbage, $^1/_4$ head celery, and 2 zucchini, all cut into bite-size chunks
    Beans ($^1/_2$ cup *each*): cooked white beans, chickpeas, and one other: either red, brown favas, or black-eyed peas (canned is fine for all)
2 cups instant couscous grains
2 tablespoons butter or olive oil
    Cinnamon, for sprinkling
    Juice of $^1/_4$ to $^1/_2$ lemon
1 to 2 tablespoons finely chopped cilantro
    Hot sauces: Zhug (page 277); Harissa (page 181)

Pasta, Rice, Polenta, and Couscous

Sauté the onion and garlic in the olive oil until they soften, then sprinkle in the paprika, cumin, ginger, coriander, cinnamon, turmeric, and cloves. Cook a few more minutes, then add the tomatoes and cook, stirring, until saucelike in consistency.

Add the stock and vegetables, cover, and simmer until the vegetables are quite tender and the sauce is very flavorful. Adjust the seasonings as needed.

Place the beans in a separate saucepan with about ¹/₂ cup of the tomato sauce and gently heat. Simmer gently while you prepare the couscous; don't let the beans become mushy.

Combine the couscous with 1 cup of cold water and let sit 10 minutes. Rub the couscous with your fingers to separate the grains, then rub in 1 tablespoon of butter or olive oil and place the couscous in a saucepan. Pour 1 cup of hot cooking liquid from the vegetables over the couscous and toss well over gentle heat until the grains swell and plump up.

Sprinkle with cinnamon, cover, and keep warm.

Reheat the vegetables and their liquid; taste for seasoning and add a squeeze of lemon juice plus extra spices, if needed.

To serve, fluff up the couscous and pile it on a platter. Serve the vegetables separately, sprinkled with cilantro, in their cooking broth with a bowl of beans on the side and both the *zhug* and *harissa,* for those who desire it.

Harissa Sauce: Combine 1 tablespoon storebought *harissa*—a potent purée of dried red chilies and spices, from a can or tube available at specialty food shops—with several cloves chopped garlic, ¹/₂ teaspoon cumin, and about ¹/₂ cup of the hot vegetable cooking liquid. Season this sauce with salt, a squeeze of lemon, and a scattering of cilantro and serve alongside the couscous.

> 463 CALORIES PER SERVING
> 11 G FAT
> 3 G SATURATED FAT
> 11 MG CHOLESTEROL
> 78 G CARBOHYDRATES
> 15 G PROTEIN
> 641 MG SODIUM

Fettucine alla Peperoni Arrosti

FETTUCINE WITH ROASTED PEPPER–GOAT CHEESE PURÉE

Serves 4 to 6

We whipped this pasta up one afternoon after shopping at the morning marketplace near the villa we rented one summer in Tuscany. It was too hot for anything overly ambitious, but we all wanted to eat something that was interesting and slightly different.

We ate a plate of licorice-scented raw fennel alongside, dressed in olive oil and lemon and studded with fat black olives. And for dessert, fresh peach sorbet with bittersweet, fragrant, brandy-soaked Amarena cherries spooned over.

4 sweet peppers, either red or yellow, or 2 of each
3 garlic cloves, chopped
3 tablespoons olive oil
1 egg, lightly beaten
1 pound fettucine
4 ounces mild goat cheese
3 to 4 tablespoons thinly sliced basil
Salt and pepper to taste

Roast the peppers over a fire until they char; place them in a plastic bag or in a pot and cover tightly. Leave for an hour, then remove the skins and rinse the peppers in cold water. Slice into strips and set aside.

Crush or purée the garlic with the peppers in a food processor or with a mortar and pestle, then add the olive oil and egg and whirl until it forms a slightly chunky sauce. Set aside.

Cook the fettucine until *al dente*. Drain and return the hot pasta to the hot pan; over medium heat toss the pasta with the pepper-egg sauce, tossing quickly so that the egg cooks and coats the pasta rather than scrambling.

Remove the pan from the heat and add the goat cheese, letting it melt as you toss, followed by the basil, salt, and pepper.

Serve hot, right away.

434 CALORIES PER SERVING
13 G FAT
4 G SATURATED FAT
45 MG CHOLESTEROL
64 G CARBOHYDRATES
15 G PROTEIN
83 MG SODIUM

Pasta, Rice, Polenta, and Couscous

FIVE

VEGETARIAN MAIN PLATES

TAGINE DU PAUVRE À LA TUNISIENNE, *Tunisian Lentil and Carrot Stew*

PASTICCIO DI VERDURA, *Garlic-Eggplant and Red Pepper Casserole with Tomatoes*

MELANZANE CON RICOTTA, *Browned Eggplant Slices Gratinéed with Fresh Tomatoes, Ricotta, and Parmesan*

IMAM BAYILDI, *Eggplant Stuffed with Onions, Tomatoes, and More Eggplant*

MOUSSAKA, *Arabian Stew of Eggplant, Zucchini, Tomatoes, and Chickpeas*

MELITZÁNES ME TYRI, *Greek Eggplant and Cheese Casserole*

TIAN OF ARTICHOKES AND TOMATOES WITH GOAT CHEESE AND OLIVES

GRATIN PROVENÇAL FERMIÈRE, *Provençal Farmer's Wife's Gratin of Potatoes, Garlic, Fresh Herbs, and Goat Cheese*

COURGE AU TOMATES ET CHÈVRE, *Sautéed Pumpkin with Tomatoes, Herbs, and Dry Goat Cheese*

FASSOULIA GIGANTES, *Greek White Beans in Tomato Sauce*

GUISO, *White Beans (or Chickpeas) Simmered with Pumpkin and Sweet-and-Spicy Red Peppers*

COCIDO DE GARBANZOS, *Chickpea and Vegetable Stew*

MINESTRA DI FARRO, CAVOLO, E FOGIOLI, *Tuscan Wheatberry, Cabbage, and Borlotti Bean Stew*

EL MATAMBRE

PIPERADE

OMELETA ME ANGINARES KE TYRI, *Flat Omelet of Artichokes and Feta Cheese*

FRITTATA PRIMAVERA, *Italian Flat Omelet Studded with Spring Vegetables*

BEID BE GEBNA TAMATEM, *Eggs Baked with Feta, Tomatoes, and Pickled Hot Peppers*

AJO CALIENTE CON HUEVOS, *Hot Garlic with Eggs*

BOSANSKA KALJA OD KAPUSA, *Cabbage Casserole with Peppers and Savory Yogurt Custard*

ESTOFAT DE QUORESMO, *Catalan Soup-Stew of Cauliflower, Romano Beans, and Chickpeas*

LENTEJAS CATALANAS, *Catalan-Style Brown Lentils*

GRILLED VEGETABLES

ESCALIVADA, *Array of Grilled or Roasted Vegetables*

AUBERGINE, FENOUIL, COURGETTES, ET LES EPINARDS AVEC COULIS DE POIVRONS ROUGES ET YAOURT SAFRAN, *Grilled Eggplant, Fennel, and Zucchini with Red Pepper Coulis and Saffron Yogurt*

ASPERGES GRILLÉES À L'AIOLI D'OLIVE, *Grilled Asparagus with Black Olive Aioli*

ARTICHAUTS GRILLÉS AVEC VINAIGRETTE MAROCAINE, *Grilled Artichokes with Moroccan Chermoula Vinaigrette*

POTIRON GRILLÉ AVEC BEURRE AU POIVRON FORTE, *Grilled Pumpkin with Red Chili Butter*

LA CALÇOTADA, *A Grilled Green Onion Feast*

THE Mediterranean table is rich with vegetable main plates, delicious dishes full of garden goodness, as enticing for omnivores as for vegetarians. Olive oil-bathed eggplant; casseroles of zucchini, tomatoes, and chickpeas; gratins of vegetables such as pumpkin, artichokes, and potatoes roasted with aromatics and lemon; all are full of the vivid flavors—and colors—so typical of food throughout the region.

Tagine du Pauvre à la Tunisienne

TUNISIAN LENTIL AND CARROT STEW

Serves 4

Called "stew of poverty" for its humble ingredients, it tastes anything but poor, with the flavors of vegetables and spices enriching the earthy lentils. Serve with chewy flatbreads and yogurt with a spicy raw vegetable salad on the side.

- ½ pound uncooked brown lentils
- 2 onions, grated
- 3 or 4 medium-size carrots, sliced
- 4 garlic cloves, chopped
- 6 tomatoes, chopped
- ¼ to ½ teaspoon *each:* cumin, cinnamon, and paprika, or to taste
  Pinch ginger, or to taste
  Several pinches cayenne pepper
- 2 tablespoons olive oil
  Salt and pepper to taste
- 1 cup vegetable broth
- ½ to 1 cup water
  Optional: Juice of ¼ lemon, or to taste

Soak the lentils in cold water to cover for an hour. Drain.

Combine the drained lentils with the grated onions, carrots, garlic, tomatoes, cumin, cinnamon, paprika, ginger, cayenne pepper, olive oil, salt and pepper, broth, and water. Bring to a boil, then reduce the heat and simmer at very low heat, covered, until the lentils and carrots are quite tender, 30 to 40 minutes. Add more liquid if the mixture threatens to burn, and leave the lid off the pot if the mixture seems too soupy.

Let sit a few minutes to meld flavors, then taste for seasoning. Serve with a squeeze of lemon if desired.

389 CALORIES PER SERVING
8 G FAT
1 G SATURATED FAT
0 MG CHOLESTEROL
61 G CARBOHYDRATES
23 G PROTEIN
67 MG SODIUM

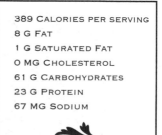

Pasticcio di Verdura

GARLIC-EGGPLANT AND RED PEPPER CASSEROLE WITH TOMATOES

Serves 4

From Puglia, Italy, comes this luscious melange of Mediterranean vegetables. Eggplant, tomatoes, and red peppers, stewed until glossy in olive oil with lots of garlic, typify the cooking of Italy's sun-washed south. It makes a marvelous main course either warm or cool, with a crisp little salad of assorted greens and herbs and a loaf of crusty bread.

While crumbs and cheese give an Italian flavor, the dish would be equally at home without them. The addition of a handful of olives at the end lends a Provençal accent, while a sprinkling of cumin spices and a green pepper added to the pot gives a North African flavor.

1 medium-size eggplant, cut into 1½-inch pieces
   Salt
1 onion, thinly sliced
¼ cup olive oil
2 red bell peppers, cut into 1½-inch pieces
4 ripe tomatoes, diced (or canned, including their juices plus a little extra from the can)
8 garlic cloves, finely chopped, plus 2 finely chopped garlic cloves for sprinkling
1 to 2 teaspoons fresh oregano or marjoram leaves, plus extra for sprinkling
1 to 2 tablespoons parsley, plus extra for sprinkling
3 to 4 tablespoons *each:* bread crumbs and grated Parmesan or Asiago cheese

Sprinkle the eggplant generously with salt and leave for 20 minutes or so, until brown droplets form on the cut edges of the eggplant. Rinse well and dry. (If you do not wish to salt the eggplant, omit this step and go directly to the next step.)

Combine everything in a heavy casserole or baking pan and bake in a 400°F oven for 45 to 60 minutes, turning with a spatula every so often so that the vegetables become tender and browned and the crumbs and cheese brown and form a thick mixture. If the vegetables seem too dry, mix in a little tomato juice and drizzle with extra olive oil.

Sprinkle with a little extra garlic, fresh oregano or marjoram, and parsley, and serve sizzling hot or let cool to room temperature.

257 CALORIES PER SERVING
16 G FAT
3 G SATURATED FAT
3 MG CHOLESTEROL
27 G CARBOHYDRATES
6 G PROTEIN
124 MG SODIUM

Melanzane con Ricotta

BROWNED EGGPLANT SLICES GRATINÉED WITH FRESH TOMATOES, RICOTTA, AND PARMESAN

Serves 4

Rich eggplant, exuberant tomatoes, and piquant cheese are hallmarks of much of the food in Naples—and of this recipe, which I forked up in a trattoria somewhere in the labyrinth of Naple's cobbled streets at a little table set outside in the warm night air.

Unlike most eggplant dishes, this simply prepared gratin is a very light-tasting one since the vegetable doesn't absorb an undue amount of oil and the flavor of the summer-ripe tomato, sweet basil, and light creamy ricotta comes through clearly.

1 medium to large eggplant, thinly sliced (but un-peeled, unless peel is very tough)
Salt as needed
3 tablespoons olive oil
6 ounces ricotta cheese
5 (or more, as desired) garlic cloves, chopped
5 ripe tomatoes, thinly sliced
4 to 6 tablespoons freshly grated Parmesan or Parmesan-type cheese (such as Sardo, Asiago, or pecorino Romano)
About ¼ cup fresh basil leaves, thinly sliced

Sprinkle the eggplant with salt on both sides and allow to sit for 30 minutes. Rinse off the bitter juices that form as droplets on the surface of the eggplant. (If you do not wish to salt the eggplant, omit this step. Salting simply reduces the amount of oil the vegetable can absorb.)

Dry the eggplant and brown on both sides in a heavy nonstick frying pan, using about 3 tablespoons of olive oil. Alternatively, you could brush the eggplant with olive oil and broil it on both sides until lightly browned.

Vegetarian Main Plates

Heat the broiler. In the meantime, arrange the eggplant slices in a baking dish and top each slice with a thin layer of ricotta, a sprinkling of garlic, a slice or two of tomato, then more garlic and a generous sprinkling of Parmesan or Parmesan-type cheese.

Drizzle the remaining olive oil over the cheese-topped eggplant, then place under the broiler until the cheese turns lightly golden brown.

Serve right away, with the fresh basil sprinkled over the top.

239 CALORIES PER SERVING
16 G FAT
4 G SATURATED FAT
17 MG CHOLESTEROL
18 G CARBOHYDRATES
10 G PROTEIN
163 MG SODIUM

Imam Bayildi

Eggplant Stuffed with Onions, Tomatoes, and More Eggplant

Serves 4 to 6

This is one of the traditional peasant dishes that is prepared in one guise or another throughout the lands that lie on the edge of the Mediterranean Sea. This version is decidedly Greek and reminds me of winters and the occasional summer spent on the island of Crete.

The ingredients are simple—eggplant, onions, tomatoes, parsley, and garlic—but combined they ooze the essential flavor of the Mediterranean. For an authentic flavor, use a fruity Greek or Cretan olive oil.

The name translates as "the priest fainted," and even though no one seems to know why the good man fell over, the explanation I have always favored is that he fell into a swoon over the deliciousness of it all.

Of course, some say he fainted because the dish used so much olive oil—and although it is not a dish to skimp on when the issue of oil is raised, you could cut back a bit if you like. If you salt the eggplant before sautéing, it will absorb less oil.

Note that sugar is added to the eggplant-tomato mixture; it doesn't make the sauce sweet but it does bring out the tomato flavor and balance the acidity. Adjust as desired.

You may serve this warm, but I think it is at its best the next day, by which time the flavors have mellowed. Leftover *imam bayildi* makes a marvelous sandwich, tucked into a crusty roll.

1 large eggplant or 2 medium-size ones
Salt as desired
1/3 cup olive oil, or as needed
2 medium-size onions, thinly sliced
8 ripe tomatoes, diced (canned is fine)
1 1/2 tablespoons tomato paste
2 teaspoons sugar, or to taste
1 cup coarsely chopped parsley
5 garlic cloves, coarsely chopped

Cut the eggplant in half and hollow out each half, leaving a 1/2-inch border around the edge. Cut the scooped-out eggplant into cubes. Salt the eggplant halves and cubes generously and leave for 30 minutes.

Brown-tinged droplets will appear all over the surface. Rinse the eggplant and blot dry.

Heat half the olive oil and brown the eggplant halves, then place in a shallow baking pan.

In another tablespoon or so of olive oil in a heavy nonstick frying pan brown the diced eggplant, then add the onion and cook until softened. Add the tomatoes, tomato paste, and sugar, and simmer for 10 to 15 minutes or until thickened. Remove the eggplant from the heat; stir in the parsley and garlic.

Heat the oven to 350°F. While it's heating, spoon the filling into each eggplant half, heaping them as high as they will go. Drizzle a little of the remaining olive oil over each eggplant half. Bake uncovered for 20 to 30 minutes or until the tops are lightly browned in spots.

Serve hot or at at room temperature

VARIATION

Aubergines Farcies

In Morocco, a similar recipe for stuffed eggplant is prepared, seasoning the onion-tomato filling with paprika, cinnamon, cumin, cayenne, and a little chopped cilantro as well.

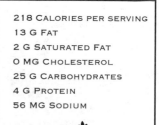

218 CALORIES PER SERVING
13 G FAT
2 G SATURATED FAT
0 MG CHOLESTEROL
25 G CARBOHYDRATES
4 G PROTEIN
56 MG SODIUM

Moussaka

ARABIAN STEW OF EGGPLANT, ZUCCHINI, TOMATOES, AND CHICKPEAS

Serves 4 to 6

I confess that this succulent stew of eggplant, zucchini, onions, and tomatoes, studded with little round chickpeas, is at its authentic best with lots and lots of olive oil. I have in fact reduced the amount considerably, but if you feel particularly wild, you can increase it to taste.

This quintessential Mediterranean stew is wonderful with chunks of bread and a crisp raw vegetable salad, a plate of feta cheese, and pungent green onions alongside. Plain buttered rice that you've tossed with a little cumin makes a good accompaniment.

1 medium-large eggplant, cut into $1\frac{1}{2}$- to 2-inch chunks
  Salt as desired
4 tablespoons olive oil, or more as desired
3 onions, peeled and sliced lengthwise
3 or 4 zucchini, cut into 2-inch long chunks
3 tablespoons chopped parsley
$2\frac{1}{2}$ to 3 cups fresh or canned tomatoes, diced; reserve the juice
$\frac{1}{2}$ teaspoon sugar, or to taste
  Greek oregano, crumbled, to taste
3 garlic cloves, chopped, or to taste
  Black pepper to taste
$1\frac{1}{2}$ cups drained cooked chickpeas

Sprinkle the chunks of eggplant with salt (optional) and leave them on a plate for 30 to 60 minutes. Rinse them well, then dry them. Brown the eggplant in a tablespoon or two of the olive oil; using a nonstick pan can keep down the amount of oil you'll need. Transfer the eggplant to a casserole or heavy pot.

Lightly sauté the onions in a tablespoon of the remaining oil until they are soft, then combine them with the eggplant. Cook the zucchini in the remaining oil until they too are golden. Add the zucchini to the casserole, along with half the parsley, the tomatoes and their juice, sugar, oregano, garlic, and black pepper.

Cover and simmer about 45 minutes or until the vegetables are very tender.

Add the chickpeas and continue to simmer another 10 to 15 minutes, then taste for seasonings. Add a little more crushed garlic, if desired, and serve hot or at room temperature, sprinkled with the remaining parsley.

213 CALORIES PER SERVING
11 G FAT
1 G SATURATED FAT
0 MG CHOLESTEROL
26 G CARBOHYDRATES
6 G PROTEIN
13 MG SODIUM

Melitzánes me Tyri

GREEK EGGPLANT AND CHEESE CASSEROLE

Serves 6 to 8

Layers of browned sliced eggplant topped with a cheese custard then baked until puffy—this delectable dish is a cross between a soufflé and a gratin and vegetable mousaka. It's simple to prepare and, once you have the béchamel sauce made, quick to toss together as well.

It is as delicious cold as it is warm, maybe even better; this is one of my favorite dishes to take along on a summer's afternoon picnic or to cut up into small bites for *meze*.

2 eggplants, sliced
 Salt as desired
 Olive oil for browning
1 tablespoon butter
1 tablespoon flour
1 cup milk
 Large pinch nutmeg
 Pinch of cayenne pepper as desired
1 cup shredded mild cheese such as Monterey Jack or mozzarella
1/2 cup grated sharp cheese such as Parmesan, Asiago, or dry Monterey Jack
4 eggs, lightly beaten

Salt the eggplant and let it sit in a strainer or on a plate for about 30 minutes, or until beads of brown moisture form on the surface of the cut eggplant. Rinse well in cold water, then pat dry with a clean towel or absorbent paper. Brown the eggplant in oil in several batches, then drain the slices on paper and set them aside.

In a saucepan heat the butter, then stir in the flour and cook a few moments. Meanwhile, in another saucepan heat the milk; then remove the flour/butter mixture from the heat and in one addition, whisk the milk into the flour mixture. Cook, stirring, over medium heat until the sauce thickens. Season with salt, nutmeg, and cayenne.

Stir both cheeses into the thick milky sauce, then add the eggs and mix well.

Arrange the eggplant in a baking dish, then pour in the cheese custard.

Heat the oven to 375°F, and bake the casserole for 35 to 45 minutes or until it is puffy and lightly golden (it will flatten as it cools).

Eat warm, or let cool and eat in squares.

219 CALORIES PER SERVING
17 G FAT
7 G SATURATED FAT
129 MG CHOLESTEROL
6 G CARBOHYDRATES
10 G PROTEIN
232 MG SODIUM

Tian of Artichokes and Tomatoes with Goat Cheese and Olives

Serves 4 to 6 as a first course or side dish

The ingredients of this dish—artichokes, tomatoes, olives, and goat cheese—taste like the end of summer: Matisse-like glimpses of the sea from shuttered windows, Mediterranean markets, and the last of the sunny vegetables before winter sets in.

A *tian* is a particularly Provençal gratin, full of Mediterranean vegetables and flavors. While this one is based on artichokes, *tians* can be made of eggplant, spinach, or zucchini instead. This one is very easy to toss together—once the artichokes are pared down to their hearts, that is. And if artichokes aren't around, it's good with just tomatoes.

Begin the meal with a salad of mixed wild greens and accompany the tian with a dish of tender pasta or potatoes cooked over an open fire.

8 artichokes, trimmed to their hearts and blanched, sliced about ½ to ¾ inch thick (or use 1 package frozen, defrosted, and drained artichoke hearts)

3 to 5 garlic cloves, finely chopped

1 teaspoon *herbes de Provence,* or as desired

2 to 3 tablespoons black olive paste

6 to 8 ripe tomatoes (must be fresh), sliced about ½ to ¾ inch thick

6 ounces goat cheese or feta cheese

4 ounces fresh bread crumbs, about ⅔ cup (3 pieces of somewhat thickly sliced country bread)

2 tablespoons grated Parmesan, pecorino, or Asiago

2 to 3 tablespoons olive oil

In a large shallow baking pan, preferably a ceramic one from Provence or Spain, arrange the blanched artichoke hearts. Sprinkle them with one-third of the garlic and one-third of the herbs, and stud with half of the olive paste.

Arrange the tomato slices so that they overlap with the artichoke hearts, and sprinkle the tomatoes with another third of the garlic and *herbes de Provence,* and with the remaining half of the olive paste. Crumble the goat cheese or feta over the tomatoes and artichokes, then sprinkle with bread crumbs, the remaining garlic and *herbes de Provence,* and Parmesan, pecorino, or Asiago. Drizzle with olive oil.

Heat the oven to 350°F. Bake the tian for about 40 minutes or until the crumb topping is golden and the tomatoes underneath are tender.

Serve right away, sizzling hot and fragrant.

260 CALORIES PER SERVING
14 G FAT
5 G SATURATED FAT
14 MG CHOLESTEROL
27 G CARBOHYDRATES
13 G PROTEIN
453 MG SODIUM

❧ Gratin Provençal Fermière

PROVENÇAL FARMER'S WIFE'S GRATIN OF POTATOES, GARLIC, FRESH HERBS, AND GOAT CHEESE

Serves 4 to 6

One year we got the idea that helping with the autumn wine grape harvest would be a marvelous way of having a holiday: not only would we find ourselves at the very heart of the Provençal soul, but we would get paid for it, too.

Twenty years later, my back is still not right. And the only really good part of the experience was the meals the farmer's wife prepared, especially this gratin of potatoes and goat cheese. (Adding the sprinkling of garlic at the end is my idea.) Using *crème fraîche* is deliciously, delightfully rich; using low- or nonfat sour cream more sensible.

You'll no doubt notice the abundant amount of garlic in the ingredients. You could cut this down if you like to about half the amount.

Since the dish is hearty, it is good served with the contrast of a crisp salad of purslane, chervil, watercress, and other interesting greens lightly dressed with olive oil and vinegar.

> 3 pounds baking potatoes, peeled and cut into chunks
> Salt and pepper to taste
> 2 onions, diced
> 2 tablespoons olive oil
> 8 to 10 garlic cloves, coarsely chopped
> 8 ounces *crème fraîche* or sour cream (low- or nonfat is fine)
> 1 log (8 ounces) goat cheese, cut into slices
> 2/3 cup shredded white cheese such as Jack, mozzarella, or Asiago
> 3 to 4 tablespoons grated Parmesan, pecorino, or other grating cheese

Cook the potatoes in rapidly boiling water until half done. Drain and sprinkle with salt and pepper.

Sauté the onions lightly in the olive oil until softened, golden, and lightly browned. Toss with the potatoes and half the chopped garlic.

Heat the oven to 350°F. In the meantime arrange half the potatoes in a baking casserole, then pour half of the *crème fraîche* or sour cream over the potatoes. Layer the goat cheese, then the remaining potatoes and *crème fraîche.*

Sprinkle with Jack, mozzarella, or Asiago, then with grated Parmesan or pecorino. Bake until the potatoes are creamy inside, and the cheese topping is lightly golden and crisped in places on top.

Sprinkle with the remaining garlic and serve right away.

465 CALORIES PER SERVING
24 G FAT
13 G SATURATED FAT
43 MG CHOLESTEROL
48 G CARBOHYDRATES
16 G PROTEIN
277 MG SODIUM

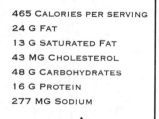

Courge au Tomates et Chèvre

SAUTÉED PUMPKIN WITH TOMATOES, HERBS, AND DRY GOAT CHEESE

Serves 4

Pumpkin is eaten throughout France in dishes ranging from soup to sautés and casseroles. In the Vaucluse, pumpkin is sautéed with lots of garlic and herbs, then left in a hot oven for about an hour to get tender, creamy, and crusty on top like a gratin.

This pumpkin dish is rich with the flavors of Catalonia and the Midi: fresh rosemary, sweet paprika, and dry goat cheese for grating.

5 garlic cloves
Salt to taste
2 pounds pumpkin, peeled and thinly sliced (about $^1/_8$ inch thick)
1 onion, chopped
2 to 3 tablespoons olive oil
5 to 7 ripe tomatoes (fresh or canned), diced
1 cup dry red or white wine
2 teaspoons chopped fresh rosemary
1 teaspoon paprika
4 ounces dry goat cheese (such as a *chabis*), coarsely shredded or grated

Crush the garlic with a pinch of salt until it forms a paste, then set aside.

Sauté the sliced pumpkin with the onion in a big, heavy frying pan in 2 tablespoons of the olive oil. When the pumpkin is lightly browned in places and half-tender, add the tomatoes, wine, half the rosemary, the paprika, and half of the garlic paste. Cover the pan and cook over medium-high heat, turning every so often, until the pumpkin is just tender.

Remove the cover and raise the heat, cooking and turning every so often until the liquid has nearly all evaporated and the pumpkin is quite tender.

Toss the remaining garlic paste into the hot vegetables, cook a few moments, add a tablespoon or so olive oil if needed, then add the cheese and continue to toss as the cheese melts.

Serve hot, sprinkled with reserved chopped rosemary.

250 Calories per serving
14 g Fat
5 g Saturated Fat
13 mg Cholesterol
23 g Carbohydrates
9 g Protein
127 mg Sodium

Fassoulia Gigantes

GREEK WHITE BEANS IN TOMATO SAUCE

Serves 4

Fassoulia—big, hearty white beans swimming in an olive oil-spiked tomato broth—to me is the essential food of Greece, although versions are doted on throughout the Mediterranean.

Fassoulia is eaten freshly simmered, ladled into bowls as soup, served with a wedge of lemon, a drizzle of olive oil, and a sprinkling of mountain herbs. Once cooled it thickens and can either be thinned out for the next day's soup or laid out on plates to be eaten at room temperature as a *meze* accompanied by chunks of crusty bread, plates of feta cheese, handfuls of bitter herbs such as arugula or purslane, cucumbers, etc.

Although rustic and peasant to its core, *fassoulia* can be turned into a sophisticated dish by the simple addition of a dollop of black olive paste and a drizzle of garlic oil (or *alli-oli*), or a few olive-spread *crostini*.

12 ounces (2 cups) raw white beans, such as *haricots blancs* (butter beans)
1 onion, chopped
1 tablespoon olive oil
2 cups diced tomatoes
   Salt, pepper, and sugar to taste
   Optional seasonings for finishing:
      Garlic oil*
      2 to 3 tablespoons black olive paste
      1 to 2 tablespoons fresh rosemary

*To make the garlic oil: purée 3 to 5 garlic cloves with a pinch of salt; I like to do this in a mortar and pestle as it releases more of the aromatic oils. Stir in 1/4 cup olive oil and set aside.

Vegetarian Main Plates

Cover the beans with cold water and bring to a boil. Cook over medium-high heat for 2 minutes, then remove from the heat and let sit in the hot water; the beans should swell and grow almost tender. Drain the beans and add 2 cups fresh water.

Place the beans in their fresh water on the stove and cook over medium-low heat, simmering gently, until the beans are just tender. Drain.

Meanwhile, lightly sauté the onion in the olive oil until it has softened, then add the tomatoes and cook together a few minutes. Add this mixture to the tender cooked beans and simmer until the beans are very tender but not falling apart. Season with salt and pepper, adding a pinch of sugar if the tomatoes are very acidic.

Serve the hot beans in bowls, each bowl garnished with a drizzle of the garlic oil, a tiny spoonful of olive paste, and a sprinkling of fresh rosemary.

361 CALORIES PER SERVING
5 G FAT
1 G SATURATED FAT
0 MG CHOLESTEROL
61 G CARBOHYDRATES
22 G PROTEIN
21 MG SODIUM

Guiso

WHITE BEANS (OR CHICKPEAS) SIMMERED WITH PUMPKIN AND SWEET-AND-SPICY RED PEPPERS

Serves 3 or 4

Throughout Spain beans and legumes are the mainstay of daily life. This dish of stewed beans and pumpkin is spiced at the last moment with a *picada*—a paste of almonds, garlic, and spices. It adds a depth of flavor to an otherwise simple dish.

The addition of sausage or salted bacon adds richness and authentic flavor, but is optional. Even in Spain, traditional ingredients are giving way to light, more healthful, meatless meals.

1 onion, chopped
2 tablespoons olive oil
Salt and black pepper to taste
1/4 red bell pepper, diced
1 tablespoon paprika
3/4 to 1 teaspoon mild red chili powder such as ancho, nora, or California
1/2 teaspoon cumin, or more to taste
Pinch cinnamon
Optional: 4 ounces Spanish chorizo or diced salted, not smoked, bacon (or pancetta)
1 pound pumpkin, peeled and cut into bite-size chunks
3 to 4 tablespoons tomato paste
1 cup dry sherry
1 cup water, or as needed
2 cups cooked drained beans—either white beans or chickpeas
3 garlic cloves
1/4 cup slivered or sliced almonds
1 green onion, thinly sliced

Lightly sauté the onion in 1 tablespoon olive oil until it is just softened and golden; salt and pepper to taste. Next, add the red pepper and cook them together a few minutes. Sprinkle with paprika, $1/2$ teaspoon of chili powder, cumin, and cinnamon and cook a few moments longer, then add the chorizo or bacon if desired, pumpkin, and tomato paste. Cover and cook over low heat a few moments.

Stir in the sherry and water, return (covered) to heat, and let cook about 15 minutes or until the pumpkin is just tender. Add the beans and simmer uncovered until the sauce thickens a little, 5 to 10 minutes.

Meanwhile, pound the garlic in a mortar and pestle or food processor, along with a generous pinch of salt, then add the almonds and the remaining chili and olive oil, pounding or whirling until a paste forms. Add the green onion and pound in or purée it with the paste.

When ready to serve, heat the pumpkin-bean mixture, then stir in the paste, warm through, and serve.

318 CALORIES PER SERVING
12 G FAT
1 G SATURATED FAT
0 MG CHOLESTEROL
38 G CARBOHYDRATES
12 G PROTEIN
117 MG SODIUM

❧ Cocido de Garbanzos

CHICKPEA AND VEGETABLE STEW

Serves 6, with leftovers

One day, while staying in a 300-year-old farmhouse on the island of Ibiza, we were served this pot of chickpeas. "A typical meal of the countryside," our host said. And later we spooned it up on the freshly white-washed terrace, shielded from the hot sun by the shade of an umbrella.

Bay leaves give the chickpeas a haunting aroma and flavor that make you realize that cooking beans from dried is really worth the effort. I often make a big pot and freeze several parcels for salads, soups, and sauces as the weeks progress.

The rosemary may not be traditional everywhere in Spain, but on Ibiza it grows wild on the hills, so fragant, so sweet, so delicious.

1 pound dried chickpeas
3 to 5 bay leaves
   Salt to taste
4 cups chicken or other stock, or broth of choice
Optional: 4 to 6 ounces flavorful ham or other smoked
   or salted meat
Optional: A pinch of mild nura or nora chili
   (or mild New Mexico chili)
1 or 2 sprigs fresh rosemary
½ celery root, peeled and diced
2 carrots, sliced
2 onions, coarsely chopped
15 cloves of garlic, whole (peeled or unpeeled, as
   you desire)
1 small to medium-size cabbage, cut into wedges
   Salt and black pepper to taste
   To serve: cooked rice or thin soup pasta, olive oil, a
   few cloves of raw garlic to crush and use as a condiment, wedges of lemon

Place the chickpeas in a container at least twice their size and add water to the top. For the best results, leave them to soak and soften overnight. If you don't have the time, bring them to a boil and cook over high heat for 5 to 10 minutes, then remove from the heat and let sit for an hour to cool and soften.

Drain the soaked chickpeas, then add fresh water to cover.

Add the bay leaves, and bring the pot to a boil. Reduce the heat and skim off the white scum that forms on the cooking surface as the beans cook. Cover the pot of beans and cook over very low heat until the chickpeas are tender, 1 to 2 hours, depending on the age of the beans and the mineral content of the water.

When the chickpeas are tender, drain but save their cooking liquid. Divide the chickpeas into two pots; fill one with cooking liquid to cover and season it with salt. Let this cool, then place in the refrigerator so that you have chickpeas to add to recipes over the next several days. From this pot you may wish to parcel off some for the freezer, too.

In the second pot place the rest of the chickpeas along with the stock or broth, optional meat if using, optional chili if using, the rosemary, celery root, carrots, onions, and garlic. Simmer for 30 minutes or so, then add the cabbage and continue to simmer for another 30 minutes until all of the vegetables are tender and the broth is well flavored. Discard the bay leaves and rosemary and serve in two courses.

As a first course, ladle the hot soup over rice or thin pasta (*fideo*); as a second course, serve the chickpeas and vegetables drizzled with olive oil, a little crushed garlic, and wedges of lemon if desired.

222 CALORIES PER SERVING
3 G FAT
0 G SATURATED FAT
0 MG CHOLESTEROL
42 G CARBOHYDRATES
12 G PROTEIN
105 MG SODIUM

Minestra di Farro, Cavolo, e Fogioli

TUSCAN WHEATBERRY, CABBAGE, AND BORLOTTI BEAN STEW

Serves 4

This Tuscan wheatberry and bean stew is a marvelous warming dish. The wheat cooks up tender and grainy, the beans are plump and rich, and the broth itself is rich with tomatoes, cabbage, onion, carrot, and garlic. Wheatberries are rich with B vitamins and fiber, making the stew as good for you as it is satisfyingly delicious.

$^3/_4$ to 1 cup (about 6 ounces) raw wheatberries
1 onion, chopped
1 carrot, diced
5 garlic cloves, coarsely chopped
1 to 2 tablespoons olive oil
1 or 2 bay leaves
$^1/_4$ to $^1/_2$ cabbage, coarsely diced or cut up into bite-size pieces
1 quart low-sodium chicken or vegetable broth/stock
$1^1/_2$ cups tomatoes, diced
$2^1/_2$ cups cooked borlotti beans; if unavailable, pinto or other pink beans
Salt and pepper
Garnish: Parmesan cheese

Place the wheatberries in a heavy saucepan with water to cover. Bring them to a boil, then reduce the heat and simmer, covered, for about an hour or until the wheatberries are chewy and tender. If overcooked they will pop; some may anyway—disregard them. As long as most of them remain intact, they are fine.

Drain the wheatberries and set them aside. This can be done a day or two ahead of time, or made way ahead and frozen.

Lightly sauté the onion, carrot, and garlic in the olive oil until softened, then add the bay leaves and cabbage and continue to cook lightly for about 10 minutes until the cabbage, too, has softened somewhat and lightly browned in spots.

Add the broth or stock and the tomatoes, bring this to a boil, then reduce the heat and simmer about 10 minutes. Add the wheatberries and beans, and continue to simmer until the soup-stew is richly flavored, about 30 minutes in all. Salt and pepper to taste.

Serve the soup-stew ladled into bowls and sprinkled generously with Parmesan; sometimes I like to set very thin shavings of Parmesan atop the soup instead to soften and warm and just slightly melt in.

514 CALORIES PER SERVING
6 G FAT
1 G SATURATED FAT
0 MG CHOLESTEROL
95 G CARBOHYDRATES
26 G PROTEIN
115 MG SODIUM

El Matambre

Serves 6 to 8

This shepherds' dish from Extremadura in Spain means "the killer," and I hope that hunger is what it is referring to. It is a hefty, filling dish of fried bread dumplings served in a tomato sauce with chopped hard-cooked egg. I like the addition of a little hot pepper to enliven it, and a sprinkling of cheese as well.

Country bread of any sort can be used—I recently made the dish using bread covered in poppy seeds, and the tiny black seeds only enhanced the bread dumplings. The herbs can vary as well—although parsley is classic, I like chopped chives, too.

8 ounces country bread, broken into bite-size chunks
8 fluid ounces milk
6 garlic cloves, crushed
3 tablespoons olive oil
2 eggs, lightly beaten
6 tablespoons chopped parsley or 3 tablespoons chopped chives; or a combination
Salt and pepper
Pinch of nutmeg
Oil for frying: to a depth of about 1/2 inch, either olive oil or a combination of olive and vegetable oil
3 or 4 green onions, including the greens, thinly sliced
1 1/2 cups tomatoes, diced (fresh or canned, including the juice)
Pinch of sugar, if needed, to balance the acidity of the tomatoes
1/4 teaspoon hot pepper flakes, or as desired
2 hard-cooked eggs, shelled and diced
Grated Parmesan or pecorino cheese

Place the bread chunks in a bowl and pour milk over them. Allow them time to absorb the milk, tossing every so often for an even coating.

Add half the garlic and half the olive oil, then mix in the eggs, parsley and/or chives, salt, pepper, and nutmeg.

Vegetarian Main Plates

Heat the oil in a heavy nonstick frying pan and, using a spoon dipped in cold water, make dumpling-like balls from the bread mixture, each about 2 inches in diameter. Fry until golden brown on each side, turning every so often until the insides of the dumplings (which start out soft and egg-soaked) are firm and cooked through. Remove from the pan with a slotted spatula and drain on absorbent paper.

Heat the remaining 1½ tablespoons of olive oil and lightly sauté the green onions in it, then add the tomatoes. (If using canned tomatoes first add the juice, cook it down, then add the diced tomatoes.) Cook about 10 minutes in total, then season with salt, pepper, and a pinch of sugar.

Serve the golden dumplings sprinkled with hot pepper flakes, blanketed with the tomato sauce, and sprinkled with hard-cooked egg and cheese. Serve right away.

328 CALORIES PER SERVING
23 G FAT
4 G SATURATED FAT
109 MG CHOLESTEROL
22 G CARBOHYDRATES
8 G PROTEIN
255 MG SODIUM

 # Piperade

Serves 4 to 6

Piperade is a creamy mixture of stewed peppers, onions, and tomatoes bound with just enough egg to hold it together. It is one of the Basque region's most famous dishes, in part because of the exceptional peppers that grow there.

Piperade is not really an omelet; it's more like a comforting bowl of delicious tomato-peppers awash in velvety, softly scrambled egg. It is a dish that is eaten in a myriad of guises throughout the Mediterranean, similar to the Spanish *pisto,* Turkish *menamen,* and North African and eastern Mediterranean *chakchouka.*

Piperade is at its best sprinkled generously with fresh basil and/or other fresh herbs and scooped up with chunks of lovely bread. For carnivores, serve with a paper-thin slice or two of silken pink prosciutto or Spanish *jamon Serrano.*

3 onions, peeled and sliced lengthwise
3 tablespoons olive oil
 Salt and pepper to taste
3 red bell peppers, sliced lengthwise
1 or 2 green bell peppers, sliced lengthwise
5 to 8 ripe tomatoes, diced
3 or 4 garlic cloves, chopped
3 eggs, lightly beaten
 Garnish: 2 to 3 tablespoons finely chopped fresh basil

Lightly sauté the onions in olive oil in a nonstick pan until the onions begin to soften; sprinkle them generously with salt and pepper, then add the red and green peppers. Continue to cook over medium-low heat, stirring every so often, letting the mixture grow soft and slightly sautéed.

When the mixture is saucelike, in about 15 minutes, add the tomatoes and half the garlic and continue to cook, letting it grow more saucelike, another 10 minutes.

Add the rest of the garlic to the pepper-tomato mixture, cook a moment, then add a few tablespoons of the pepper-tomato mixture to the eggs, then pour it all back into the peppers-tomatoes-onions in the pan.

Stir and scramble over low heat as the eggs lightly set and form a cloak for the peppers and tomatoes. Taste for seasoning.

Serve right away, sprinkled with basil.

VARIATION

Chakchouka
Add ½ to 1 fresh chili pepper to the mixture and sprinkle in cumin to taste. Instead of basil, sprinkle with cilantro.

187 CALORIES PER SERVING
10 G FAT
2 G SATURATED FAT
107 MG CHOLESTEROL
20 G CARBOHYDRATES
6 G PROTEIN
44 MG SODIUM

Omeleta me Anginares ke Tyri

FLAT OMELET OF ARTICHOKES AND FETA CHEESE

Serves 4 to 6 or more

The first time I visited Europe I bought an old VW in Holland and headed south on a long slow adventure to the Mediterranean. The car had frequent and serious problems, so the first people I met in almost every country were auto mechanics. And since I spent an inordinate amount of my budget on repairing this car, they were extremely friendly people. This was the first meal I ate in Greece, courtesy of my auto mechanic's mother.

6 medium-size artichokes or 12-ounce package of frozen artichokes
2 to 3 tablespoons olive oil
3 garlic cloves, chopped
6 to 8 eggs, lightly beaten
Salt and pepper
6 ounces feta cheese, diced or cut into bite-size pieces
Sprinkling of fresh herbs: thyme and marjoram

Prepare the artichokes: cut them into halves or quarters, then blanch and drain them. If using frozen artichokes, don't bother blanching—simply defrost them and drain.

Sauté the artichokes in half the olive oil in a heavy nonstick frying pan until the artichokes are lightly golden in spots. Next, add the garlic. Cook a few moments until the garlic smells fragrant, then remove the artichokes from the heat and let them cool slightly.

Season the beaten eggs with salt and pepper, then add the artichokes and mix in well.

Heat the remaining oil and pour in the artichoke-egg mixture, then scatter the feta into the still-liquid mixture.

Gently cook a few minutes over medium-low heat until the bottom sets and the top begins to firm up. You can pick up the edges and let the top, still-liquid eggs roll underneath to cook, if you like. Continue cooking until the eggs are cooked through the middle.

Heat the broiler and place the half-cooked flat omelet underneath the heat. Cook until the top is flecked with light brown color. Remove from heat and serve sprinkled with thyme and marjoram.

251 CALORIES PER SERVING
16 G FAT
6 G SATURATED FAT
238 MG CHOLESTEROL
16 G CARBOHYDRATES
15 G PROTEIN
494 MG SODIUM

Frittata Primavera

ITALIAN FLAT OMELET STUDDED WITH SPRING VEGETABLES

Serves 4

This multicolor vegetable frittata—yellow eggs studded with bits of pale green zucchini, red pepper, and bright green peas—is savory and delicious. It can be served as part of an *antipasto* or as a main course, and its satisfaction belies its ease of preparation.

1   medium-size zucchini, diced
2   tablespoons olive oil, or as desired
     Salt and pepper to taste
2   garlic cloves, chopped
1   medium to large or 2 small to medium onions, chopped
1   red bell pepper, roasted and cut into strips, diced
1/4 cup young peas (fresh or frozen)
     Large pinch dried mixed Italian herbs or *herbes de Provence*
3   eggs, lightly beaten

In a heavy nonstick frying pan lightly sauté the zucchini in a small amount of the olive oil until just golden in spots and tender. Remove the zucchini from pan, season it with salt and pepper, and toss it with the garlic. Set this aside.

Sauté the onion in 1 to 2 teaspoons of the olive oil until softened and lightly golden in spots. Season with salt and pepper and add to zucchini along with the red pepper, peas, and mixed Italian herbs or *herbes de Provence*.

Pour the eggs into the vegetable mixture and let sit for 5 to 30 minutes.

Heat a teaspoon or two of olive oil in the frying pan and, when hot, add the vegetable-egg mixture, spreading it evenly with a spoon or spatula.

Cook over medium-low heat until the bottom lightly browns and the top is no longer runny; pop under the broiler to cook the top until just firm and lightly flecked with golden brown.

Serve the frittata hot, warm, or at cool room temperature.

163 CALORIES PER SERVING

11 G FAT

2 G SATURATED FAT

160 MG CHOLESTEROL

11 G CARBOHYDRATES

7 G PROTEIN

58 MG SODIUM

Beid be Gebna Tamatem

EGGS BAKED WITH FETA, TOMATOES, AND PICKLED
HOT PEPPERS

Serves 4

Eaten throughout the Middle East and Balkans in varying guises, this simple dish of feta cheese and tomatoes seasoned with paprika and pickled chilies, then baked with an egg or two, is one of the most delicious and comforting dishes I can think of eating. It's especially good when the weather is hot, and it really is at its most charming and cozy self when made in individual casseroles with ceramic lids that each person can lift off so as to inhale the enticing aroma.

This dish is one of my comfort foods; a dish that, if you have enough meals at my house, I will eventually feed you. It is my favorite meal after a long plane flight or a hectic work day and as likely as I am to feed it to others, I am equally likely to make a bowlful for myself on nights when I am eating solo.

Good bread is really necessary with this dish, to dunk into the savory juices. A good first course is a crisp herb salad or cooked greens such as the Greek *Horta Vrasta* (page 9) and a plate of brown rice-stuffed *Dolmathes* (page 30).

12 ounces feta cheese, cut into thick slices
 4 to 6 ripe tomatoes, cut into slices or wedges
 1 tablespoon olive oil or butter
 2 garlic cloves, finely chopped
 2 to 4 pickled chilies such as jalapeños; about 3 tablespoons if sliced
 4 or 8 eggs
   Sprinkling of paprika and thyme

Preheat the oven to 400°F.

Arrange the feta cheese and tomatoes in 4 individual casseroles, drizzle with half the olive oil or dot with half the butter, and bake for 5 to 8 minutes or long enough to heat through and lightly cook the tomato.

Sprinkle the tomatoes and cheese with the garlic and pickled chilies, then break one or two eggs into each casserole, spooning up a little of the feta-tomato mixture over the edge of the eggs.

Sprinkle with paprika and thyme and the remaining oil or butter, then cover the casseroles with either their lids or with foil. Bake until the eggs set, about 8 minutes.

Serve right away, steaming hot, with chunks of country bread for dipping.

~~ Ajo Caliente con Huevos

HOT GARLIC WITH EGGS

Serves 4

Actually, this dish is more like hot bread and tomatoes with lots of garlic and a poached egg on the side. It's delicious for a summery brunch, although I was served it in a Seville *tapas* bar as a *tapa*. The original had almost double the amount of olive oil and was, indeed, luscious. Choose the amount of oil you can live with.

Since this is a dish that depends on strong tomato flavor, it is at its best when made with height-of-summer, ripest-of-ripe tomatoes. Perhaps canned tomatoes would work; but this dish really tastes best when the weather is hot enough to ripen the tomatoes.

10 garlic cloves
   Salt to taste
3 to 4 tablespoons olive oil, or as desired
1 to 1 1/2 pounds ripe tomatoes, peeled and diced
4 ounces stale country bread (about 4 or 5 slices), cut or broken into small bite-size pieces
4 poached eggs
   Sprinkling to taste: fresh marjoram, basil, or oregano

Place the garlic in a mortar and pestle or food processor. Sprinkle with salt, then crush. Remove about a third of the crushed garlic and mix it with 1 tablespoon olive oil. Set aside.

Heat 1 tablespoon olive oil in a heavy frying pan, then add the remaining crushed garlic and cook a few moments.

When the garlic is golden, add the remaining olive oil and about a third of the tomatoes. Stir together and cook until tomatoes are saucelike, then push the mixture over to one side of the pan and add another third of the tomatoes. Cook over high heat until the tomatoes are saucelike, then mix with bread and add the remaining tomatoes to pan. Cook until the bread and tomatoes are a solid, tomatoey mass.

Vegetarian Main Plates

Remove from heat, season with salt and pepper, then stir in the crushed garlic–olive oil mixture. Serve several spoonfuls with a poached egg alongside, or nestle into ramekins and serve each topped with a poached egg and sprinkled with herbs.

277 Calories per serving
16 G Fat
3 G Saturated Fat
212 MG Cholesterol
23 G Carbohydrates
10 G Protein
315 MG Sodium

Bosanska Kalja Od Kapusa

CABBAGE CASSEROLE WITH PEPPERS AND SAVORY YOGURT CUSTARD

Serves 4 to 6

Along the coast of the former Yugoslavia are some of the most exquisite of Mediterranean landscapes: tiny islands dot the sea, sandbar beaches glide into the shallow azure sea, and Medieval fortresses and castles overlook harbors, clinging perilously from cliffs that rise from the water.

This cabbage dish is utterly Balkan and distinctly Mediterranean. It is a favorite lunch dish, one you smell in the streets at midday and as you walk up the floors of an apartment building. Each family has its own version; many include meat, but many—such as this one—do not.

Parboiling the cabbage gives it a silky texture, and helps eliminate the skunky scent that cabbage can sometimes have. Take care to simmer the cabbage with tomatoes for long enough so that it develops a rich flavor. For vegans and those who don't particularly like the tang of yogurt, you can serve the cabbage without its tart custard. It's almost as good.

Crusty bread and a plate of feta cheese sprinkled with paprika and olive oil would be a typical accompaniment, as would a salad of sliced green peppers, onions, radishes or turnips, and cucumbers.

2 small to medium cabbages or 1 large one (2½ to 3 pounds in total), thinly sliced

2 onions, thinly sliced

5 garlic cloves, chopped

2 tablespoons olive oil

2 tablespoons paprika

1 red bell pepper, diced

8 ounces (1 cup) diced tomatoes (canned is fine), including juices

1 to 2 tablespoons fresh chopped marjoram, or to taste

Pinch of sugar, if needed

Salt and pepper to taste

12 ounces yogurt

2 eggs, lightly beaten

Parboil the cabbage and cook it for about 5 minutes or until it begins to turn translucent; drain.

Lightly sauté the onions and half the garlic in the olive oil until the onions soften, then sprinkle them with paprika and add the red bell peppers and tomatoes. Cook a few moments.

Add the drained cooked cabbage to the mixture, stir to mix well, then add half the marjoram, a pinch of sugar, and salt and pepper to taste.

Cover and cook for 30 minutes, stirring every so often, until cabbage is very tender and flavorful. There should be virtually no liquid left; if there is, remove the lid and cook a few minutes until the liquid cooks out. Remove from the stove, add the remaining garlic, then taste for seasoning. Set aside a moment.

Whisk the yogurt to remove any lumps, then whisk in the egg.

Arrange the cabbage in a baking pan or casserole, then pour the yogurt-egg mixture evenly over it.

Preheat the oven to 375°F. Bake for 15 to 25 minutes or until the custard is firm.

Serve right away or let cool slightly. Sprinkle with the remaining marjoram before serving.

209 CALORIES PER SERVING
9 G FAT
2 G SATURATED FAT
110 MG CHOLESTEROL
27 G CARBOHYDRATES
10 G PROTEIN
172 MG SODIUM

Estofat de Quoresmo

CATALAN SOUP-STEW OF CAULIFLOWER, ROMANO BEANS, AND CHICKPEAS

Serves 4 to 6

This Lenten soup blends the *mayorquina,* a soup of cabbage and tomatoes prepared in Perpignan (where the castle of the kings of Majorca is still to be seen), and the French Catalan stew of cabbage and white beans, *l'ouillade.*

    While both are usually served as a soup ladled over crusty bread and deliciously sopped with olive oil, I have instead turned it into a stew by adding cauliflower and green beans, and thickening the sauce with a spicy, garlicky *picada* of ground almonds.

  8 garlic cloves, chopped

  1 onion, thinly sliced

$^1\!/_2$ red bell pepper, chopped

  1 small cauliflower, cut into florets

  3 to 4 tablespoons olive oil

  2 bay leaves

14 ounces ($1^1\!/_2$ cups) tomatoes, diced, plus their juices
Several sprigs *each:* fresh marjoram, thyme, and basil (or pinches of each, dried, or $^1\!/_4$ teaspoon *herbes de Provence*)

$^1\!/_8$ teaspoon fennel seed
Pinch sugar, if needed, to balance the acidity of the tomatoes

  3 cups low-sodium chicken or vegetable stock

$^1\!/_2$ pound green Romano beans, trimmed, then cut into bite-size pieces

$^1\!/_2$ to $^2\!/_3$ cup cooked chickpeas

  2 pinches saffron threads

  3 tablespoons ground almonds (almond meal), preferably toasted

  1 teaspoon vinegar or more, to taste
Several shakes hot pepper seasoning (Tabasco, etc.)

Vegetarian Main Plates

Sweat about three-quarters of the garlic with the onion, red bell pepper, and cauliflower in 2 tablespoons of the olive oil for about 15 minutes or until the vegetables are softened.

Add the bay leaves, tomatoes, herbs, fennel seed, pinch of sugar, and stock and bring to a boil. Reduce the heat and simmer slowly over very low heat for 30 minutes or so.

Add the Romano beans and chickpeas and simmer while you make the *picada*.

To make the *picada:* In a mortar and pestle (which releases more flavor than does a food processor), pound the saffron threads into a powder. Add the reserved garlic and continue to pound with a pinch of salt, until it forms a sticky paste. Add the almonds, reserved olive oil, vinegar, and hot pepper seasoning, and pound or stir to mix well.

Stir this mixture into the hot soup, then ladle the soup into bowls, offering lemon juice and/or olive oil to drizzle into each bowl as desired.

193 CALORIES PER SERVING
10 G FAT
1 G SATURATED FAT
0 MG CHOLESTEROL
22 G CARBOHYDRATES
8 G PROTEIN
162 MG SODIUM

Vegetarian Main Plates

Lentejas Catalanas

CATALAN-STYLE BROWN LENTILS

Serves 6

Although one tends to think of the Mediterranean as perpetually warm and languorous, when winter hits it can hit shockingly hard. This lentil dish is especially warming, one I appreciated on a frigid January day as I spooned it up for lunch. The *picada* adds layers of flavor while thickening the lentils in a subtle way.

1 cup dried brown lentils

3 or 4 garlic cloves

$1/4$ teaspoon salt

Large pinch saffron

$1/4$ cup slivered blanched almonds ($3^1/2$ ounces), lightly toasted in an ungreased frying pan

1 slice country style bread (not sourdough), lightly browned in a teaspoon or two of olive oil until golden and crisp, then cut into bite-size pieces

1 tablespoon chopped fresh parsley or basil

Enough olive oil to form a paste

Salt and pepper to taste

Place the lentils in a saucepan with cold water to cover by about an inch. Bring to a boil over medium heat, then reduce the heat and let simmer for about 30 minutes. Remove from the fire and leave, covered, to cool. The lentils should become tender but not mushy and there should be a little extra liquid, but the lentils should not be swimming. If the lentils appear dry or wrinkled, add extra hot water to them.

In a mortar and pestle or food processor, crush the garlic with salt and saffron, then add the almonds, bread, parsley or basil, and about a tablespoon of water.

When a rough but evenly chopped mixture is formed, add a spoonful or so of olive oil—just enough so that the mixture forms a thick paste.

Heat the lentils over medium-high heat so that the liquid is nearly evaporated (pour some off if it is very watery). Stir in the savory paste, stirring well so that it thickens the sauce of the lentils. Cook for only a minute or two, long enough to thicken the sauce but not dissipate the seasonings.

Taste for salt and pepper and serve right away.

185 CALORIES PER SERVING
6 G FAT
1 G SATURATED FAT
0 MG CHOLESTEROL
23 G CARBOHYDRATES
11 G PROTEIN
128 MG SODIUM

GRILLED VEGETABLES

Throughout the Mediterranean one of the dominating scents is that of burning wood, and the aroma of food cooking over the embers. Whether it's Italy, the south of France, Tunisia, Israel, the coast of the former Yugoslavia, Egypt, Greece, or Turkey, there is always that elusive tantalizing smell in the air.

The art of roasting and grilling vegetables is an important part of the Mediterranean culinary tradition. The vegetables' charred skins yield tender, almost creamy flesh; they can be diced and eaten with no more than a glistening of olive oil, or they can be mashed into salads, puréed into soups, or julienned and tossed into pastas.

Onions, leeks, zucchini, peppers, fennel, potatoes, sweet potatoes, artichokes, asparagus, endive, and radicchio all are roasted and grilled, too.

Often they are served the next day, as part of another dish. In Greece, tomatoes are often roasted over the grill in tavernas, where there is always a fire going for *souvlakia* and the like, until the tomato skins are scorched and their flesh intensified by the fire, then turned into next-day tomato sauce: *salsa domatas kapsalismeni.* And who has not sat at a little table shaded from the hot Mediterranean sun and spooned up smoky, savory eggplant salad?

In Catalan Spain you might find escalivada, a feast of vegetables cooked on the grill, dressed in olive oil, lemon or vinegar, and lots of fresh herbs, or La Calçotada, the Catalonian springtime binge of green onions, cooked until their skins char and then served with a spicy dipping sauce, *romescu.*

Escalivada

ARRAY OF GRILLED OR ROASTED VEGETABLES

Serves 4

When the weather is less than perfect for cooking outside, this Catalan vegetable feast may be prepared in a big pan in the oven.

6 garlic cloves, chopped
3 tablespoons olive oil
1 to 2 tablespoons red wine vinegar
   Salt and pepper
   Large pinch mixed dried herbs or thyme
1 eggplant, cut into halves
1 *each:* red, yellow, and green bell peppers
4 whole heads of garlic
2 fennel, each cut into halves
2 zucchini, cut into lengths or halves
4 ripe tomatoes
2 red onions, cut into quarters

Prepare the dressing: Combine the 6 garlic cloves, olive oil, vinegar, salt and pepper, and herbs.

Arrange the vegetables in a large baking pan and drizzle half of the dressing over them.

Prepare the fire and when the coals are covered in white ash, place the vegetables on the grill. Cook, turning, until the outsides of the vegetables are lightly charred and the insides are tender.

Remove the vegetables from the grill and douse them with the remaining dressing. Serve on a platter accompanied by a plate of lovely goat or sheep cheese, a salad of *frisée* and green olives, and crusty bread.

341 CALORIES PER SERVING
12 G FAT
2 G SATURATED FAT
0 MG CHOLESTEROL
58 G CARBOHYDRATES
11 G PROTEIN
97 MG SODIUM

Aubergine, Fenouil, Courgettes, et les Epinards avec Coulis de Poivrons Rouges et Yaourt Safran

GRILLED EGGPLANT, FENNEL, AND ZUCCHINI WITH RED PEPPER COULIS AND SAFFRON YOGURT

Serves 4

August in Saint-Tropez: it was the feast of St. Laurent. Near the woods there was dancing under the plane trees, which had been strung with fairy lights. Little bistros set up tables in the warm summer night air and served the lightest of vegetables, cooked over an open grill, chic and refreshing on a sultry Côte d'Azur night.

5 garlic cloves, finely chopped
Pinch saffron threads
Pinch salt
1/2 cup yogurt
1 onion, chopped
1 tablespoon olive oil
5 ripe tomatoes or 1 cup diced tomatoes (canned is fine)
Large pinch *herbes de Provence*
1 roasted red bell pepper, diced
Salt and pepper to taste
1 medium-size eggplant, sliced into steaks
2 zucchini, sliced diagonally
2 bulbs of fennel
Garnish: 1 tablespoon fresh basil leaves, thinly sliced

Make the garlic-saffron yogurt: crush 1/2 clove of the garlic with the saffron and salt, either in a mortar and pestle or food processor. Add the yogurt and whirl until it forms a pale yellow color. Chill until ready to use.

Make the tomato-pepper *coulis:* lightly sauté the onion and remaining garlic in the olive oil until they are softened, then add the tomatoes and cook until sauce-like. Stir in the *herbes de Provence,* then add the red bell pepper. Cook together a few minutes; season with salt and pepper, and purée to a smooth consistency.

Arrange the sliced eggplant, zucchini, and fennel on a cookie sheet; brush them with olive oil and sprinkle them with salt and pepper.

Start a fire. When the coals are covered with white ash, about 40 minutes, grill the vegetables on both sides until they are browned.

To serve: spoon a puddle of red pepper and tomato *coulis* onto each plate. Arrange the eggplant, zucchini, and fennel on each plate in a pleasing manner. Garnish with a sprinkling of basil and a drizzle or dollop of the pale golden yogurt—I like to arrange tiny little droplets around the plate like a string of pearls.

200 CALORIES PER SERVING
5 G FAT
1 G SATURATED FAT
2 MG CHOLESTEROL
36 G CARBOHYDRATES
8 G PROTEIN
136 MG SODIUM

Asperges Grillées à l'Aioli d'Olive

GRILLED ASPARAGUS WITH BLACK OLIVE AIOLI

Serves 4

Fresh green stalks of asparagus taste so fine cooked over the grill: it brings out their grassy flavor and crisp-tender texture. Adding a dollop of salty black olive paste to the garlicky mayonnaise of Provence, *aioli*, makes a luscious purple-black-gray sauce, its flavor evocative of spring in villages throughout France's Mediterranean coast.

Serve, as a vegetable course, a huge pile of asparagus—the bigger the better. At the height of asparagus season, there is no finer supper, with crusty bread alongside and a plate of goat cheeses and fruit for dessert.

For a lower fat, more austere dish, omit the olive *aioli* and serve the grilled asparagus with wedges of lemon and a flurry of chopped basil.

1   bunch green asparagus, trimmed of their tough ends
4   tablespoons olive oil
3   garlic cloves, chopped
2   tablespoons dry white wine
2   teaspoons vinegar, or to taste
2   teaspoons chopped fresh rosemary
    Salt and pepper to taste
3   tablespoons black olive paste
4   tablespoons purchased mayonnaise
1/4 teaspoon lemon juice, or to taste

Marinate the asparagus in half the olive oil, half the garlic, the wine, vinegar, and half the rosemary. Season with salt and pepper and leave while you make the olive *aioli*.

Stir the remaining garlic, remaining olive oil, and remaining rosemary into the olive paste, then add a little at a time to the mayonnaise, mixing to combine well.

Season with lemon to taste. It should form a purple-black sauce; if it separates, stir vigorously to recombine or add a touch more mayonnaise for emulsification. Keep chilled until ready to serve.

Grill the asparagus until crisp tender, 2 to 3 minutes on each side.

Serve with a bowl of the olive *aioli* for dipping.

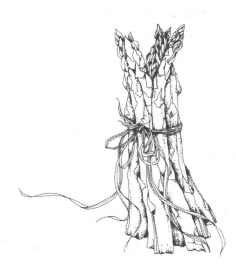

290 CALORIES PER SERVING
29 G FAT
3 G SATURATED FAT
8 MG CHOLESTEROL
7 G CARBOHYDRATES
4 G PROTEIN
387 MG SODIUM

Artichauts Grillés avec Vinaigrette Marocaine

GRILLED ARTICHOKES WITH MOROCCAN CHERMOULA VINAIGRETTE

Serves 4

Cooking over a fire brings out the smoky best in artichokes. It is the ancient way of cooking artichokes from Sicily throughout the Mediterranean. In Sicily it might be served with a spicy fresh tomato sauce, in southern France with a garlicky *aioli,* and in Morocco with the following *chermoula* vinaigrette.

4 medium-size artichokes, cut into halves and trimmed of their chokes; peel and keep the stems as well
4 garlic cloves, chopped
1/2 teaspoon *each:* paprika and cumin
1/4 cup lemon juice
1/2 cup olive oil
3 to 5 ripe tomatoes, diced
3 to 4 tablespoons *each:* chopped parsley and chopped cilantro
Salt and cayenne pepper as desired

Start the fire and let the coals burn until they are coated with white ash.

Blanch the artichokes and their stems; drain and set aside.

Mix the garlic, paprika, cumin, lemon juice, olive oil, tomatoes, parsley and cilantro, and salt and cayenne pepper. Brush a small amount of this onto the cut sides of the artichokes.

Grill the artichokes over the hot coals, turning every so often, until the outside leaves are browned but the inside (cut side) are only lightly browned in spots and tender.

Serve the artichokes hot with the remaining sauce-relish.

327 CALORIES PER SERVING
28 G FAT
4 G SATURATED FAT
0 MG CHOLESTEROL
20 G CARBOHYDRATES
5 G PROTEIN
124 MG SODIUM

Vegetarian Main Plates

Potiron Grillé avec Beurre au Poivron Forte

GRILLED PUMPKIN WITH RED CHILI BUTTER

Serves 4

Pumpkin is delicious when brushed with olive oil and cooked in big slabs on the grill. A dab of lightly spicy red chili butter is a gorgeous gilding, but not essential.

- 1 pound pumpkin or hubbard squash, seeded and cut into $1/2$- to $3/4$-inch slices
  Olive oil for brushing
- 4 garlic cloves, chopped
  Salt and pepper
- 3 tablespoons softened butter
- 1 tablespoon mild red chili powder such as ancho or nora
- $1/4$ teaspoon cumin
- 1 tablespoon chopped cilantro

Start a fire; when the coals are covered with white ash, you are ready to cook.

Brush the pumpkin with the olive oil, sprinkle with half of the garlic and salt and pepper to taste.

Grill over medium-hot coals until lightly browned in spots on each side and just tender when cut through.

Meanwhile, combine the remaining garlic with softened butter, mild red chili powder, cumin, and cilantro. Season with salt and pepper.

Remove the pumpkin from the grill and serve each slice with a nugget of chili butter to melt in.

146 CALORIES PER SERVING
12 G FAT
6 G SATURATED FAT
25 MG CHOLESTEROL
10 G CARBOHYDRATES
2 G PROTEIN
117 MG SODIUM

La Calçotada

A GRILLED GREEN ONION FEAST

Serves 4 to 6

This feast of grilled young onions (*calçots*) was once the prelude to a family feast in the fields, taken in the first flush of spring. These days, the calçotada is celebrated in restaurants and civic social clubs throughout the area surrounding the Catalonian town of Tarragona. The town of Valls, just north of Tarragona, is said to have originated the onion fest, and restaurants there serve thousands of eager onion eaters each day of the season (roughly from January to April).

The appearance of the first green onion shoots is a harbinger of warm weather, a symbol of hope at the end of winter and a promise of the warmth to come.

La Calçotada is traditionally served with a variety of sauces for dipping: *alli-oli* and the following *romescu*—strong with the fumes of pounded garlic and hot pepper. If the *romescu* is too intense, thin with a few spoonfuls of sherry.

1/4 ancho chili
2 or 3 garlic cloves
Salt to taste
3 tablespoons toasted, ground almonds (almond meal)
1/2 slice stale country-type bread
2 tablespoons olive oil
1 tablespoon lemon juice
2 ripe tomatoes, diced
2 bunches green onions, young leeks, or green garlic, trimmed, rubbed with a little olive oil, and sprinkled with salt

Lightly toast the ancho chili, then place it in a bowl and pour in hot water to cover. When plump, remove from its bath, discard the seeds and veins, and purée with garlic, salt, almonds, bread, olive oil, lemon juice, and tomatoes. Taste for seasoning and set aside.

Barbecue or grill the green onions, leeks, or garlic over high heat until they are charred on the outside and tender inside. Cut the green onions into 2-inch lengths.

Serve the onions piled in a heap with *romescu* sauce for dipping.

96 CALORIES PER SERVING
7 G FAT
1 G SATURATED FAT
0 MG CHOLESTEROL
7 G CARBOHYDRATES
2 G PROTEIN
25 MG SODIUM

Vegetarian Main Plates

SIX

MEAT, POULTRY, AND FISH

MEAT AND POULTRY

BLANC DE POULET AVEC CITRONS PRESERVÉS, *Chicken Breasts with Preserved Lemons and Rosemary*

POLLO ALLA DIAVOLO, *Chicken Wings with Mustard and Spice Coating*

DJEJ BIL HAMUS, *Moroccan Poached/Simmered Spiced Chicken Thighs with Lemony Chickpea Sauce*

KEBABPCHKA OR KEFTHEDES, *Savory Balkan Meatballs of Turkey and Soy*

CONIGLIO ALLA TOSCANO, *Rabbit Tuscan Style*

PORC PROVENÇAL, *Medallions of Pork Loin Marinated in Provençal Flavorings, Roasted or Grilled*

PAPAKI ME MOUSTARTHAS, *Grilled Duck Breast with Herbs, Rosemary, and Mustard*

CARDO CON JAMÓN, *Cardoon with Shreds of Spanish Ham*

TAGLIATA CON RUCOLA E RADICCHIO, *Thin Slices of Grilled Beef with Arugula and Radicchio Salad*

ARNI ME FASSOLIA, *Braised Lamb with Romano or Runner Beans*

FISH AND SEAFOOD

MOROCCAN GRILLED FISH BROCHETTES

PESCE AGLIO, POMODORI SECCHI, *Poached Swordfish with Herbs and Sun-Dried Tomatoes*

BAKED SALMON WITH GARLIC, CILANTRO, AND TOMATOES

LOTTE AUX ARTICHAUTS ET FÈVES, *Roasted Monkfish with Artichokes and Favas*

IN THE Mediterranean meat and poultry are not the focus of the meal as they are in the rest of Europe. Instead, meals are usually based on vegetables, grains, salads, and fresh cheeses, with small amounts of meat and poultry included occasionally in everyday meals. Large meat and poulty dishes are traditionally reserved for holidays and celebrations.

Modern Mediterranean meals stay close to this tradition, depending on which country you are in. Often a meal begins with an assortment of salads for a *meze* or *tapa,* soup or pasta.

The second course is usually a modest portion of meat or poultry, simply prepared by grilling, sautéing, or stewing. Often a small amount of meat or poultry is stretched by a large amount of vegetables. Chicken simmers with garden vegetables and a handful of olives, then is scattered with fragrant herbs, thin strips of meat are grilled then tossed with greens, lamb might be coated in spices and steamed or roasted, rabbit might be stewed or grilled. And always the flavor of lemon is never far from the pot.

Unlike meat and poultry, fish, hauled up from the briny depths of the sea, is an essential food of the Mediterranean. Fish and shellfish appear often on the Mediterranean table, delighted in and treated with great reverence. Whatever region you are in will yield its flavor to the fish: garlic, olive oil, lemon, tomatoes, and herbs.

Often fish and shellfish are simply stewed into a one-pot meal such as Zarzuela (page 270), bouillabaisse, or zuppa di pesche.

Blanc de Poulet avec Citrons Preservés

CHICKEN BREASTS WITH PRESERVED LEMONS AND ROSEMARY

Serves 4

Along with the pine forest scent of fresh rosemary, the preserved lemons give a refreshing flavor to the marinade in this recipe.

If you are just discovering the Moroccan salt-preserved lemon, you are in for a treat: pungent lemony skin; salty, silky flesh; and the thickened, honeyed liquid it's preserved in. If preserved lemon is unavailable, use fresh lemons or a combination of the juice and its fresh chopped fruit with salt to taste.

4 boneless chicken breasts, skin on
½ preserved lemon (see Salted Lemons, page 278), diced or mashed with a fork, plus 2 tablespoons of the preserving juice
6 to 8 garlic cloves, chopped
2 sprigs fresh rosemary, leaves removed and chopped (about ½ to 1 teaspoon)
  Juice from 2 fresh lemons
1 to 2 tablespoons chopped fresh parsley

205 CALORIES PER SERVING
8 G FAT
2 G SATURATED FAT
83 MG CHOLESTEROL
3 G CARBOHYDRATES
30 G PROTEIN
630 MG SODIUM

Combine the chicken with the preserved lemon, the preserved lemon juice, half of the garlic, and the rosemary. Leave to marinate for 2 hours at room temperature or overnight in the refrigerator.

Prepare the fire. When the coals are white-ashed, sprinkle the chicken with the remaining garlic, place the chicken on the grill, and cook 3 to 4 minutes on each side. Do not overcook!

Serve right away, the chicken drizzled with fresh lemon juice and sprinkled with parsley. To eat, remove the skin if you wish.

Pollo alla Diavolo

CHICKEN WINGS WITH MUSTARD AND SPICE COATING

Serves 4

Coated with mustard and spices and roasted to a crisp, these little wings are a delectable culinary souvenir from a picnic dinner on an Italian beach. The ingredients are gathered from all over the Mediterranean, and the mustard imparts its spunky, devilish spiciness.

If you're in the mood to start a fire and cook outdoors, these are also delicious grilled instead of baked.

2   pounds chicken wings
    Juice of 1 lemon or lime
1/2 teaspoon *each*: cinnamon and cumin
1/2 teaspoon dried basil leaves or marjoram
2   tablespoons paprika
    Salt and pepper to taste
3   to 5 tablespoons mild Dijon-type mustard
1   tablespoon olive oil

Cut the chicken wings into two parts each, the little drumstick and the wing tips. Alternatively, you can purchase the wings cut up like this or leave them in one piece.

Toss the chicken with the lemon or lime juice, cinnamon, cumin, basil or marjoram, paprika, salt, pepper, mustard, and olive oil.

Preheat the oven to 375°F. Arrange the chicken on a baking sheet and bake for 35 to 40 minutes, turning several times, until the chicken is sticky and crusty and browned. If the chicken is not crispy, raise the heat to 400°F for the last 10 minutes.

Remove from the pan and blot gently on absorbent paper. Serve right away and eat hot.

VARIATION

Use small fish in place of the chicken wings and cook the little fish over an open grill.

340 CALORIES PER SERVING
23 G FAT
6 G SATURATED FAT
90 MG CHOLESTEROL
2 G CARBOHYDRATES
29 G PROTEIN
238 MG SODIUM

❧ Djej Bil Hamus

MOROCCAN POACHED/SIMMERED SPICED CHICKEN THIGHS WITH LEMONY CHICKPEA SAUCE

Serves 4

I like to make this with skinless chicken thighs because with the skin removed, the dark meat can absorb its spicy rub all the better. And while the original is usually prepared with a whole chicken, I find that dark meat stands up best to the steady heat of the pot whereas white meat goes dry and dull.

Serve the chicken, chickpeas, and sauce ladled over steamed rice or over split and toasted pita bread with a dollop of yogurt alongside.

6 to 8 garlic cloves, coarsely chopped or sliced
Salt to taste
1 teaspoon ground ginger
Pepper to taste
1 tablespoon olive oil
2 pounds chicken thighs, skins removed but bones left in
1/4 cup *each*: chopped fresh parsley and cilantro
1/2 teaspoon turmeric
2 cinnamon sticks, each about 2 inches long, or 1 stick 4 to 5 inches long
1 onion, grated
Several large pinches saffron threads
4 cups chicken broth
2 cups water
3 cups cooked drained chickpeas
Juice of 2 lemons

In a mortar and pestle crush 3 cloves of the garlic with a large pinch of salt, then work in the ginger, black pepper, and olive oil. Rub this on the chicken and leave to marinate at room temperature for 2 hours or overnight in the refrigerator.

Place the marinated chicken thighs in a heavy saucepan with the reserved garlic, half the parsley and cilantro, the turmeric, cinnamon stick(s), grated onion, saffron, chicken broth, and water. Bring this to a boil, then reduce the heat and simmer very slowly over low heat for about 40 minutes or until the chicken is very tender.

Add the chickpeas and cook through, about 10 minutes, letting the chickpeas absorb the flavor of the broth.

Drain the chickpeas and chicken; set the mixture aside and keep it warm.

Boil down the broth until it forms an intensely flavored, well-reduced sauce, about 1½ cups in total.

Adjust the spice seasonings, salt and pepper, etc., then stir in the lemon juice. Return the chicken and chickpeas to the sauce, warm through for a minute or so, then serve sprinkled with the reserved parsley and cilantro.

355 CALORIES PER SERVING
8 G FAT
1 G SATURATED FAT
63 MG CHOLESTEROL
44 G CARBOHYDRATES
29 G PROTEIN
167 MG SODIUM

Kebabpchka or Kefthedes

SAVORY BALKAN MEATBALLS OF TURKEY AND SOY

Serves 4

These meatballs are very savory, very delicious. In the Mediterranean and Balkan regions they may be authentically prepared with ground veal or pork, but I find that a combination of turkey and texturized vegetable or soy protein tastes wonderful, without the guilt.

Serve with a Mediterranean salad of chopped raw cucumber, tomato, pepper, onion, and feta cheese, all sprinkled with lots of fresh mint or oregano, and chewy pita or crusty French bread.

1	pound ground turkey
1/2	cup texturized vegetable protein
1	onion, finely chopped
6	to 10 garlic cloves, coarsely chopped
1	egg, lightly beaten
	Salt and pepper to taste
	Dash allspice
1	teaspoon soy sauce
1/2	teaspoon fresh thyme or several pinches dried thyme
	Flour for dusting
1	tablespoon olive oil, if needed

Combine the turkey with the texturized vegetable protein, onion, garlic, egg, salt and pepper, allspice, soy sauce, and thyme. Form the mixture into walnut-size balls, then roll them in flour.

Heat the oil in a nonstick pan, then add the turkey-soy balls and cook, shaking every so often, until lightly browned on all sides.

VARIATION

Balkan Stuffed Red Peppers

In the Balkans the peppers used for stuffing are smaller than ordinary full-size bell peppers, with a spicy but less feisty bite than a jalapeño. They have great flavor and look nice, too.

If you can find smallish red and green peppers or very mild chilies such as yellow wax, use them. Stuff them with the above-described filling, then arrange them in a baking dish and pour over them enough stock to reach a depth of about $1/2$ to $3/4$ inch. Cover and bake for 45 minutes or until the peppers are tender and the filling cooked through.

Remove the stuffed peppers from the pan and pour the liquid into a saucepan. Bring the liquid to a boil and cook it down until it reduces to an intensely flavored sauce with an almost glazelike consistency. Stir in a cup of yogurt, pour this sauce over the stuffed peppers, then return the stuffed peppers to the oven and bake for about 10 minutes or long enough to heat the yogurt through and rewarm the dish. Serve sprinkled with paprika, hot or at cool room temperature.

307 CALORIES PER SERVING
16 G FAT
4 G SATURATED FAT
109 MG CHOLESTEROL
13 G CARBOHYDRATES
27 G PROTEIN
262 MG SODIUM

Coniglio alla Toscano

RABBIT TUSCAN STYLE

Serves 4

Rabbit is super lean, with a woodsey flavor that goes well with a variety of assertive, strong flavors. It can be grilled, baked, or stewed, but regardless of how it is cooked it is a good idea to marinate rabbit. Marinating the rabbit gives it succulence, which is important because rabbit, being super lean, can dwindle into dryness. Here the marinated rabbit is browned, then simmered in red wine and tomatoes and served scattered with sweet basil. You can vary the dish quite a bit: add green and/or black olives in the last few minutes of cooking, or accompany the rabbit with a few grilled sausages and serve it over polenta or fat pappardelle noodles.

Then again, if you are sentimental about bunnies, and who among us doesn't have those flashes of irrational bunny love, you can make the dish with duck or chicken, with the skin removed.

    1 rabbit, cleaned and cut into 10 to 12 pieces
  1/4 cup red wine vinegar
    1 cup dry red wine such as Zinfandel
  1/4 cup brandy
    5 garlic cloves, sliced
    2 onions, sliced
    5 fresh sage leaves or 1/2 teaspoon dried sage
    1 sprig fresh rosemary
    2 pieces of lemon peel, about 1 inch each
    3 to 5 tablespoons olive oil, or as desired
    1 tablespoon flour
    2 cups diced tomatoes (canned is fine; include
       the juice)
   10 fresh basil leaves
       Salt and pepper to taste

Combine the rabbit with the vinegar, wine, brandy, garlic, onions, sage, rosemary, and lemon peel and leave in a large bowl, well covered, overnight. Turn once or twice if you happen to remember.

Remove the rabbit from the marinade. Remove the solids from the marinade and dice them. Discard the stems and seeds.

Strain the liquid into a shallow stove-top casserole and add the rabbit, then simmer until the rabbit is done and the liquid has evaporated.

Add the olive oil to the rabbit, cook a few minutes, then sprinkle it with flour and continue to cook until the flour is cooked. Add the diced marinade vegetables, the tomatoes, and half the basil, then cover and cook slowly over very low heat until the rabbit is very tender. Taste for salt and pepper and serve the rabbit with its sauce, sprinkled with the remaining basil.

SAGE

416 Calories per serving
21 G Fat
5 G Saturated Fat
107 MG Cholesterol
15 G Carbohydrates
40 G Protein
55 MG Sodium

Porc Provençal

MEDALLIONS OF PORK LOIN MARINATED IN PROVENÇAL FLAVORINGS, ROASTED OR GRILLED

Serves 6 to 8

Pork has been bred to be a very lean creature, indeed. So lean it is, that you must marinate it to keep it moist and flavorful. The following marinade cloaks the slices of pork and seals in the juices; you can then cook the pork slices over hot coals or pan-brown them.

1 pork loin, 3 pounds or so, sliced ¼ to ½ inch thick
Grated rind of 1 orange
Juice of 1 orange
½ to 1 tablespoon chopped fresh tarragon
10 bay leaves
10 to 15 garlic cloves, coarsely chopped
1 cup dry white wine
2 tablespoons brandy
3 tablespoons olive oil
Salt and pepper to taste

Mix the sliced pork with the remaining ingredients. Cover and leave to marinate overnight in the refrigerator.

Prepare the grill. When the ash is white, you are ready to cook.

Remove the meat from the marinade (discard the marinade since it contains juices from the raw pork). Cook the pork over the coals, turning every so often, until the flesh is pale pink and turning white. This should only take a few minutes on each side. The meat should still be juicy, not overcooked and dry.

Serve right away.

VARIATION

The marinated pork may be pan-browned in a nonstick frying pan. Remove the meat from the pan. Defat the marinade and pour it into the pan. Boil it down until it makes a concentrated sauce. Taste for seasoning and serve, poured over the little pork medallions.

286 Calories per serving
16 G Fat
5 G Saturated Fat
109 MG Cholesterol
1 G Carbohydrates
32 G Protein
81 MG Sodium

Papaki me Moustarthas

GRILLED DUCK BREAST WITH HERBS, ROSEMARY, AND MUSTARD

Serves 4

While duck is a fatty bird, its breast, once the skin is removed, is lean and meaty rather than rich and greasy. In the following dish of grilled duck that I once ate in Greece, the duck breast is marinated in a garlicky emollient, then coated with mustard and grilled. It makes a superb summer supper, especially following a selection of light vegetable *meze* or *tapas* or a chilled soup or crisp salad.

Or you could turn the grilled duck into a warm salad by arranging the hot duck on top of a selection of vinaigrette-dressed leaves and grilled vegetables such as asparagus or mushrooms.

Duck breast is at its best served rare; always slice it thin, against the grain, so that each bite is tender (since like all lean meats, it can be a bit tough or chewy).

> 4 duck breasts, bones removed
>   Salt and pepper to taste
> 5 garlic cloves, chopped
> 1 teaspoon *herbes de Provence*
> 1 tablespoon chopped fresh rosemary
>   Juice of 1/2 lemon
> 1 tablespoon olive oil
> 2 to 3 tablespoons strong Dijon-type mustard

Combine the duck breasts with salt, pepper, garlic, and *herbes de Provence* and leave overnight in the refrigerator.

Toss the duck with the rosemary, lemon, olive oil, and mustard and leave another 1 to 2 hours.

Cook either over the grill or in a heavy ridged or flat pan until just cooked on each side but pink inside, about 5 minutes on each side. Carve thinly against the grain and serve, garnished with sprigs of fresh rosemary.

149 CALORIES PER SERVING
7 G FAT
2 G SATURATED FAT
72 MG CHOLESTEROL
1 G CARBOHYDRATES
20 G PROTEIN
155 MG SODIUM

Meat, Poultry, and Fish

Cardo con Jamón

CARDOON WITH SHREDS OF SPANISH HAM

Serves 4

Spanish ham, *jamón*, is salty and dry, delicious not only as an appetizer in weather that is sultry and hot, but also shredded as a seasoning in addition to or in place of salt.

This dish is my friend Paul's, from the kitchen of his 300-year-old mountain farmhouse on the island of Ibiza, where we've shared many sweet meals. Cardoons are large vegetables that look like giant celery and taste somewhat like artichokes. They are doted on throughout the Mediterranean, especially in Italy, Spain, North Africa, and Provence.

Serve as a first course *tapa* or as a side dish with crusty bread to scoop up the bits of cardoon, *jamón*, and vinaigrette sauce.

8 stalks of cardoon
2 ounces *jamón* or prosciutto, cut into strips or
  coarsely chopped
2 tablespoons olive oil
1 to 2 teaspoons balsamic vinegar
  Squeeze lemon juice
  Salt and pepper as desired, to taste

Peel off the outer tough strings from the cardoon and trim the edges. Cut it into bite-size lengths, about 1 to 2 inches, and blanch the cardoons in salted boiling water until they are just tender, about 10 minutes. Drain.

Toss the warm cardoons with the *jamón* or prosciutto, olive oil, balsamic vinegar, lemon juice, and salt and pepper to taste.

Serve at warm room temperature.

142 CALORIES PER SERVING
10 G FAT
1 G SATURATED FAT
0 MG CHOLESTEROL
9 G CARBOHYDRATES
5 G PROTEIN
553 MG SODIUM

Tagliata con Rucola e Radicchio

THIN SLICES OF GRILLED BEEF WITH ARUGULA AND RADICCHIO SALAD

Serves 4

Genoa: A warren of narrow walkways and cobbled streets that only a tiny Fiat or perhaps a motor scooter could pass through. Some of the pathways are dead-ends, others lead you to a long flight of stone stairs taking you to another street. Follow, follow, and the narrow little streets open onto charming piazzas. At the end of the day bars put out tables and chairs in these squares and crowds gather to sip, nibble, and chat before heading home or to a restaurant for the evening meal.

Ancient stone buildings covered with bills and notices: concerts, festivals, flea markets, and "Liguria-on-line." People are amused by us, they are interested and want to chat.

In the restaurant a young man leans over from a nearby table. "What is that?" he asks when the waiter brings my *tagliata con rucola e radicchio*. "It is beautiful." And so it was, and delicious too.

A *tagliata* is a large piece of meat, such as lean flank steak, marinated and then grilled. It is served warm, in thin slices cut against the grain. In Genoa my *tagliata* came on a bed of delightful salad leaves.

8 garlic cloves
Several pinches salt (about $1/8$ to $1/4$ teaspoon)
3 tablespoons olive oil
$1 1/2$ tablespoons vinegar or lemon juice
$1/2$ to 1 teaspoon mixed dried herbs or rosemary or thyme
1 flank steak
Several handfuls *each:* arugula leaves and radicchio leaves, torn into bite-size pieces
2 tablespoons fresh basil, thinly sliced, or as desired
Salt and pepper to taste

In a mortar and pestle crush the garlic with a large pinch or two of salt. When it forms a paste, work in 2 tablespoons of the olive oil, then 2 teaspoons of the vinegar or lemon juice and the dried herbs.

Rub this mixture all over the meat and leave it to marinate for 2 hours at room temperature or preferably in the refrigerator overnight.

Prepare the grill: when the coals are covered in a white ash, place the flank steak on the grill and cook it on each side until it has reached the desired doneness, turning every so often. It is best when rare and will probably take 10 minutes on each side, but this depends on the heat of the coals and the thickness of the meat. You will need to check it yourself once or twice.

Remove the flank steak to a carving platter and allow it to sit and rest for a few minutes before carving.

Toss the arugula with the radicchio and the basil. Dress it with the remaining olive oil and vinegar or lemon juice; salt and pepper to taste.

Slice the flank steak against the grain, then arrange each portion of sliced beef (3 to 4 ounces) on a bed of the salad and serve right away.

247 CALORIES PER SERVING
15 G FAT
5 G SATURATED FAT
64 MG CHOLESTEROL
2 G CARBOHYDRATES
25 G PROTEIN
112 MG SODIUM

Arni me Fassolia

BRAISED LAMB WITH ROMANO OR RUNNER BEANS

Serves 4 to 6

This is the stew that is prepared in endless variations, in endless tavernas, throughout the islands and mountains of Greece. Big fat runner or Romano beans are very nice in the tomato-rich stew; so, too, is lightly browned eggplant, blanched zucchini, or leaves of spinach or chard.

Blotting off the fat from browning helps keep the fat level down; in addition, you could make the stew a day ahead and leave it in the refrigerator overnight—just skim off the fat that has chilled to a firm waxy substance. (This stew, like most others, tastes best when prepared a day before serving.)

2 pounds boneless lamb chunks, such as shoulder or leg, or 3 pounds bone-in lamb (shoulder chops, etc.)
Salt and pepper to taste
4 tablespoons olive oil
2 onions, thinly sliced lengthwise
3 cups diced tomatoes, including their juices
1 tablespoon honey
2 tablespoons tomato paste dissolved in 2 tablespoons water
1 cup meat broth or stock
1 bay leaf
2 tablespoons cumin
1/4 teaspoon *each:* cinnamon and allspice or cloves
2 teaspoons dried oregano leaves, crumbled
1 to 2 pounds Romano or runner beans, trimmed and cut into bite-size pieces
1/4 cup chopped fresh parsley
2 tablespoons lemon juice
1 garlic clove, chopped

Sprinkle the lamb chunks with salt and pepper, then quickly brown them in 2 tablespoons of the olive oil. Remove the meat from the pan and blot it lightly with paper towels. Pour off the fat from the pan.

Sauté the onion in the same pan in 1 tablespoon olive oil, then add the tomatoes, honey, tomato paste, meat broth or stock, bay leaf, cumin, cinnamon, allspice or cloves, and oregano. Return the meat to the pan. Bring to a boil, then reduce the heat to very low and simmer, covered, or bake in a 325°F oven until the meat is tender, about 45 minutes.

Blanch the beans for 1 minute, then drain and add them to the pan along with the remaining tablespoon of olive oil and half the parsley. Simmer a few minutes longer. Taste for seasoning, then stir in the lemon juice and add a dash more honey, if needed.

Combine the parsley and garlic, and stir in just before serving.

Serving Suggestion
For a lower-fat dish, let the meat cool, then spoon off excess oil.

485 CALORIES PER SERVING
33 G FAT
11 G SATURATED FAT
105 MG CHOLESTEROL
19 G CARBOHYDRATES
29 G PROTEIN
145 MG SODIUM

In the Mediterranean seafood is one of the great pleasures of the table. Prepared simply—grilled, sautéed, or simmered—it is often served with no more than a handful of herbs and a squeeze of sour lemon.

Moroccan Grilled Fish Brochettes

Serves 4

While the fish is grilling, grill sliced eggplant and peppers—red and/or green—alongside as well as wedges of parboiled, lightly marinated potatoes, all sprinkled with cumin, paprika, olive oil, and lemon and served with a bowl of hot pickled peppers or chopped onions.

   This makes great cookout fare, perfect for a summer supper at the beach. A selection of fresh salads such as raw fennel in lemon vinaigrette, ripe sliced tomatoes and basil, and artichokes with olive oil and garlic would all be delicious starters.

> 5 garlic cloves, chopped
> 1/2 teaspoon *each:* paprika and cumin
>   Several pinches cayenne pepper
> 1/2 to 1 teaspoon salt, or to taste
> 4 tablespoons olive oil
> 2 tablespoons lemon or lime juice
> 2 tablespoons *each:* chopped fresh parsley and chopped fresh cilantro
> 1 1/2 pounds firm-fleshed white fish, cut into 1- to 2-inch cubes
> 1 lemon, cut into wedges

Combine the garlic, paprika, cumin, cayenne, salt, olive oil, lemon or lime juice, and 1 tablespoon each of the parsley and cilantro. Add the fish cubes and toss together to coat them all.

Leave the fish to marinate in this mixture for 2 hours at room temperature or overnight in the refrigerator.

To grill: Thread the fish cubes on metal skewers or bamboo skewers that have soaked for 30 minutes in cold water.

Cook the fish brochettes over charcoal until they are lightly browned on each side, about 7 to 8 minutes in total.

Serve sprinkled with remaining parsley, cilantro, and offer lemon wedges and a bowl of hot sauce such as *harissa* (page 181) or garlic *zhug* (page 277), or a saucer each of paprika and cayenne pepper.

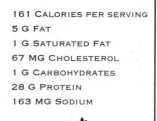

161 CALORIES PER SERVING
5 G FAT
1 G SATURATED FAT
67 MG CHOLESTEROL
1 G CARBOHYDRATES
28 G PROTEIN
163 MG SODIUM

Pesce Aglio, Pomodori Secchi

POACHED SWORDFISH WITH HERBS AND SUN-DRIED TOMATOES

Serves 4

This luscious and easy-to-prepare dish can be made with tuna instead of swordfish, and could, if you like, include artichoke hearts.

4 swordfish steaks, about 1½ pounds in total
1 tablespoon olive oil
3 garlic cloves, chopped
½ teaspoon *herbes de Provence*
   Salt and pepper to taste
⅓ to ½ cup dry white wine
8 sun-dried tomatoes, coarsely chopped or julienned
1 lemon, sliced thin

Heat the oven to 375°F.

Rub the swordfish steaks with oil and garlic, then sprinkle them with *herbes de Provence,* salt, and pepper. Place them in a baking pan just large enough to hold them in one layer with an inch or so in between each steak.

Add the wine to the pan, then sprinkle the sun-dried tomatoes and lemon slices over the fish. Cover with foil. Bake until the fish is just cooked through, 10 to 15 minutes.

Serve the fish with a little of the sun-dried tomatoes, lemon slices, and pan juices poured over.

252 CALORIES PER SERVING
10 G FAT
2 G SATURATED FAT
63 MG CHOLESTEROL
6 G CARBOHYDRATES
33 G PROTEIN
270 MG SODIUM

Meat, Poultry, and Fish

Baked Salmon with Garlic, Cilantro, and Tomatoes

Serves 4

This recipe is from Tunisia, from a Spanish cantor with a passion for food and cooking. He was the keeper of Kashrut when I catered for parties in kosher kitchens, and as we cooked he shared stories and recipes from his exotic childhood. For celebrations, I prepared huge whole salmon, but the following scaled-down version is equally good.

Sometimes I make a double portion of the spicy cilantro mixture and rub half into the salmon, saving the remainder to mix with diced tomatoes and serve as a salsa-like relish with the fish.

$^{1}/_{2}$ fresh green chili such as a jalapeño, chopped
4 garlic cloves, chopped
1 bunch cilantro, chopped
$^{1}/_{4}$ to $^{1}/_{2}$ teaspoon ground cumin
$^{1}/_{4}$ cup lemon juice (juice of 1 or 2 lemons)
1 salmon fillet, about 2 pounds
2 tablespoons olive oil
   Salt and pepper
2 tomatoes, sliced

Combine the chili, garlic, cilantro, cumin, and lemon juice; set aside.

Brush the salmon fillet with olive oil, sprinkle with salt and pepper, then place it on a heavy-duty aluminum foil sheet. Spread the cilantro mixture on the salmon, then top with a layer of sliced tomatoes.

Fold the edges of the foil over so that they meet each other, then seal them tightly. Place the parcel on a baking sheet.

Preheat the oven to 400°F. Bake the fish until the salmon is firm, about 20 minutes. Unwrap the fish carefully, as steam can burn the unwary. Serve the salmon and its cooking juices right away.

360 CALORIES PER SERVING
19 G FAT
3 G SATURATED FAT
107 MG CHOLESTEROL
6 G CARBOHYDRATES
40 G PROTEIN
97 MG SODIUM

Lotte aux Artichauts et Fèves

ROASTED MONKFISH WITH ARTICHOKES AND FAVAS

Serves 4

Monkfish is an ugly beast of a fish, its face as frightening as an ogre. But it is the monkfish's tail that fishmongers sell and diners covet, with its flesh firm and mild, tasting remarkably like lobster.

Monkfish, also known as *lotte* or anglerfish, is a quintessentially Mediterranean fish. If unavailable, use a succulent shellfish such as lobster tails or scallops, or in the lower-rent district, cod.

8 ounces fava beans, shelled

4 artichokes, trimmed of their outer leaves

1 or 2 monkfish tail fillets, cut into 4 portions (about 2½ pounds altogether), tough membrane and grainy side strip removed (have your fishmonger do this for you)

1 head garlic, divided into cloves (2 cloves cut into slivers)

Salt and pepper

2 tablespoons olive oil

2 cloves chopped garlic

1 cup fish or chicken broth

Juice of 1 lemon

1 tablespoon chopped fresh basil and/or parsley

Blanch the fava beans, then rinse in cold water and skin them. Set them aside.

Blanch the artichoke hearts, then remove them from the heat and cut them into quarters. Discard their inner chokes and set aside.

Make incisions all over the monkfish fillets and insert garlic slivers as if you were preparing a roast. Salt and pepper the filets, then tie each with string to keep it together during roasting.

Preheat the oven to 350°F. While the oven is heating, warm 1 tablespoon of the olive oil in a heavy frying pan and add the fish. Brown the fillets quickly on all sides, then surround them with the whole garlic cloves. Slide the frying pan into the oven, and roast the fillets for about 15 minutes; remove from the oven.

While the fish is baking, heat the chopped garlic in the remaining tablespoon of olive oil and add the favas and artichokes. Pour in the broth and bring to a boil. Cook over very high heat until it reduces to a strong-flavored liquid. Add the lemon.

Remove the monkfish from the pan and slice; arrange on a serving platter with the favas and artichokes. Add the reduced broth to the pan and cook over high heat, then pour it over the fish and vegetables. Serve right away, sprinkled with basil and/or parsley.

369 CALORIES PER SERVING
12 G FAT
2 G SATURATED FAT
68 MG CHOLESTEROL
21 G CARBOHYDRATES
48 G PROTEIN
216 MG SODIUM

Rougets et Haricots à la Vinaigrette d'Olives Noires Provençals

PROVENÇAL PAN-BROWNED SNAPPER, WHITE BEANS, AND BLACK OLIVE VINAIGRETTE

Serves 4

Lunch in Valbonne, sitting outside at a little table set in the market square under arches shading us from the heat of midday; the marketplace was just packing up and my purchases were settled on the ground around my feet, where a small pack of dogs had also gathered.

We ate roasted vegetables, little salads, and the following pan-browned red snapper surrounded by tender white beans, splashed with a little black olive vinaigrette. It was the essence of Provence, the essence of the Mediterranean.

3 garlic cloves, chopped
2 tablespoons black olive paste
$1/2$ to 1 teaspoon chopped fresh rosemary, or to taste
$1/4$ cup olive oil, plus 1 to 2 teaspoons for rubbing onto the fish
1 to $1 1/2$ tablespoons red wine vinegar, or to taste
$1 1/2$ pounds red snapper filets, with skin on
    Salt and black pepper to taste
1 cup cooked white cannellini or similar beans, drained (canned is fine; rinse well)
    Garnish: 1 tablespoon chopped fresh parsley

Combine half the garlic with the olive paste, rosemary, $1/4$ cup olive oil, and vinegar. Set it aside.

Rub the snapper with salt and pepper, then with the remaining olive oil. Heat a nonstick frying pan, sprinkle the filets with the remaining garlic, and pan brown the snapper filets, on the skin side first, then on the second side, cooking until they are just opaque.

Meanwhile, arrange a border of white beans on each plate or on a serving platter. When the fish has cooked, place it in the center of the beans, then drizzle the top of the fish and the beans with the vinaigrette. Serve right away, sprinkled with parsley.

339 CALORIES PER SERVING
19 G FAT
2 G SATURATED FAT
45 MG CHOLESTEROL
12 G CARBOHYDRATES
30 G PROTEIN
277 MG SODIUM

❧ Scampi alla Griglia

LEMON-MARINATED GRILLED PRAWNS WITH LEMON-TOMATO-HERB SALSA

Serves 4

These prawns are pure Mediterranean in character, marinated so that the olive oil and lemon permeates every bite. Vary the herbs and you will vary the flavor of the dish.

You don't need to add tomatoes to your salsa—lemon and herbs do well on their own. Or you can omit the salsa altogether.

1½ pounds large shrimp or prawns, in their shells with their heads removed
6 tablespoons olive oil
5 tablespoons lemon juice
5 garlic cloves, chopped
2 teaspoons chopped fresh parsley
2 to 3 teaspoons chopped fresh herbs such as fennel, thyme, rosemary, oregano, or marjoram
Salt and black or cayenne pepper to taste
3 ripe tomatoes, diced
2 or 3 lemons, cut into wedges

Combine the shrimp or prawns with half the olive oil, half the lemon juice, half the garlic, and half the herbs. Season with salt and black or cayenne pepper to taste. Leave to marinate for an hour.

Meanwhile, light the grill. When the coals are covered with white ash, they are ready, about 40 minutes. While you're waiting for the coals to heat, make a salsa of the diced tomatoes, remaining oil, remaining lemon juice, remaining garlic, and remaining herbs. Season with salt and pepper.

Remove the shrimp or prawns from the marinade and grill them over the hot coals. When they come off the grill, serve them with the salsa spooned around and with the lemon wedges.

VARIATION

Gambas al Ajillo

For this classic Spanish *tapa,* marinate the prawns or shrimp as in the preceding recipe, omitting the herbs and the salsa. Remove the shrimp or prawns from their marinade and dry with absorbent paper or a clean towel.

In a frying pan, heat 3 to 5 cloves chopped garlic in a little of the olive oil from the marinade; add the shrimp or prawns and cook until they are lightly colored and turning pink. Remove from the heat and serve right away, sprinkled with parsley.

261 CALORIES PER SERVING
14 G FAT
2 G SATURATED FAT
219 MG CHOLESTEROL
10 G CARBOHYDRATES
25 G PROTEIN
261 MG SODIUM

❧ Zarzuela

SPANISH FISH AND SEAFOOD STEW

Serves 4

Throughout the Mediterranean you will find variations on this theme: a big cauldron of fish and shellfish in a broth redolent with wine, garlic, and tomatoes. This one is Spanish.

$\frac{1}{2}$ pound uncooked shrimp, in their shells
3 to 4 tablespoons olive oil
5 garlic cloves, coarsely chopped
16 mussels, scrubbed
1 pound firm-fleshed white fish (such as monkfish, eel, cod, or bass)
$\frac{1}{2}$ pound cleaned squid, tentacles diced, bodies sliced into rings
$\frac{1}{4}$ cup brandy
1 onion, chopped
1 teaspoon paprika
$1\frac{1}{2}$ cups diced tomatoes (canned is fine, including the juices)
1 tablespoon tomato paste
1 bay leaf
Pinch thyme or mixed dried herbs
$\frac{1}{2}$ cup *each:* dry white wine and fish or chicken stock
Pinch salt
2 or 3 pinches saffron threads
3 tablespoons chopped fresh parsley

Lightly sauté the shrimp in half the olive oil and half the garlic for about 1 minute until the shrimp begin to turn pink, then remove the shrimp and garlic with a slotted spoon.

In the same oil, cook the mussels until they begin to open, about 8 minutes, then remove to the plate with the shrimp. Add the fish to the pan, brown slightly, then add the squid. Brown a few minutes together, then remove from the heat and pour in the brandy. Ignite the brandy, taking care not to singe your eyebrows. When the flames die down, remove the contents to another container.

Add the remaining olive oil to the pan and lightly sauté the onion until it softens, then sprinkle in the paprika and cook a few moments. Add the tomatoes, tomato paste, bay leaf, and thyme or mixed dried herbs and continue to cook a few minutes until saucelike, then pour in the wine and boil until the sauce reduces down to about half its volume.

Stir in the fish or chicken stock and the reserved shellfish and fish. Cover and cook over very low heat for a few minutes.

While this is cooking, in a mortar and pestle pound the remaining garlic with a pinch of salt, saffron, and parsley, then add a few spoonfuls of the fish broth until it makes a smooth sauce.

Add this to the fish, simmer a few minutes longer, and serve.

346 Calories per serving
13 g Fat
2 g Saturated Fat
260 mg Cholesterol
11 g Carbohydrates
41 g Protein
282 mg Sodium

Pescado con Perseil

SPANISH COD WITH A PARSLEY CRUST

Serves 4

Chopped parsley and garlic, mixed with bread crumbs and olive oil, make a lovely cloak for cod or, indeed, any white-fleshed fish fillet or steak.

   The mixture is good, too, tucked into the open shells of mussels, then popped under the broiler to crisp up.

1½ pounds cod fillets, skin removed
   Salt and black pepper to taste
6 garlic cloves, crushed
3 tablespoons olive oil
4 tablespoons lemon juice
1 cup fresh bread crumbs
2 tablespoons chopped fresh parsley

Sprinkle the cod with salt, pepper, half the garlic, and half the olive oil. Let it sit at room temperature for an hour or overnight in the refrigerator.

   Heat the oven to 350°F. Sprinkle the cod with lemon juice, then mix the remaining garlic and olive oil with the bread crumbs and parsley and sprinkle it over the fish. Spoon any of the olive oil from the bottom of the pan over the crumbs. Bake for 15 to 20 minutes or until the fish just flakes when prodded with a sharp knife or fork.

VARIATION

Spanish Fish and Mussels with Parsley and Crumbs
Add 2 pounds of scrubbed mussels to the pan and re-duce the amount of fish to 1 pound, cut into 4 pieces. Sprinkle the fish with only half of the parsley mixture and, when the mussels open up, sprinkle them with the remaining parsley and crumbs.

263 CALORIES PER SERVING
12 G FAT
2 G SATURATED FAT
67 MG CHOLESTEROL
10 G CARBOHYDRATES
30 G PROTEIN
157 MG SODIUM

OLIVES, PICKLES, AND ZESTY CONDIMENTS

OLIVES, pickles, and zesty condiments are eaten throughout the Mediterranean, often purchased from a stall or shop, at other times put together with a few pungent ingredients, a few fresh herbs, and a glistening of olive oil to hold it all together.

The following are just a few of my favorites; others are attached to recipes scattered throughout the book, and still others are for sale on grocers' shelves.

Pomodori Secchi e Marinate

PLUMP HERB-MARINATED SUN-DRIED TOMATOES

Makes about 2 cups

Marinating your own sun-dried tomatoes is worth the slight effort demanded: the tomatoes are sweet and tender, with fresh and vivacious rather than long-preserved flavor.

In addition, dried tomatoes are so easy to find these days and last nearly forever in their dried leathery state.

You can vary the seasonings to taste: red wine vinegar gives a sharp flavor, sherry vinegar a slightly unexpected nuttiness, and balsamic vinegar emphasizes the sweetness of the tomatoes. Similarly for herbs: thyme, oregano, marjoram, and sweet basil are all magnificent fresh, and in the winter oregano, thyme, and *herbes de Provence* are terrific as well.

1 package (¹/₂ pound) sun-dried tomatoes
  Salt to taste, if needed (some dried tomatoes, especially those from Italy, are already salted)
3 tablespoons olive oil, or as desired
1 tablespoon vinegar of choice
3 garlic cloves, chopped
  Large pinch of dried thyme, dried *herbes de Provence,* or several tablespoons fresh herbs to sprinkle when serving

Place the sun-dried tomatoes in a saucepan and cover with water. Bring to a boil, then reduce the heat and simmer for about 10 minutes or until they soften.

Drain the tomatoes if they have softened; if they are not quite soft yet, let them sit in the hot liquid and continue to steep and soften another 5 minutes or so.

Sprinkle the drained tomatoes with salt (if they are unsalted), olive oil, vinegar, garlic, and dried herbs if using. Let cool.

Toss tomatoes several times in their seasonings. Serve sprinkled with fresh herbs if desired.

143 CALORIES PER ¹/₄ CUP
6 G FAT
1 G SATURATED FAT
0 MG CHOLESTEROL
18 G CARBOHYDRATES
5 G PROTEIN
32 MG SODIUM

Zhug

CHILI-GARLIC PASTE/SAUCE

Makes about ½ cup

This Israeli condiment of Yemenite descent reeks deliciously of garlic, cilantro, and spices. It is delicious spread onto thin flat breads, judiciously dabbed into a falafel-filled pita or a plate of tomato-sauced spaghetti, or thinned as an accompaniment to soups or couscous.

- 3 garlic cloves
  Large pinch salt
- 2 or 3 small hot fresh chilies, cut up, or 4 or 5 small dried hot red chilies, soaked for 30 minutes in boiling water to cover, then cut up
- 1 teaspoon lemon juice, or to taste
- ¼ teaspoon cumin, or to taste
- ¼ teaspoon paprika
  Optional: Pinch ground cardamom
- 1 tablespoon tomato paste
- 1 to 2 tablespoons chopped fresh cilantro
- 3 to 4 tablespoons water

Crush the garlic with salt in a mortar and pestle or food processor, then add the chilies and purée into a paste. Mix in the lemon juice, cumin, paprika, ground cardamom if desired, tomato paste, cilantro, and water.

Taste for seasoning; store for up to a week in the refrigerator.

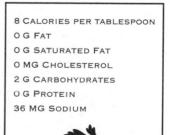

8 CALORIES PER TABLESPOON
0 G FAT
0 G SATURATED FAT
0 MG CHOLESTEROL
2 G CARBOHYDRATES
0 G PROTEIN
36 MG SODIUM

Salted Lemons

10 preserved salted lemons

Moroccan salted lemons are seductive: fragrant and tangy, their scent is distinctly that of lemon but subtler, tamed to a sensual aroma rather than an acidic hit.

You see them for sale in trays and bottles throughout the Middle East, and also throughout the south of France where large populations of North Africans dwell. They are a part of the cuisine of Nice, as well, and you are apt to find them flavoring soups, stews, vinaigrettes, or simmered bean dishes. As a salad ingredient they are fantastic.

Luckily, too, they are easy to make. I put up only small amounts as I am not fond of preserving things for long periods of time—I am frightened of poisoning people. But these lemons, with their generous salting, pose no danger although they are necessarily salty.

Although traditionally only the peel is eaten, I find that the whole little lemon is delicious. I have also been told that they can accumulate a white scum that is harmless, and indeed this seems to be the case. Just scrape or rinse it off.

> 10 lemons, unsprayed and preferably organic
>   Several tablespoons sea salt
> 8 ounces lemon juice
>   Several canning jars large enough to accommodate the lemons (Wash the jars in hot, soapy water and rinse well. Pour boiling water over the jars and let them sit in hot water until ready to fill.)

Wash the lemons well, then cut each lemon into 6 or 8 wedges. Although they are traditionally left attached, I usually leave them in halves so that I can get them into the jars more easily.

Press salt into the cut surfaces, pressing salt into every crevice you can, then place the lemons in the prepared canning jars. Into the top of each jar add 2 to 3 tablespoons sea salt, $1/3$ cup lemon juice, then boiling water to reach the top.

Cover and leave to age. After 2 weeks they are pretty good; at 3 to 4 weeks, sublime.

17 CALORIES PER LEMON
0 G FAT
0 G SATURATED FAT
0 MG CHOLESTEROL
7 G CARBOHYDRATES
1 G PROTEIN
2235 MG SODIUM

Tahina Sauce

Serves 4 to 6

Tahina is a creamy purée of sesame seeds, available in natural food shops and supermarkets. It is spiced with garlic and lemon, then eaten throughout the Middle East with a wide variety of vegetables and herbs. It is a requisite sauce for *falafel,* and combined with mashed chickpeas makes *hummous,* with grilled eggplant, *baba ghanoush.*

Tahina dips grace the tables of weddings and Bar Mitzvahs, late-night cafés, and afternoon teas on *kibbutz.* Although we tend to think of pita as the classic bread for dipping, slices of crusty bread such as baguettes are very nice dipped into the nutty, spicy sauce.

1 cup *tahina* (sesame seed paste), well stirred
3 garlic cloves, finely chopped
Juice of 1 or 2 lemons
Salt and black and red cayenne pepper to taste
¼ cup water, or enough for the consistency desired
¼ teaspoon cumin, or to taste
Pinch coriander powder, turmeric, or curry powder
Garnish: olives, chopped cilantro, a few drops *zhug* or Tabasco, a drizzle of olive oil

Mix the *tahina* with the garlic, lemon juice, salt, and black and red cayenne pepper, then stir in the water and mix until it forms a creamy consistency. First it will thicken and become pastelike, then it will thin out and become creamy. If it is to be used for a sauce, add extra water and make a thinner sauce.

Season with cumin and with coriander, turmeric, or curry and taste for seasoning. Use as desired or serve swirled onto a plate for dipping, garnished with olives, chopped cilantro, hot pepper seasoning, and olive oil.

243 CALORIES PER SERVING
22 G FAT
3 G SATURATED FAT
0 MG CHOLESTEROL
10 G CARBOHYDRATES
7 G PROTEIN
46 MG SODIUM

Salsa de l'Ail

GARLIC SAUCE

Yields about ½ cup

This potent, garlicky brew is delicious dribbled onto grilled vegetables or fish, crisp baked potatoes, or stewed chicken.

This recipe was shared with me by a peasant woman, Maria, who lives in a hillside village outside of Grasse and adores garlic.

> 4 garlic cloves
> ¼ to ½ teaspoon salt, or as desired
> 1 tablespoon olive oil
> 1 to 3 teaspoons vinegar
> ½ cup water, or as desired

Crush the garlic and salt in a mortar and pestle; this releases the oils in a pleasing way. When chopped, the garlic does not respond in the same way and will be harsh.

Slowly work in the olive oil, then the vinegar, then finally the water. It should form an emulsion.

18 CALORIES PER TABLESPOON
2 G FAT
0 G SATURATED FAT
0 MG CHOLESTEROL
1 G CARBOHYDRATES
0 G PROTEIN
67 MG SODIUM

Preserved Lemon Zhug

This fragrant chile relish is a first cousin to salsa. It is aromatic with spices and tangy with preserved lemon—delicious with grilled or browned fish. If you have no preserved lemon, use fresh lemon or lime juice mixed with grated lemon or lime zest to taste.

How much hot pepper to use is also a matter of personal taste. Choose ones that are hot but not too juicy, such as Thai or cayenne. Any hot chile can be used; however, consider their pungency and fire when you judge the amount.

3 or 4 garlic cloves, finely chopped or crushed
2 or 3 hot peppers, thinly sliced or chopped
1½ cups fresh or canned tomatoes, diced; include the juice
½ onion, finely chopped
⅛ to ¼ teaspoon cumin
Seeds from 2 cardamom pods
3 tablespoons chopped fresh cilantro
Small pinch of sugar, if needed
¼ preserved lemon, diced
2 to 3 tablespoons juice from preserved lemon or fresh lemon juice
Salt to taste if using fresh lemon

Purée the garlic with the hot peppers, then stir in the tomatoes, onion, cumin, cardamom, cilantro, sugar if needed, and preserved lemon. Do not purée further; a chunky consistency is preferable.

Adjust the seasoning with juice from preserved lemon, more cumin, and salt if needed.

4 CALORIES PER TABLESPOON
0 G FAT
0 G SATURATED FAT
0 MG CHOLESTEROL
1 G CARBOHYDRATES
0 G PROTEIN
49 MG SODIUM

Almond-Thickened Garlic Sauce

Serves 4

Thick, creamy garlic sauces are eaten throughout the Mediterranean, from the garlic-egg-olive oil *aioli* of Provence, to Greece's *skortalia,* to Spain's *alli-oli,* an emulsion of garlic and olive oil whipped into a frenzy without benefit of egg or other emulsifying agents.

The eastern Mediterranean has similar sauces, such as this creamy amalgam of garlic, almonds, and bread with olive oil, a little apple and mint thrown in. It is an unlikely combination that is absolutely delicious and refreshing, especially with baked beets eaten cool as a salad. Since I feel decidedly undecided about using raw eggs, *aioli* is something I make only rarely, when I am sure of the source of the egg. This sauce, which uses the ancient Mediterranean technique of thickening with almonds and bread, eliminates the problem.

The apple, fruit vinegar, and mint give a decidedly Moorish-Spanish accent to this quintessentially Mediterranean sauce.

$^1/_2$ cup slivered almonds
4 garlic cloves, chopped
1 slice country bread
$^1/_4$ cup olive oil
A few drops of almond extract or essence
Juice of 1 lemon
1 apple, cored but unpeeled, diced
Salt to taste
Raspberry or other fruit vinegar to taste
$^1/_2$ teaspoon dried mint, or as desired

Crush the almonds and garlic until a paste or coarse meal forms; set it aside. Pour cold water over the bread, then squeeze it dry and add it to the almond-garlic mixture. Whirl the ingredients together in a blender or pound in a mortar until a paste forms, then gradually add the olive oil, almond extract or essence, lemon juice, and apple; process until a thick emulsion is achieved.

Season with salt, vinegar, and dried mint.

255 Calories Per Serving
21 G Fat
3 G Saturated Fat
0 Mg Cholesterol
15 G Carbohydrates
4 G Protein
54 Mg Sodium

Spicy Moroccan Butter

Makes about 1 cup

Soft butter spiced with the flavors of North Africa—it's delicious melted onto pasta, spread onto crusty bread, or tossed with couscous.

1 large dried mild red chili (such as the new world ancho, guajillo, New Mexico, or the European nura or nora), lightly toasted, then deveined and seeded
5 to 8 green onions, thinly sliced
3 to 5 garlic cloves, chopped
1 tablespoon *each:* paprika and cumin
1 teaspoon coriander
2 tablespoons *each:* chopped fresh parsley and mint
3 to 4 tablespoons chopped fresh cilantro
1 stick softened butter
  Salt
  Tiny dash lemon or lime juice

Grind the toasted chile to a powder in a cleaned coffee grinder. Alternatively, you can rehydrate the chile and purée it in a blender or mortar and pestle.

Mix the powder or paste well with the green onions, garlic, paprika, cumin, ground coriander, parsley, mint, and cilantro and purée together.

Work the chile-spice paste into the softened butter, then season it with salt and lemon or lime juice.

This keeps well for 3 to 4 days covered in the refrigerator and may be frozen, although the herbs will wilt and become limp in both flavor and texture.

61 CALORIES PER TABLESPOON
6 G FAT
4 G SATURATED FAT
17 MG CHOLESTEROL
1 G CARBOHYDRATES
0 G PROTEIN
64 MG SODIUM

Pesto/Pistou

Makes about 1 1/2 cups, enough for 6 servings of pasta

Lou Pistou is Provence's fragrant balm of pounded garlic and basil, known as *pesto* across the border and further along the Ligurian coast around Genoa.

Pistou is quintessentially Niçoise and *pesto* is aromatically Genoese—in fact, there are disagreements as to who exactly gave whom this sweet herbal sauce.

The two always had close ties, as Nice has been a part of France only since 1860. During the 500 years prior to that (except for the French rule of 1792–1814) Nice belonged to the House of Savoy, whose kingdom was the Kingdom of Sardinia, which included at various times much of northern Italy, much of the boot, and islands, too.

When making *pesto* or *pistou,* remember that this fragrant basil paste must be made to taste. Each basil will have its own perfume, each green paste will need more or less oil, will require more or less salt, and will dictate whether or not to include cheese.

Many people, myself included, add a bit of parsley—say, 1/2 cup—to the basil mixture. I find that it lightens the *pesto* and is more digestible, too.

Nuts are another variable. Walnuts are favored in Liguria, pine nuts in Provence, pistachios in Sicily. I like to make my *pesto* without any nuts at all, as I find that the nuts can taste tired long before the basil does. For a hit of nut flavor, I like to scatter a handful of pine nuts or almond slivers over the finished dish.

Pesto/pistou is one of those things that keeps extremely well in the freezer. Make a big batch and enjoy it for months.

2 garlic cloves, chopped
  Salt to taste
1/4 cup olive oil, or more as needed
2 cups torn or cut-up fresh basil leaves or 2 cups basil plus 1/2 cup parsley
  Optional: 1/4 to 1/2 cup grated cheese such as Parmesan, pecorino, Romano, or Asiago

Sprinkle the garlic with salt, then crush it in a mortar and pestle or food processor. Add the olive oil and basil leaves, pounding or processing until it forms a thick, fragrant green paste.

Add the cheese as desired.

VARIATION

Add ¼ cup slivered almonds, pine nuts, or walnuts, pounding them into the paste at the beginning before you work in the basil.

FIVE TRADITIONAL DISHES WITH PESTO

Gnocchi and Green Beans with Gorgonzola Pesto
Cook potato gnocchi until just tender, adding young green beans at the last moment so that they just cook through but remain bright green in color. Toss with several ounces of diced gorgonzola cheese and several tablespoons *pesto*.

Fettucine Verde alla Pistou   Toss green *al dente* pasta with *pesto* and a tablespoon of mascarpone, *fromage frais,* or ricotta cheese. Serve sprinkled with pine nuts and shredded basil.

Tomato-Pesto Eggplant Halves   Brown small (Japanese) eggplant halves, on their cut sides first, then turn over and add onions, diced tomatoes, and garlic to the pan and simmer the bottoms of the eggplant. Once the eggplant is tender all the way through and the tomato sauce is thick and savory, serve with the cut, browned tops spread with *pesto*.

Minestrone alla Genovese or Soupe au Pistou   Prepare a light, quickly simmered soup of white beans, tomatoes, zucchini, green beans, a little celery, carrots, and cabbage. Serve with a spoonful of pasta and a swirl of *pesto* added at the last minute.

Grilled Goat Cheese with Favas and Pesto   Cook fresh fava beans, peeled of their tough skins, by simmering with onions and garlic until tender. Stir in a tablespoon or two of *pesto,* top with slices of goat cheese, then broil until the cheese lightly melts and is flecked with golden brown.

21 CALORIES PER TABLESPOON
2 G FAT
0 G SATURATED FAT
0 MG CHOLESTEROL
0 G CARBOHYDRATES
0 G PROTEIN
0 MG SODIUM

 # Olivada

OLIVE PASTE FROM THE RIVIERA

Makes about 1 cup

Regardless of where exactly the Riviera begins—is it Marseilles? Toulon?—and where it ends . . . somewhere along the Tuscan coast, perhaps . . . you will find variations of this olive spread. It is delicious spooned onto pizza, fire-roasted potatoes, or hard-cooked eggs and tomatoes for a summer lunch.

1 garlic clove, finely chopped
1 cup pitted black oil-cured or Kalamata olives
1/4 cup olive oil, or as needed
1/4 teaspoon *herbes de Provence*
1 tablespoon fresh rosemary, chopped

Combine the garlic and olives in a food processor and purée, adding enough olive oil as you go along to form a smooth paste.

Season with *herbes de Provence* and rosemary.

53 CALORIES PER TABLESPOON
6 G FAT
1 G SATURATED FAT
0 MG CHOLESTEROL
1 G CARBOHYDRATES
0 G PROTEIN
221 MG SODIUM

Olives, Pickles, and Zesty Condiments

La Saoussa dai Oliva

POUNDED OLIVE AND CAPER SAUCE

Makes about ²/₃ cup

This piquant sauce, with its garlicky perfume and earthy, salty olives, is extremely good with anything grilled, such as sliced eggplant or artichokes, with a bowl of *aioli* alongside. It's also very nice with sliced hard-cooked egg and tomatoes as a simple summer starter.

3   cloves garlic, peeled and coarsely chopped
3   tablespoons black olive paste
1   tablespoon capers, rinsed
     Pinch dry mustard
     Pinch or two *herbes de Provence*
     Juice of ¹/₄ lemon
¹/₄ cup olive oil

Crush the garlic in a mortar and pestle or in a food processor, then work in the olive paste, capers, mustard, *herbes de Provence,* and lemon juice, and pound or whirl until the mixture has the consistency of a chunky paste.

Work in the olive oil. With time it will separate; simply stir it together again.

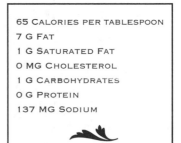

65 CALORIES PER TABLESPOON
7 G FAT
1 G SATURATED FAT
0 MG CHOLESTEROL
1 G CARBOHYDRATES
0 G PROTEIN
137 MG SODIUM

EIGHT

STREET FOOD

SAVORY PASTRIES
TYROPITA OR BOREKS, *Cheese- and Herb-Filled Filo Pastries*

TARTE AUX LÉGUMES MÉDITERRANÉS, *Mediterranean Pepper and Tomato Tart with Capers and Green Olives*

COCA DE BALEARES, *Savory Pepper, Black Olive, and Pine Nut Tart from the Balearic Islands*

LA SOCCA, *Thin Crepe of Chickpea Batter*

SANDWICHES
FOCACCIA ALLA VERDURE, *Rosemary Focaccia Filled with Grilled Vegetables, Sautéed Greens, and Cheese*

PAN BAGNAT, *Côte d'Azur Salad-Filled Sandwich Roll*

SOUVLAKIA FROM A GREEK ISLAND

BREAD, FOCACCIA, FOUGASSE, AND PIZZA DOUGH

PANE RIPIENE

PIZZA
CLASSIC MARGHARITA

PIZZA FROM A LITTLE STREET IN AIX EN PROVENCE

PIZZA BIANCA

PIZZA ALLA MELANZANE E PESTO

PIZZA DI VERDURA E FORMAGGIO

SAVORY SNACKS
SUPPLI AL TELEFONO, *Italian Cheese-Filled Rice Croquettes*

FALAFEL

BREK OR BRIK, *Crisp Triangle Pastries*
HARIRA, *Lemon-Scented Hearty Lentil Soup*
BEID MASLUG, *Moroccan Eggs from the Marketplace,*
  with Toasted Cumin and Salt

SNACKS and little meals, eaten in the streets and markets of much of the Mediterranean, add to the sensual appeal of its street life.

Mediterraneans know something I have long known: it is nice to see people eat. Usually someone will wish you a good appetite in the language of whichever country you happen to be in.

Street foods make ordinary streets come to life: they smell enticing and make people stop, nibble, engage each other in a little conversation. Street foods might be accompanied by loud cries, such as that for *socca,* the tinkle of bells for ice cream, or simply the voices of people milling happily. Street vendors offer wares by displaying gaily colored seductive signs, sometimes garish, other times charming, and often street foods typify the flavors of the country.

Sometimes street food is the very simplest of edibles such as the nuts, seeds, and dried fruits that are extremely popular throughout the Mediterranean. You see signs posted on buses and in cinemas: "Don't Spit Seed Shells onto the Floors."

Street food is not home food. It is food that is sociable and perhaps a bit naughty, cooked by methods that are often difficult for a home kitchen to set up. Braziers of hot charcoal, for example: the scent of food cooked over these little barbecues perfumes the entire Mediterranean, regardless of whatever is being cooked over the coals.

Fried foods are also favored as street foods. True, frying is far from healthful, but such dishes can be fat-reduced to a less dietarily threatening level at home, using a tiny amount of olive oil in a nonstick pan.

In the streets and marketplaces of Tunisia you will find one of my favorite crisp street foods: the *brik* or *brek*, crisp-browned pastry filled with herbs, meat or fish, and often an egg. Bite into it and the yolk spurts out provocatively, making a delicious sloppy sauce for the pastry. Then there is the Middle East *falafel* (known in Egypt as *taamia*, and made with broad beans instead of chickpeas).

Think of pizza, eaten from the street in most every town in Italy and throughout France's Mediterranean coast as well. Throughout Provence there are even pizza trucks with portable wood-burning ovens that drive throughout the area every night, something like an ice cream truck but these dispatch smoky, crusty, enticing pizza covered with toppings that range from grilled vegetables and local cheeses to the North African sausage *merguez*.

Everywhere there are fried potatoes: I especially remember a bag of tasty ones, crisp and potatoey, accompanied by slices of fried eggplant and a pickled hot pepper or two as a condiment. The Viccuria marketplace in Palermo is famous for its stalls of fried foods: huge vats of boiling oil with a wide variety of ingredients that are cooked in them. Whole eggplant is one of my favorites—take several home and add them to pasta for a simple convenience food. Or see what the vendor fishes out of the cauldron next and buy it, wrapped up in paper for wandering and nibbling.

Street food is snack food, often sloppy food, made to be eaten individually or in a large sociable group. It is made to be eaten while you walk along the street or sit in the park, while you shop or daydream, to be eaten with your fingers, out of a paper, or perhaps from a bowl, but never from a proper place setting. It just wouldn't taste right.

Sometimes street food is as basic as a cone of boiled chickpeas spiced with cumin from a Moroccan market, grilled fish and slabs of eggplant with a spicy hot chili sauce, or hard-boiled eggs with a spicy dipping mixture.

In the Mediterranean fruit is frequently sold on the street: cactus pears peeled and cleaned of their spikes; chunks of fresh coconut in Rome, kept sweet and refreshing with a constant stream of clear, cool water; ripe pineapple on sticks, so sweet and juicy it drips from your chin as you bite into it. One of my favorite fruits to eat in the street is melon. In the summer in Italy you'll find stalls selling *cocomero* or *auguria*, ripe watermelon that seems sweeter and more flavorful than any on earth and so refreshing in the blistering heat.

These are often the first flavors you associate with a place and time—later they are never quite the same as they were in that faraway land.

Then you wander into your kitchen and begin to cook up some memories of your holiday in the Mediterranean.

Street Food

SAVORY PASTRIES

Savory pastries might be made at home sometimes, but they are street food to me—things that I love buying from street vendors in the Mediterranean while wandering through winding streets en route to my next adventure.

≈ Tyropita or Boreks

CHEESE- AND HERB-FILLED FILO PASTRIES

Serves 10 to 12 as a little *meze,* 6 to 8 as a main course (one big pie)

Crisp pastries filled with various combinations of different types of cheeses are a favored treat throughout much of the Middle East. Often sold from bakeries that specialize in a variety of pastries, *tyropitas* were my favorite street snack when I lived in Greece, although spinach was a close second and making the decision was never easy.

If you like, use all olive oil rather than the combination of olive oil and butter called for in the recipe; you can really cut down the amount—just dab it on lightly instead of brushing it.

12 ounces feta, crumbled

½ cup cottage cheese or ricotta cheese
 1 egg, lightly beaten
    Pinch *each:* nutmeg and black pepper
 3 to 5 green onions, thinly sliced
 2 tablespoons fresh dill, coarsely chopped
 1 tablespoon fresh tarragon, coarsely chopped
    (or ½ teaspoon dried)
 1 to 2 tablespoons fresh mint, chopped
 1 tablespoon fresh cilantro or Italian parsley, chopped
 2 to 3 tablespoons melted butter
 2 to 3 tablespoons olive oil
 1 pound filo dough

(CONTINUED)

Preheat the oven to 435°F.

Mix the feta with cottage or ricotta cheese, egg, nutmeg, black pepper, green onions, dill, tarragon, mint, and cilantro or parsley.

Combine the melted butter and olive oil.

For individual *meze*-sized pastries: carefully take a sheet of filo dough and lightly brush with the butter–olive oil mixture. You don't need much, as it will spread quite a bit as it bakes. Fold in half to make filo double thick—it's easier to work with. At one of the corners place a spoonful or two of the cheese mixture, then fold over and over again, enclosing the filling completely as you fold the dough, brushing a bit of butter and oil on the pastry as you go along.

Place the pastry parcel on a baking sheet and repeat until you run out of filling or dough. (Any leftover dough can be stored well-wrapped in the refrigerator for up to a week, and frozen [or refrozen] for up to 3 months. Leftover filling must be refrigerated and should be used within a day or two: it may be spooned into an omelet or spread onto thin slices of baguette, topped with grated cheese, then broiled until melted and crisp.)

For one big pie: brush a baking sheet with melted butter/oil and layer one sheet of filo dough, brush lightly with butter/oil, then add another sheet of filo until you have 6 to 8 layers of filo. Spread the cheese mixture, fold over the edges while you add 6 or so top layers of filo, brushing lightly with butter/oil as you go.

Bake for 20 minutes or until golden brown and crisp. Serve hot, although in Greece they are often served at room temperature.

243 CALORIES PER SERVING
13 G FAT
6 G SATURATED FAT
48 MG CHOLESTEROL
22 G CARBOHYDRATES
9 G PROTEIN
564 MG SODIUM

THREE DELICIOUS TRADITIONAL FILO PASTRIES/PIES

Spanakopita (Greek Spinach and Cheese Filo Pie) Instead of the assorted herbs, add a cup or so of spinach—cooked, squeezed dry, and chopped—to the cheese and proceed according to the recipe.

Kolokopita (Grated Zucchini and Cheese Pie) To make this specialty of Turkish Jews, add 1 cup coarsely shredded zucchini (which you've drained to rid of excess water) to the cheese and herb mixture. You may adjust the herbs to include marjoram, etc.

Brik au Pommes de Terre (Tunisian Potato Pastry) Brown 2 chopped onions in olive oil until softened, then add 3 cloves chopped garlic and 2 tablespoons chopped parsley and warm with the onions a few moments. Remove from heat and mix with 2 boiled then mashed large baking potatoes (1 pound) and 1 lightly beaten egg. Season well with salt and pepper, and use this as a filling for filo dough. Potato-filled *brik* can either be baked on a baking sheet or fried until golden brown.

❧ Tarte aux Légumes Méditerranés

MEDITERRANEAN PEPPER AND TOMATO TART WITH CAPERS AND GREEN OLIVES

Serves 4 to 6

Crisp shortcrust or yeast dough covered with a layer of golden sautéed onions—and often tomatoes, sometimes peppers, too—then dotted with black olives and sprinkled with herbs is one of Nice's most famous, traditional pastries.

   The following tart is a composite of the Provençal *pissadeliere,* Italian pizza, Balearic *coca,* with a bit of Catalan *piperade* thrown in. Make it in individual little tarts if you like for easy eating, or in one large cookie sheet for a more street food-like feeling.

2   onions, thinly sliced lengthwise
2   tablespoons olive oil
1   *each:* red and green bell peppers, cut into 2-inch
      strands (approximately)
8   to 10 ripe tomatoes, sliced
5   garlic cloves, chopped
2   tablespoons tomato paste
      Large pinch sugar
1   tablespoon chopped fresh parsley
1   tablespoon capers, rinsed
1/8 to 1/4 teaspoon *herbes de Provence*
6   to 8 pimiento-stuffed green olives, sliced
      Shortcrust dough for 1 pie shell, rolled out to fit
      on a cookie sheet or in about 15 tartlet shells;
      or 1 recipe yeast dough for Bread, Focaccia,
      Fougasse, and Pizza Dough (page 308)
      Freshly grated Parmesan, Asiago, pecorino, or aged
      goat cheese for sprinkling

Lightly sauté the onions in olive oil until just softened, then add the peppers and cover, sweating them by cooking over low, low heat until they are tender.

Remove the cover and add the tomatoes, then cook a few minutes longer until the tomatoes are tender and saucelike.

Add the garlic, tomato paste, sugar, parsley, capers, *herbes de Provence,* and olives; remove from heat and let cool.

Preheat the oven to 375 to 400°F. Spread the cooled filling over rolled-out crust, then bake for 35 to 45 minutes or until the crust is golden brown around the edges. Sprinkle the baked tart with cheese and serve.

VARIATION

Mediterranean Aubergine Tart
Reduce the amount of peppers to ½ each and add 1 diced, browned eggplant to the saucelike filling mixture.

289 CALORIES PER SERVING
16 G FAT
3 G SATURATED FAT
0 MG CHOLESTEROL
33 G CARBOHYDRATES
5 G PROTEIN
341 MG SODIUM

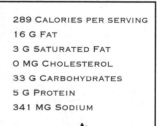

Coca de Baleares

SAVORY PEPPER, BLACK OLIVE, AND PINE NUT TART FROM THE BALEARIC ISLANDS

Serves 6 to 8

Coca is a pizza-like flat tart from the Balearic islands of Majorca, Minorca, Ibiza, and For-mentara. It can be based on a short crust or yeast dough and prepared with savory fillings like the one in this recipe or with sweet fillings like fruits.

One of the ways that a savory *coca* differs from a pizza is that a coca doesn't have a tomato sauce base nor is cheese a necessary topping.

3 *each:* red and yellow bell peppers, thinly sliced
1 onion, thinly sliced
5 garlic cloves
3 tablespoons olive oil
  Pinch of sugar
  Salt and pepper to taste
1 cup fresh or canned tomatoes, diced
3 tablespoons fresh herb mixture such as oregano, marjoram, and thyme
1 recipe yeast dough such as the one for Bread, Focaccia, Fougasse, and Pizza Dough (page 308) or 1 recipe pie crust (store-bought is fine)
10 to 15 black oil-cured olives, pits removed, halved
1 to 2 tablespoons pine nuts

Slowly sauté the peppers, onion, and half the garlic in the olive oil in a nonstick frying pan, cooking until the peppers are softened but not browned, about 15 minutes. Season with sugar, salt, and pepper, then add the tomatoes and continue to cook another 15 to 20 minutes. Set aside to cool, then add the remaining garlic and the fresh chopped herbs to the peppers and tomatoes.

Heat the oven to 400°F.

Press the dough or crust into an approximately 15-inch pizza or tart pan, then fill it with the cooled pepper-tomato mixture. Sprinkle with the halved olives and pine nuts.

Bake for 20 to 30 minutes or until the crust is lightly golden and cooked through and to bake the peppers and tomatoes into a strongly flavored filling.

342 CALORIES PER SERVING
11 G FAT
2 G SATURATED FAT
0 MG CHOLESTEROL
52 G CARBOHYDRATES
9 G PROTEIN
137 MG SODIUM

La Socca

THIN CREPE OF CHICKPEA BATTER

Serves 4

Prepared from chickpea batter sizzled in huge, olive oil-anointed copper baking pans, *la socca* is scraped from the hot pan into wide strips, then piled into a paper cone for out-of-hand snacking.

La socca is the traditional midmorning snack (*casse-croute*) of manual workers, market gardeners, and vendors, the quintessential snack of the region, indeed, in much of the Mediterranean (called *cade* in Toulon, *faina* in Sardinia, *farinata* in Genoa, *cecina* in Tuscany).

"*Tout caud*" is the cry of socca, and as soon as the pan is out of the oven a crowd gathers, whether it is in a marketplace, a building site, or café. Often the *socca* is prepared in woodburning ovens nearby and rushed to the scene on the back of a bicycle. Crowds usually swarm over it until the last bit is scraped up and the bicycle has disappeared to return with yet another panful.

My favorite is found along the streets of the other market, the one past the train station that spills onto the neighboring streets, where the *socca* is greasy and wonderful. As you rest your feet from the rigors of negotiating the seemingly endless market, sprinkle the strips of chickpea pancake with black pepper and sip a glass of cool rosé alongside.

Some add white flour to the batter, while others add egg for a crepe-like delicacy. All are delicious, but to be at its best, try preparing *socca* over a woodburning fire, for the whiff of smoke is perfect with the vegetal flavor of the chickpea flour.

1 to 1½ cups cold water or more, enough to make a
   batter as thick as crepe batter or whipping cream
1 teaspoon salt
2 tablespoons olive oil, plus a little extra for the pan
1 cup chickpea flour
   Freshly ground black pepper to taste

Slowly whisk water, salt, and olive oil into the chickpea flour, mixing until it forms a smoothish batter; it will still have a few lumps and resemble a slightly lumpy crepe batter. Sieve or strain the batter to smooth out the lumps.

Heat a shallow frying pan or crepe pan—heavy cast iron, steel, or lined copper works well. Into the hot pan drizzle 2 to 3 teaspoons olive oil and swirl around to disperse evenly. Pour or ladle in ¼ to ½ cup batter and swirl around the hot oiled pan, letting the batter roll up onto the sides and then back down again.

Let it cook over medium-high heat a few moments, as it turns from wet to slightly firm. You'll want to cook the bottom to a crusty brown but not burned consistency.

The top of the pancake will probably still be damp. Place under a hot broiler or in the upper quarter of a hot oven for a minute or two to cook the top; the pancake is done when no longer moist.

Cut into squares or wide strips using a spatula and scrape out of the pan (it will stick slightly in spots). Serve sprinkled with freshly ground black pepper.

231 CALORIES PER SERVING
17 G FAT
2 G SATURATED FAT
0 MG CHOLESTEROL
15 G CARBOHYDRATES
5 G PROTEIN
537 MG SODIUM

Focaccia alla Verdure

ROSEMARY FOCACCIA FILLED WITH GRILLED VEGETABLES, SAUTÉED GREENS, AND CHEESE

Serves 4

If focaccia is not available, use *ciabatta, fougasse,* or any Mediterranean-type country bread or roll for this succulent sandwich.

At Il Café-Bar you will find *panini* (crusty sandwiches) filled with spinach and cheese, roasted peppers, grilled eggplant and cheese, chunky omelets, or tangy marinated vegetables. Sometimes a sandwich bar might be called a *focacceria,* with the sandwiches stuffed into *focaccia,* hot and fresh, slit into half and filled plump.

There can be lots of jostling with the crowd during busy times, as each hungry person tries to decide what to choose, and the counterperson does his or her best to accommodate.

The following sandwich is a rather luxe version of the classic, although much plainer, sandwich you find in nonpretentious sandwich bars throughout Italy.

It is wonderful to make a day or two after a barbecue since you'll have a nice assortment of vegetables to pop between the covers of the bread. As for which cheese is better, fresh mozzarella or goat cheese, they are both terrific. And, I might add, sheep's milk cheese is too.

1 bunch chard or spinach
4 to 6 tablespoons olive oil
3 garlic cloves, chopped
  Salt and pepper to taste
4 large squares focaccia, split to make two layers
1 tablespoon red wine vinegar, or to taste
2 tablespoons chopped fresh rosemary
6 to 8 ounces fresh mozzarella or goat cheese, sliced
  Selection of grilled vegetables: several slices *each* of eggplant, zucchini, onions, peppers, tomatoes, etc.
  Garnish: 20 to 25 black olives such as Niçoise or Kalamata

Blanch the chard or spinach and squeeze dry. Chop, then warm in a tablespoon of olive oil. Remove from heat and add 1 clove chopped garlic and salt and pepper to taste.

Lightly toast the focaccia, then sprinkle it with a little olive oil, garlic, a few drops of vinegar, and rosemary.

Arrange a thick layer of mozzarella or goat cheese on the bottom of each focaccia. Broil until the cheese melts, then top with a layer of chard or spinach and bits of the roasted vegetables, dressing it all with olive oil, garlic, rosemary, and drops of vinegar as you pile it on.

Close up and enjoy right away, garnished with the pungent black olives.

540 CALORIES PER SERVING
27 G FAT
7 G SATURATED FAT
24 MG CHOLESTEROL
54 G CARBOHYDRATES
20 G PROTEIN
1193 MG SODIUM

Pan Bagnat

CÔTE D'AZUR SALAD-FILLED SANDWICH ROLL

Serves 4

Known by a myriad of spellings, including *pan bagne, pan bagnia,* and *pain bagna,* this hefty sandwich roll filled with crisp salady things literally translates, in the patois of the region, as bathed bread for the fact that the bread is bathed in the luscious juices of the salad filling.

Legend has it that originally the bread halves were first dipped—bathed—in the salty Mediterranean sea before being slathered with olive oil and stuffed (these days the bacteria count in the sea—at least on some beaches—is too high to dip even your toes, let alone rounds of bread).

But the *pan bagnat* is quintessential Niçoise street food. You find it at little stands and kiosks, bakeries, and cafés wrapped in paper and piled high in the morning, usually disappearing by noon. Although the traditional sandwich includes a few chunks of anchovy or tuna, this version is all-vegetable, the fishy bits optional.

4 large crusty rolls
6 tablespoons to 1/2 cup olive oil, or as desired
3 tablespoons to 1/4 cup red wine vinegar, or as desired
1/4 to 1/2 teaspoon dried oregano leaves
8 to 10 garlic cloves, finely chopped or crushed
1 red bell pepper, thinly sliced
1 green bell pepper, thinly sliced
4 ripe tomatoes, thinly sliced
1/2 red onion, thinly sliced and separated into rings
4 leaves curly leaf lettuce, cleaned and dry, or 1/2 cup cooked and dried green or Romano beans
12 leaves or so fresh basil, thinly sliced
2 hard-cooked eggs, peeled and cut into quarters or slices
8 to 12 black flavorful olives, pitted and halved
Optional (although authentic): 1 can (4 ounces) of tuna fish or 8 anchovies

Cut the rolls in half lengthwise, and pull out a little of the insides (save for other use, to thicken soup or gazpacho, etc.). Drizzle a bit of olive oil and vinegar on each cut side and sprinkle with oregano and garlic.

Let the dressing sink in for a few minutes, then begin layering the bottoms of the rolls with the other ingredients: peppers, tomatoes, onion, lettuce or green beans, basil, egg, and olives, drizzling with olive oil, vinegar, and garlic in between. (If using the tuna or anchovies, add them evenly to the sandwiches.)

Cover with second half of roll, press down, and chill until ready to eat. This is at its best 2 to 3 hours after preparation, when the juices have soaked in but the rolls are not sodden.

682 CALORIES PER SERVING
29 G FAT
5 G SATURATED FAT
107 MG CHOLESTEROL
89 G CARBOHYDRATES
18 G PROTEIN
955 MG SODIUM

Souvlakia from a Greek Island

Serves 4

When I lived on the island of Crete, I was extremely fond of *souvlakia* and confess to spending an inordinate amount of time tasting examples in the search for the ultimate recipe. My requirements were strict but reasonable: lean meat that was tender and lemony, fresh pita bread, tangy fresh thick yogurt, lots of salad, and so forth. The following is my rendition, one I've prepared in the ensuing decades whenever I feel nostalgic.

My favorite stall in Aghios Nicholaos sprinkled hot paprika over their *souvlakia;* I mix cayenne with paprika for mine.

12 ounces lean lamb, cut into cubes
 5 garlic cloves, chopped
   Salt and pepper
   Juice of 1/2 lemon
 2 tablespoons olive oil
 4 ounces yogurt
 2 ounces feta cheese, crumbled
 1 cucumber, peeled and diced
1/2 onion, chopped or thinly sliced
 1 green bell pepper, diced
 3 tomatoes, diced
 2 tablespoons chopped fresh parsley
 4 pita breads
 1 tablespoon paprika
1/4 to 1/2 teaspoon cayenne pepper, or to taste

Combine the lamb with 4 cloves of garlic, salt and pepper, lemon juice, and olive oil. Leave it to marinate in the refrigerator overnight.

Start a fire on a charcoal grill.

Combine the yogurt and feta cheese with the remaining garlic and set this aside. Combine the cucumber, onion, green pepper, tomatoes, and parsley. Season with salt and pepper and set aside.

Lightly spray the pita breads with a little water unless they are very fresh.

Remove the lamb from the marinade and thread onto metal skewers or bamboo skewers that you have soaked in cold water for 30 minutes. Grill the kebabs quickly over the hot coals for 4 to 6 minutes per side; lamb is best, to my taste, when rare or at least pink.

Combine the paprika with the cayenne pepper.

Warm the pita breads on the grill quickly, then spread each with a swipe of the yogurt-feta mixture. Place a kebab on top of the pita and pull off the hot grilled meat. Top with salad mixture and finally a sprinkling of the hot paprika. Roll up to close and eat right away.

431 CALORIES PER SERVING
16 G FAT
6 G SATURATED FAT
81 MG CHOLESTEROL
39 G CARBOHYDRATES
33 G PROTEIN
508 MG SODIUM

Bread, Focaccia, Fougasse, and Pizza Dough

Makes 1 loaf, 4 individual-size pizzas, or about 12 rolls

This is a good basic dough for breads, rolls, focaccia, *fougasse,* or pizza. For bread and rolls, shape as you would any standard bread or roll; for pizza follow the directions below.

Focaccia (in Liguria) and *fougasse* (in Provence) are large, flat, leaf-shaped breads, often flavored with a variety of savory ingredients. Try a few tablespoons of chopped rosemary leaves added to the dough or ¼ cup black and/or green olives. Sun-dried tomatoes or nuggets of Roquefort or sheep (feta) cheese add piquancy, too.

1 teaspoon *each:* active dry yeast and sugar
1¼ cups lukewarm water
1 teaspoon salt
2 tablespoons olive oil
1 pound bread flour, or as needed

Stir together the yeast, sugar, and water, then let stand until it becomes foamy. Stir in the salt and oil, then add the flour, a little at a time, stirring with a big wooden spoon until most has been absorbed and the dough forms a ball.

Place the dough on a floured board and knead until soft and smooth but still firm, about 5 minutes, adding more flour as needed to keep the dough from sticking.

Place the dough in an oiled bowl and cover well with plastic wrap, leaving enough room for dough to rise. I often just put the oiled dough in a largish plastic bag and put that into the bowl. Leave in the refrigerator for a long rise until doubled or tripled in size, 8 to 12 hours. You can keep it for up to about 4 days in the refrigerator—simply punch it down each time it rises. To rise at room temperature, allow 1 to 2 hours.

To make pizza: flatten the dough out very thin with oiled hands, stretching as much as you can. Lay the dough out on a baking sheet and top and bake as desired (see below). For *calzone*, place the filling only on one side of the dough, then fold the other half over to enclose the filling. Bake as for pizza, allowing extra time for the thickness of the *calzone*.

To make bread, rolls, or focaccia: Roll or form a loaf of punched-down dough, place on a baking sheet or in a pan, and let rise until doubled, then bake at 425°F as desired. The bread is ready when the crust is golden brown and sounds hollow when tapped on its underside. The length of baking time will depend on the size and thickness of what you are baking. For a crisper crust, place a pan of boiling water in the bottom of the oven. The steam helps create a crisp crust. Alternatively, you can spray water directly into the oven several times, using a sprayer for plants; repeat several times during the first 5 to 10 minutes of baking.

159 CALORIES PER SERVING
3 G FAT
0 G SATURATED FAT
0 MG CHOLESTEROL
28 G CARBOHYDRATES
5 G PROTEIN
1 MG SODIUM

Pane Ripiene

Serves 4

Literally, *pane ripiene* means stuffed bread. The bread is hollowed out, dredged with luscious olive oil-dressed vegetables, lots of garlic, any leftover grilled vegetables you might have, thinly sliced fresh tomatoes, and herbs, with a little cheese added just in case you need more flavor. It is typically brash and full of southern Italian flavors and—what more can you ask for—it is best made a day ahead of time.

1 baguette, cut in half lengthwise, and hollowed out (use filling for making gazpacho or other bread-thickened soup or sauces)
Olive oil for drizzling
Vinegar for sprinkling
Chopped garlic to your heart's desire
Leftover grilled vegetables: sautéed eggplant, peppers, zucchini
5 to 8 whole leaves of basil or 1 teaspoon fresh marjoram leaves
4 ripe tomatoes, thinly sliced
8 to 10 oil-cured or other flavorful black olives, pitted and halved
Optional: 4 marinated sun-dried tomatoes, chopped
Thinly sliced mild white cheese such as mozzarella

Drizzle the cut sides of the bread with olive oil, vinegar, and garlic.

Layer with grilled vegetables, herbs, tomatoes, olives, sun-dried tomatoes (if using), and cheese.

Wrap up tightly and leave overnight in refrigerator. Slice and serve as desired.

396 CALORIES PER SERVING
15 G FAT
5 G SATURATED FAT
16 MG CHOLESTEROL
48 G CARBOHYDRATES
15 G PROTEIN
699 MG SODIUM

PIZZA

Pizza has been eaten in Naples for centuries; petrified pizzas have been dug up from the ruins of Pompeii.

But while Neapolitans were eating this chewy, flatbread topped with tomato and cheese, it was Queen Margharita of Italy, wife of King Umberto I, who made it famous throughout the rest of Italy.

On a state visit to Naples she was taken through the little winding streets and stopped at the Pizzeria Brandi, which enthusiastically created a pizza in her honor. Topped with the colors of the Italian flag: red tomatoes, white mozzarella, and leaves of green basil, it was named after the Queen.

Pizza Margharita is perhaps the most famous pizza throughout the world to this day, and the pizzeria, still in business, has a commemorative plaque hanging outside, put up in 1989 to mark the centennial.

Naples is still the best place to eat pizza: crisp-crusted, tender-fleshed dough, tasting slightly of the smoke from the wood-burning oven. Pizza is never eaten at home, always in a café or street stall and always at night as an informal meal or late night snack. A newcomer to Naple's pizza passion is *pizza fritti*, a sort of *calzone* that is fried to a golden sizzle in boiling oil rather than baked. High fat, definitely, but it seems to have captured the hearts and stomachs of much of Naples.

BAKING PIZZA

Pizza can be made with either a thick or thin crust; no doubt you have your favorite. Regardless, it is the quality of the dough that dictates the quality of the pizza—the most delicious toppings will be lost on sodden, cardboard-like crust.

For a good-quality dough, use bread flour. It has more flavor and gives the dough more body. Traditional pizzerias add a bit of the leftover pizza dough to each new batch as a sort of sourdough starter.

Let it rise slowly, several times; I like to leave it in the refrigerator over the course of several days. The softer and more moist the dough, the lighter and crisper your crust will be.

Be sure to leave a margin around the edges so that the filling doesn't spill over, and so that you have a nice, crusty contrast to the rich center filling.

Make sure the oven is thoroughly preheated and very hot before placing the pizza inside.

Baking pizza on a baking stone helps give it a crisper crust and more of a pizza-oven effect. If you've no pizza stone (I don't), place a flat ceramic pan filled about halfway with boiling water in the bottom of the oven. The steam helps create a crisp crust.

Pizza can also be baked in a covered grill, where it picks up the delicious scent of the smoke. Place the pizza in its pan directly on the hot grill, cover, and let cook about 5 minutes depending on how hot the grill is. Check every few minutes and retrieve when the dough is baked through and the toppings have melted and lightly browned.

Classic Margharita   Smear the flat dough with a thin layer of good-quality tomato paste or very thick sauce. Make a layer of thin slices of ripe tomatoes, sprinkle with crushed dried oregano leaves and a little chopped garlic, and top with sliced mozzarella. After baking, drizzle with olive oil and sprinkle each pizza with a few torn leaves of fresh sweet basil.

Pizza from a little street in Aix en Provence   Make the sauce: crush garlic with salt and saffron, using a mortar and pestle or food processor, then add ¹/₂ cup tomato paste, ¹/₂ cup diced tomatoes (canned is fine, including their juices), and a large pinch of *herbes de Provence*. Brush the dough with oil, spread on some sauce, then top to taste with: capers, a few black Mediterranean olives, and if desired a few strands of roasted peeled pepper strips. Top with a grating of mozzarella, a sprinkling of Parmesan, and bake.

Pizza Bianca   White pizza, named for its lack of tomato topping. Brush the stretched-out pizza dough with olive oil, then top with marinated artichoke hearts, chopped garlic, chopped fresh marjoram, shredded mozzarella, and grated Parmesan, pecorino, or Asiago. Drizzle with more olive oil and bake.

Pizza alla Melanzane e Pesto   I ate this not long ago in Genoa, where fresh herbs are in abundance and *pesto* was offered on every menu for nearly every meal.

Smear the flattened dough with a generous amount of tomato sauce or *passata*, and top with chopped garlic and eggplant slices that have been browned (either on a grill, under the broiler, or in a frying pan) and brushed with olive oil. Top with a sprinkling of mozzarella and Parmesan, then bake. When it comes out, serve with dollops of *pesto*.

Pizza di Verdura e Formaggio   Spread the dough with tomato sauce, then top with spinach (cooked, squeezed, and chopped), chopped garlic, crumbled marjoram, dollops of either goat cheese or gorgonzola, and a sprinkling of mozzarella and Parmesan. Drizzle with oil and bake.

Suppli al Telefono

ITALIAN CHEESE-FILLED RICE CROQUETTES

Serves 4

Whenever you have a thick leftover *risotto*, consider these crisp cheese-filled morsels from the south of Italy. When the cheese heats it melts and strings; the *telefono* of its name refers to the strings of cheese, which look like telephone wires.

Authentic *suppli* are deep-fried in hot oil; I make them in a nonstick pan with a tiny bit of oil and they are very good.

Suppli can be made ahead of time and reheated in the oven.

1/2 pound mozzarella cheese, cut into bite-size pieces
   Leftover *risotto* (about 2 cups)
   Flour for dredging
 2 eggs, lightly beaten
2/3 to 1 cup bread crumbs, or as needed for coating the
   rice balls
   A small amount of oil for frying

Coat each square of cheese with cold leftover *risotto,* then dredge each in flour. Leave to firm up for an hour if possible.

Dip each floured rice ball in egg, then quickly into the crumbs. Leave to dry at least 30 minutes if possible.

Heat a heavy nonstick pan over medium heat, add a teaspoon or two of oil and the crumb-and-rice-coated cheeses.

Cook, turning once or twice, until they are golden brown. Serve right away. They are delicious when hot and melted, murderous when cold.

345 CALORIES PER SERVING
13 G FAT
7 G SATURATED FAT
139 MG CHOLESTEROL
35 G CARBOHYDRATES
20 G PROTEIN
335 MG SODIUM

Falafel

Serves 6 to 12, depending on whether guests eat a whole or half-filled pita; any left-over falafel balls can be frozen, as can the dough itself.

Falafel was probably my first introduction to Mediterranean food, my favorite snack on the way back from afternoon art classes in Jerusalem.

The little balls of ground chickpeas were squeezed into the hot boiling fat before my eyes, then scooped out browned, sizzling with spicy flavor and tucked into tender, soft, warm pita bread. Salads were piled high, *tahina* squirted on, and when asked *"horeef?"* (hot peppers) I always answered, "Yes, yes, yes!" Biting into a freshly made *falafel*, my teeth crunched the salads while the *falafel* balls were still just hot enough to slightly burn my tongue if I wasn't careful. Each bite was different, with pickled peppers, crisp potato chips, and strands of sauerkraut sharing the pita with the more usual chopped cucumbers, tomatoes, and cabbage.

The important thing about *falafel* is that they are freshly made, not cold and sitting around for hours or—horrors—days at a time. The pita must be soft and fresh and so tender that the contrast nearly catches your breath.

Alas, the little *falafel* stands run by Arabs, serving hot, freshly cooked *falafel* packed into a pita with care, have more and more been replaced by large do-it-yourself *falafel* stands, where the patties and salads are piled high and each person greedily rather than thoughtfully puts together his or her own.

Preparing *falafel* at home is a great way to enjoy eating them without the deep-fat frying involved. You can easily make little patties and brown them in the tiniest bit of oil in a nonstick frying pan. I recommend using a packaged *falafel* mix, mixed according to package directions, with a little extra cilantro added to the dough, the patties rolled in sesame seeds before browning.

1 package *falafel* mix
Water as called for in package directions
¼ cup chopped fresh cilantro
½ cup sesame seeds
A small amount of vegetable oil for browning
6 pita breads, cut into halves
1 cucumber, diced
3 tomatoes, diced
¼ cabbage, red or green, shredded
¼ cup, or to taste, Zhug (page 277); or *harissa*
1 cup prepared Tahina Sauce (page 279)
Pickled peppers, sauerkraut, or other pickles as desired

Mix *falafel* according to package directions; stir in the cilantro and chill until the mixture is firm.

Roll the mixture into balls, then roll each ball in sesame seeds to cover, pressing the seeds into the *falafel* dough, then flatten the balls slightly for even cooking.

Heat a nonstick frying pan with a tiny bit of oil, then add the *falafel* patties. Brown over a medium heat, turning once or twice, until the patties are crisp, cooked through, and golden brown.

Pop into soft pita breads right away, add vegetables, *zhug* and *tahina* sauces, and eat. If you need to keep them warm to serve all at once, place the browned *falafel* on a cookie sheet and keep them warm in a 300°F oven for up to 15 minutes or so.

222 Calories per serving
7 G Fat
1 G Saturated Fat
0 MG Cholesterol
29 G Carbohydrates
8 G Protein
442 MG Sodium

Brek or Brik

CRISP TRIANGLE PASTRIES

Yields 1 *brik*

This crisp Tunisian pastry is filled with all manner of things and sold in markets and street stalls from Morocco to Israel. I remember buying *brik* from a stall in which you chose the filling, after which the freshly made pastry was quickly wrapped around the filling and the whole thing tossed into boiling oil for just a moment, long enough to cook the pastry to a golden hue.

The most delicious filling to my mind is a smear of spicy chili-garlic *zhug* or *harissa,* or for omnivores, a nugget of spicy raw lamb or a chunk or two of tuna. Then comes a raw egg. As the pastry fries the egg poaches; it is thrilling to bite into the crisp flaky pastry and have the lovely running egg yolk explode in your mouth, along with a dab or two of sizzlingly spicy *zhug* sauce.

Authentically, *brik* is prepared with freshly made *malsouqa* pastry leaves, but filo dough gives luscious results and is easy to use.

Instead of frying, lower the fat content by heating a baking sheet in the oven, then quickly topping a piece of oil-brushed filo dough with the filling and the egg, then quickly wrapping it up. Fast, onto the hot baking sheet, then fast, into the hot oven. Bake about 8 minutes and the egg whites should have firmed up, the yolks runny.

For each brik

1 tablespoon *Zhug,* plus more to taste (see page 277)

1/4 cup hot stock or water

Pinch *each:* caraway seed, cumin, and cilantro

Juice of 1/4 lemon

Salt to taste

1 sheet filo dough

If baking, several tablespoons olive oil

Optional (for omnivores): 1 tablespoon ground lamb or several chunks of tuna

Garnish: chopped fresh cilantro, cumin, and chopped garlic for sprinkling

If frying, oil

1 egg

Combine *zhug* paste with stock or water, caraway, and cumin and bring to boil. Simmer for 5 minutes, then remove from heat and stir in the cilantro and lemon juice. Salt to taste and set aside.

Fold the filo dough in half so that it forms a long rectangle. If baking, brush the dough with a little olive oil.

Smear a little of the remaining *zhug* paste to taste onto the filo dough, add meat (if using), and sprinkle with cilantro, cumin, and garlic.

If frying, heat the oil until hot enough for frying (a cube of bread will sizzle and turn golden brown nearly immediately).

When the oil is hot enough to fry or the baking sheet is hot enough to burn your fingers, open the egg into a saucer. Quickly slip it onto the spot of *zhug* and filling on the pastry.

Immediately fold the pastry over to enclose the egg in a small triangular shape and continue folding over and over so that each side is closed and your triangle completely encloses the egg.

Quickly place the parcel in the hot oil or on the hot baking sheet before the egg has a chance to break through the delicate dough.

If frying, fry the pastry until golden on one side, then turn and fry the other side. Place on absorbent paper to drain excess grease. The egg will probably be very lightly poached at this point and will need a bit more cooking.

If baking, place the pastry in a 425°F oven for about 8 minutes, or until golden brown.

Repeat until you have as many *brik* as desired.

To reheat, place the pastries on a baking sheet and bake in a 350°F oven for about 5 to 8 minutes or until heated through. Keep an eye on the eggs so that their yolks don't cook until firm.

Serve hot with spicy sauce prepared with *zhug* for dipping.

228 CALORIES PER SERVING
15 G FAT
3 G SATURATED FAT
213 MG CHOLESTEROL
14 G CARBOHYDRATES
9 G PROTEIN
208 MG SODIUM

Harira

LEMON-SCENTED HEARTY LENTIL SOUP

Serves 4

Harira is the traditional dish served to break the daytime fast during the Moslem month-long observance of Ramadan. It is eaten as soon as the sun sets and voices of prayer are heard from the minarets or radios, signaling the end of the daylight abstention.

Authentic *harira* is made with a lamb stock, but a vegetable broth makes a good, if lighter, *harira*, too.

Thickening the *harira* is traditionally done with a paste of yeast and sometimes flour, sometimes rice cooking liquid. It does give a certain richness to the soup, but I prefer a lighter, clearer-flavored bowlful and have omitted this step in my recipe. I do, however, sometimes add a little asafetida or nutritional yeast, to taste.

Similarly, a sprinkling of cilantro at the end is fresh and invigorating. In Morocco any of a wide variety of herbs might be used—chervil, watercress, or purslane, especially. If any are on hand, by all means scatter these herbs over each bowlful.

2 or 3 medium onions, chopped
2 tablespoons olive oil
1/2 teaspoon *each:* ground ginger and cumin
1/4 teaspoon turmeric
6 cups defatted lamb stock or vegetable broth
2 tablespoons tomato paste
3 tablespoons *each:* red lentils (Indian *dahl*) and brown/green lentils
3 tablespoons chopped fresh cilantro, plus extra for sprinkling
2 tablespoons chopped celery leaves (or, if unavailable, celery heart)
1 1/2 teaspoons freshly and coarsely ground black pepper
4 to 6 garlic cloves, peeled and coarsely cut up
1/3 cup orzo
2 eggs, lightly beaten
1 1/2 tablespoons lemon or lime juice
1/8 teaspoon cinnamon, or to taste
1 lemon or lime, cut into wedges

Sauté the onions in olive oil until golden and lightly browned, then sprinkle in ginger, cumin, and turmeric, cooking another moment or two to bring out the flavors of the spices.

Stir in the stock or broth, tomato paste, red and brown/green lentils, cilantro, celery leaves or heart, black pepper, and garlic. Bring to a boil, then reduce the heat and simmer uncovered until the lentils are just cooked through, about 30 minutes.

Add the orzo and cook over medium heat about 10 minutes or until they are just tender, then beat in the eggs and lemon or lime juice. Beat well, letting the egg string into tiny delicate strands. Season with a sprinkling of cinnamon.

Serve each bowlful with a scattering of cilantro and wedge of lemon or lime for each person to squeeze in.

315 Calories per serving
12 G Fat
2 G Saturated Fat
107 MG Cholesterol
41 G Carbohydrates
13 G Protein
742 MG Sodium

Beid Maslug

MOROCCAN EGGS FROM THE MARKETPLACE, WITH TOASTED CUMIN AND SALT

In many Middle Eastern markets, such as in Tunisia or Beirut, hard-cooked eggs are a staple street food. Whenever I'm in these markets and feeling hungry, there always seems to a nearby street stall selling little cones of twisted paper filled with Moroccan eggs and dipping spice—nothing could seem more appealing.

I sometimes like a little hot stuff such as *harissa* or *zhug* dabbed onto my egg, too.

Per person
1/2 teaspoon cumin seeds
1/2 teaspoon salt, preferably sea salt
1 hard-cooked egg
Optional: a pinch of cayenne pepper

Lightly toast the cumin seeds in an ungreased pan until they smell fragrant; take care not to let them burn.

Grind the toasted seeds in a mortar and pestle or under a rolling pin. The old man in the market who showed me how to toast cumin used an old, empty wine bottle, which I've since found useful for rolling all sorts of spices in addition to cumin.

When the cumin is ground, combine it with the salt.

Serve the eggs with the cumin-salt alongside for dipping, and offer a sprinkling of cayenne if desired.

VARIATION

Fry eggs in olive oil until the edges are just browned and slightly crisp but the yolks are still soft, then season with cumin, paprika, cayenne, and oregano. Serve sunny-side up or over easy, sprinkled with chopped cilantro and, if you like, green onions. Serve crusty bread or pita for dipping into the rich spicy eggs with a fresh tangy ripe tomato and green pepper salad on the side.

81 CALORIES PER SERVING
6 G FAT
2 G SATURATED FAT
213 MG CHOLESTEROL
1 G CARBOHYDRATES
7 G PROTEIN
1128 MG SODIUM

SWEETS

THREE YOGURT SWEETS

YIAÓURTI ME MÉLI, *Greek Yogurt with Honey and Toasted Pistachios*

FRAISES AU YAOURT, *Rose and Vanilla Yogurt with Strawberries*

BANANOTEEM LEBEN, *Banana and Raisins in Vanilla Yogurt*

SUE KREITZMAN'S AMAZING LOWFAT TIRAMISÙ

FRUIT DESSERTS

PESCHE E LAMPONE AL FORNO, *Roasted Peaches with Raspberries*

PÊCHES ET NOIX, *Nectarines or Peaches with Sugar-Toasted Walnuts*

POMEGRANATE SEEDS WITH LYCHEES, MANGOES, AND MINT LEAVES

COMPOTE AUX FRAISES, *Red Wine and Strawberry Compote with Cardamom and Sorbet or Frozen Yogurt*

FROMAGE BLANC AVEC PÊCHES ET PISTACHES, *Vanilla-Almond Ricotta with Peaches, Pistachios, and Cognac*

PASTRIES AND TARTS

CROSTADA DI RICOTTA, *Ricotta Cheesecake*

MOORISH ALMOND FINGERS

TARTE AU CITRON, *Provençal Lemon Tart*

TARTE AUX FIGUES ET AMANDES, *Fresh Fig and Almond Tart*

ICES, SORBETS, AND OTHER FROZEN SWEETS

WHEN I think about dessert in the Mediterranean, I think about fruit, ripe and dripping with honeyed juices. Not long ago in Provence we hiked several miles up the hillside to the local village for lunch. On the way down we had dessert, eaten from tree to tree, vine to vine, berry patch to berry patch. Soft persimmons and pink-fleshed figs fell at our feet; a variety of grapes were ours for the picking, from husky wild berries to sweet little grapes perfumed with the scent of blossoms. We ate the last of the raspberries and then discovered the first golden apples of the season.

Everything was exquisitely fresh, absolutely in season, and no amount of embellishment could have made it more delicious. On the other hand, that evening we had pastries from Monsieur Ernest's of Cannes, perhaps the most amazing pastries I have ever eaten. So delicate, with the gossamer texture of sugary things whirled into lighter than light creations. Each bite made us feel lighter and lighter until I felt I might fly away. It was blissful.

Then there are the traditional Mediterranean desserts from the East: the syrup-drenched pastries and cakes, crisp shortbreads, and crunchy cookies. And the Greeks enjoy an unusual sweet-snack: preserves or thick jams made from roses, quince, vanilla, mastic (a fragrant resin), even eggplant, eaten from a spoon with a glass of cold water. I always enjoyed watching both children and grown-ups sipping and nibbling on this, while they sat on long wooden benches during the weekly movie (usually a spaghetti Western) in our Cretan village. Some licked the spoon then sipped the water, others stirred the sweet preserves into the water, making a sweet cooling drink.

And what about *gelato, granita,* and other ice creams? Are there any that are more deliciously refreshing than those of the Mediterranean? Not only are fruits, chocolate, nuts, and preserved fruit used in these frozen concoctions, but also coffee, flower waters, bits of nougat, crumbled amaretti, and seed brittles.

But all of these are sweets that one buys. There is less of a tradition of made-at-home sweets. Butter and cream are not traditional ingredients in the Mediterranean kitchen, at least not until recently.

But there are many little sweets, quickly prepared from simple ingredients, often from fruit, that are prepared in the home: ricotta cheese in Italy, for instance, dusted with sugar and finely ground espresso or mixed with lemon peel and sugar.

When I find myself in the Mediterranean at dessert time, I always return to the sweet refreshment of fruit, best illustrated by the following sweet I sampled in Spain: *zumo de naranja con frutas frescas:* a bowl of sweet seasonal fruit awash in freshly squeezed orange juice, with a little sugar on the side to spoon in as we pleased.

FIVE SIMPLE MEDITERRANEAN FRUIT DESSERTS

Ripe figs cut open, garnished with raspberries, and drizzled with anisette.

Melone al Marsala: A good reason to get out your melon-baller. Make balls of a good ripe cantaloupe, sprinkle with a tablespoon of sugar, and add a good splash of Marsala. Chill well. (The name *cantaloupe*, by the way, is derived from the castle of Cantalupo, in whose vicinity this melon was first grown in Europe.)

A favorite in Israel: Utterly ripe watermelon served in icy cold chunks with a wedge of salty feta on the side.

Peaches, Amaretti Crumbs, and Fromage Frais: In custard pots or bowls layer sliced ripe peaches (peeled or unpeeled) with crumbled amaretti or crisp macaroons and any fruit-flavored *fromage frais* or combination of *fromage frais* mixed with fruit yogurt. Let chill and eat when the crumbs have softened and flavored it all.

Ripe mangos drizzled with lime juice and scattered with raspberries, each serving accompanied by tiny scoops of raspberry sorbet, mango sorbet, and vanilla frozen yogurt, all drizzled with orange liqueur.

Yiaóurti me Méli

GREEK YOGURT WITH HONEY AND TOASTED PISTACHIOS

Serves 4

Greek yogurt is not easily found in the United States; when I crave its richness, I mix ordinary lowfat yogurt with lowfat sour cream.

$^1/_4$ to $^1/_2$ cup shelled pistachio nuts
2 tablespoons sugar
1 cup yogurt (lowfat is fine)
1 cup sour cream (lowfat is fine)
   Honey (preferably a dark and flavorful unfiltered herb honey), as desired
   Sprinkling of cinnamon

Lightly toast the pistachio nuts in a heavy ungreased frying pan; during the last few minutes sprinkle with sugar, giving it long enough to caramelize slightly. Pour onto a plate and let cool.

Mix the yogurt with the sour cream, stirring until very smooth. Chill until ready to serve.

When ready to eat, sprinkle each portion with toasted pistachios and drizzle honey and a sprinkling of cinnamon over each bowl according to taste.

180 CALORIES PER SERVING
12 G FAT
5 G SATURATED FAT
28 MG CHOLESTEROL
14 G CARBOHYDRATES
6 G PROTEIN
64 MG SODIUM

Fraises au Yaourt

ROSE AND VANILLA YOGURT WITH STRAWBERRIES

Serves 6

For a richer dish, combine the yogurt with an equal part of lowfat sour cream.

> 1 basket strawberries, washed, husked, and sliced
> 1/4 to 1/2 cup sugar, or to taste
> 1 quart (approximately) plain yogurt
> 1/2 teaspoon vanilla extract
> 1 tablespoon rose water

Mash the strawberries until they are chunky, then mix them with the sugar.

Stir the yogurt until it is smooth, then add it to the strawberries along with the vanilla and rose water. Chill until ready to serve.

150 CALORIES PER SERVING
3 G FAT
2 G SATURATED FAT
9 MG CHOLESTEROL
24 G CARBOHYDRATES
8 G PROTEIN
108 MG SODIUM

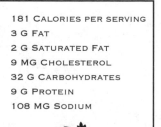

Bananoteem Leben

BANANA AND RAISINS IN VANILLA YOGURT

Serves 6

When I lived on an Israeli kibbutz we regularly ate versions of this—although it's very simple to prepare it tastes very satisfying. I like the way the raisins plump up as they chill with the yogurt.

1 quart plain yogurt or mixture of yogurt and sour
   cream (lowfat or nonfat is fine)
¼ to ½ cup sugar, or to taste
1 teaspoon vanilla extract
2 bananas, diced
¼ cup raisins, or more if desired

Stir the yogurt until it is smooth, then add the sugar and vanilla and mix well. Stir in the bananas and raisins and chill until ready to serve.

181 CALORIES PER SERVING
3 G FAT
2 G SATURATED FAT
9 MG CHOLESTEROL
32 G CARBOHYDRATES
9 G PROTEIN
108 MG SODIUM

Sue Kreitzman's Amazing Lowfat Tiramisù

Serves 6 to 8

I have eaten two amazing *tiramisùs*. The first was about 15 years ago in a little Florentine trattoria, and it was ecstasy by the spoonful. Rich *mascarpone* fluffed into gossamer lightness with whipped farmhouse eggs layered with coffee- and rum-soaked ladyfingers. It was terrible for the arteries and full of expensive and/or hard to get ingredients, and by the time salmonella in raw eggs became a concern I decided *tiramisù* was probably a thing of the past, at least as far as my table was concerned.

Then I had lunch with Sue Kreitzman, Europe's premier lowfat cookery writer, and had the second of the terrific *tiramisùs*. In fact, when she brought out the cocoa-dusted creamy treat, I thought she might have suspended her lowfat food style for dessert. It was so lovely, creamy, and enchanting.

The answer, however, was this: a lowfat version of the original, but in its own right even more delicious. Instead of the more usual coffee, the cookies had been dipped in orange juice and liqueurs, making a tangy contrast to the richer cheese. And we felt light and lithe afterward instead of weighed down.

16 or so ladyfingers or other sponge cookies
1/4 cup orange juice
2 tablespoons *each*: peach liqueur, orange liqueur, and brandy
12 ounces ricotta cheese
6 ounces low- or nonfat sour cream; or combination nonfat sour cream and nonfat cream cheese
1/4 cup sugar, or to taste
1/2 to 1 teaspoon vanilla extract, or to taste
1 to 2 tablespoons unsweetened cocoa
2 teaspoons sifted powdered sugar

Arrange the ladyfingers in the bottom of a 12 × 7 baking dish.

Mix the orange juice with the liqueurs and spoon this over the ladyfingers.

In a food processor whirl the ricotta and low- or non-fat sour cream until smooth, then add the sugar and vanilla. Taste for sweetness.

Spoon the creamy cheese over the soaked ladyfingers, sprinkle with cocoa and powdered sugar, then cover with plastic and chill for at least 2 hours.

226 Calories per Serving
3 G Fat
1 G Saturated Fat
45 MG Cholesterol
38 G Carbohydrates
8 G Protein
304 MG Sodium

Pesche e Lampone al Forno

ROASTED PEACHES WITH RASPBERRIES

Serves 4

Peaches and raspberries make a delightful combination in both color and flavor. Roasting brings out the deeper flavors of the peaches; adding raspberries keeps the taste lively and vivacious.

> 4 ripe but firm peaches
> 1/2 cup sugar, or as desired
> 2 tablespoons unsalted butter
> 1/2 cup dry white wine
> 1/2 cup fresh raspberries
> A few drops of almond or vanilla extract

Peel the peaches: cut a cross at the stem end, then plunge each peach into boiling water. Leave a few minutes, then remove with a slotted spoon and submerge into cold water, preferably water to which you have added a few ice cubes. Slip off the skins.

When cool enough to handle, arrange the peaches in a baking dish. If you like, you may cut them into halves and remove their pits, but I think they are rather unusual and nice left whole.

Heat the oven to 400°F. While it is heating, toss the peaches with sugar and dot with butter, add wine to the pan, then roast for 20 to 30 minutes.

When the peaches are tender, lightly glazed in parts, and almost ready to eat, add raspberries to the baking dish. Return the dish to the oven for another 10 minutes or so to warm the raspberries with the peaches.

Remove peaches and raspberries from oven and add a few drops of almond or vanilla extract to the juices. Spoon the juices over the peaches and eat either hot over cool ice cream or frozen yogurt, or eat them cool with thick Greek yogurt.

199 Calories per serving
6 G Fat
4 G Saturated Fat
17 MG Cholesterol
35 G Carbohydrates
1 G Protein
2 MG Sodium

Pêches et Noix

NECTARINES OR PEACHES WITH SUGAR-TOASTED WALNUTS

Serves 4

This dish of slightly sweet walnuts paired with ripe nectarines or peaches is so simple but so good: evocative of summer mornings in the south of France, where the territory of walnuts just gives way to that of almonds and olive oil. This sweet makes me think of bowls of *café au lait* and thick slices of crisp bread spread with jam, but it's also very good for dessert with rich yogurt, such as Greek sheep's milk yogurt, or with a lovely ice cream—dark cherry or jasmine tea ice cream is very nice, as is fragrant vanilla.

The important thing is to toast the walnuts lightly, then sprinkle them with sugar and keep them tossing over low heat until the sugar melts. Take care at this stage that the sugar doesn't burn, as sugar is very delicate that way, and burnt sugar will ruin the nuts completely.

$^2/_3$ cup shelled walnuts, in small pieces
5 to 6 tablespoons sugar
4 nectarines, sliced

Lightly toast the walnuts in a heavy ungreased frying pan until the nuts are fragrant and slightly darker in color.

Sprinkle the sugar over the walnuts, then lower the heat and continue to cook, tossing the nuts until the sugar melts and coats the nuts. Remove from the heat.

Arrange sliced nectarines or peaches on a plate and scatter the sugar-toasted walnuts over them.

245 CALORIES PER SERVING
12 G FAT
1 G SATURATED FAT
0 MG CHOLESTEROL
34 G CARBOHYDRATES
4 G PROTEIN
2 MG SODIUM

Sweets

Pomegranate Seeds with Lychees, Mangoes, and Mint Leaves

Serves 6 to 8

Tropical fruit are grown in abundance in Spain these days—exotic fruit such as lychees and loquats in addition to the traditional ancient fruit of the Mediterranean such as pomegranates.

This pan-Mediterranean fruit salad, which I've eaten in guises throughout the region from the Italian islands to North Africa, and from Ibiza to Israel, is terribly refreshing, especially after a hearty meal of pasta or couscous. Garnish with a handful of fragrant mint leaves, slightly crushed between your hands to release their sweet aroma.

The pomegranate is an ancient Mediterranean fruit, with legends and folklore accompanying it wherever in the region you find yourself. It is often seen as a symbol of fertility, granting the eater an abundance of children—their number the same as the seeds in the fruit.

It is a sacred fruit of Judaism, one of the seven fruit found in the Promised Land by the Hebrews fleeing Egypt's bondage. Jewish tradition says that we should all be obligated to perform good deeds, their number matching the number of seeds inside the pomegranate.

2 or 3 ripe red pomegranates
1 cup fresh lychees, peeled and stones removed (canned is fine)
2 ripe mangoes, peeled and cut from the pit
3 or 4 kiwis, peeled and diced or sliced
   About ½ cup other summery or tropical fruit: diced ripe pineapple, pitted loquats, star fruit, etc.
2 to 3 tablespoons sugar, or to taste
2 to 3 tablespoons orange liqueur such as Grand Marnier or strawberry liqueur such as Fraise de Bois
2 to 3 tablespoons brandy or cognac

Remove the seeds from the pomegranates and set aside. Discard the skin and pith.

Toss the seeds with the remaining fruit, then dress with the sugar, liqueur, and brandy or cognac.

Chill until ready to serve, up to 3 or 4 hours—any longer and it tends to get into a flavor muddle.

140 CALORIES PER SERVING
1 G FAT
0 G SATURATED FAT
0 MG CHOLESTEROL
33 G CARBOHYDRATES
1 G PROTEIN
5 MG SODIUM

Compote aux Fraises

RED WINE AND STRAWBERRY COMPOTE WITH CARDAMOM AND SORBET OR FROZEN YOGURT

Serves 4

The combination of cardamom, red wine, and strawberries is such a simple yet harmonious combination it is nearly breathtaking. This chic little dessert tastes utterly of summer in the south of France.

1 cup red wine
1/4 cup sugar
1/2 to 3/4 teaspoon fresh ground cardamom seeds, or to taste
2 tablespoons good-quality strawberry preserves, such as Bonne Maman
3 cups strawberries (2 baskets)
Vanilla or peach frozen yogurt or sorbet

Combine the red wine, sugar, and cardamom in a saucepan and bring the mixture to a boil. Reduce the heat and simmer for 5 to 10 minutes. Remove from the heat and stir in the preserves.

Place the strawberries in a bowl, then pour the hot spiced wine over them. Cool the mixture to room temperature, then chill it until very cold, about 4 hours.

Serve each bowlful with a scoop of frozen yogurt or sorbet.

128 CALORIES PER SERVING
0 G FAT
0 G SATURATED FAT
0 MG CHOLESTEROL
27 G CARBOHYDRATES
1 G PROTEIN
5 MG SODIUM

Fromage Blanc avec Pêches et Pistaches

VANILLA-ALMOND RICOTTA WITH PEACHES, PISTACHIOS, AND COGNAC

Serves 4

This dessert is almost *tiramisù*-like with its layer of soaked sponge cake and its sweet creamy topping. The topping here is lighter, however, inspired by the queen of lowfat *tiramisù*, Sue Kreitzman. It combines a light, fresh cheese such as ricotta *(fromage blanc)* with a dash of *fromage frais,* lowfat cream cheese, or low- or nonfat sour cream rather than a heavy, high-fat cheese such as the Italian *mascarpone.*

4 slices sponge or other lowfat simple cake
3 tablespoons cognac, brandy, or concentrated fruit juice
1 to 2 tablespoons orange juice, peach liqueur, or schnapps
2 cups ricotta cheese
$^1/_2$ cup *fromage frais* or nonfat or lowfat sour cream
$^1/_4$ cup sugar or other sweetener to taste
2 tablespoons raspberry preserves
 Dash *each:* vanilla and almond extract
 Optional: 1 tablespoon cognac
2 or 3 ripe peaches, peeled and diced
2 tablespoons unsalted pistachio nuts

Place a piece of cake at the bottom of each of four individual bowls. Drizzle with the cognac, brandy, or fruit juice and the orange juice, peach liqueur, or schnapps.

Stir the ricotta to make it smooth and mix it with the *fromage frais* or nonfat or lowfat sour cream. Mix in the sugar, raspberry preserves, vanilla extract, almond extract, and cognac, then stir in the peaches and pistachios. Pour over the pieces of cake. Chill until ready to serve.

426 CALORIES PER SERVING
13 G FAT
7 G SATURATED FAT
78 MG CHOLESTEROL
56 G CARBOHYDRATES
21 G PROTEIN
270 MG SODIUM

Crostada di Ricotta

RICOTTA CHEESECAKE

Serves 6 to 8

This Sicilian ricotta cheese tart is not as rich and heavy as the cheesecakes I grew up with. It is lightly sweet, tangy with cheese, and a little piece is very satisfying after a savory meal.

3 tablespoons Marsala
$1/4$ cup golden raisins
$1/4$ cup toasted slivered almonds or shelled unsalted pistachios
2 cups ricotta cheese
1 cup sugar, or to taste
3 eggs, lightly beaten
$1/8$ teaspoon cinnamon
$1/2$ teaspoon vanilla, or more to taste
$1/4$ teaspoon almond extract or essence
3 tablespoons flour
Pinch of salt
Grated zest of 1 well-washed lemon
Juice of 1 lemon
1 pie crust for deep-dish 9- to 12-inch pie pan or 15 × 9-inch baking pan

Mix the Marsala with the golden raisins and leave them to plump up for 30 minutes.

Combine the almonds or pistachios with the ricotta, sugar, eggs, cinnamon, vanilla, almond extract or essence, flour, salt, lemon zest, and lemon juice.

Pour into a deep-dish pie shell, leaving at least $1/2$ to $3/4$ inch of space on top so that the mixture doesn't puff up and out of the dish.

Heat the oven to 350°F. When it is up to temperature, bake the cheesecake for 1 to $1 1/4$ hours. Cool 20 minutes; eat either warm or chilled.

385 CALORIES PER SERVING
17 G FAT
6 G SATURATED FAT
100 MG CHOLESTEROL
46 G CARBOHYDRATES
12 G PROTEIN
247 MG SODIUM

Sweets

Moorish Almond Fingers

Serves 4 to 6

These North African pastries are dusted with cinnamon and sugar, brittle-crisp on the outside, and filled with a delicious almondy ooze; every bite presents a delightful contrast in textures.

Enjoy with a cup of strong, dark coffee at tea time or after a couscous dinner when you feel particularly indulgent.

8 ounces almond paste or 8 ounces ground almonds mixed with $1/3$ cup honey and a dash of almond extract

1 egg, lightly beaten

3 tablespoons orange flower water

4 tablespoons softened unsalted butter
    Dash almond extract

3 to 5 tablespoons sugar, or to taste (different almond pastes have varying degrees of sweetness and will need different amounts of sugar)

$1/4$ pound filo pastry

2 tablespoons, approximately, unsalted butter for brushing (or half butter, half vegetable oil)

2 teaspoons cinnamon, for sprinkling

2 tablespoons sifted powdered sugar, for sprinkling

Combine the almond paste with egg, orange flower water, butter, almond extract, and sugar. Mix well until smooth.

Lay out 1 sheet of filo dough, then brush lightly with butter or oil-butter mixture. Lay another sheet on top, then place several tablespoons of the almond mixture along one edge, fold over the edges to enclose the filling, then roll up like a cigar. Repeat until all filo and filling is used up.

Heat the oven to 350 to 375°F. While the oven is heating, arrange the pastries on an ungreased baking sheet, then bake until golden, about 10 to 15 minutes.

Sprinkle with cinnamon and sifted powdered sugar. Enjoy warm or at room temperature.

295 CALORIES PER SERVING
19 G FAT
8 G SATURATED FAT
69 MG CHOLESTEROL
27 G CARBOHYDRATES
5 G PROTEIN
107 MG SODIUM

❧ Tarte au Citron

PROVENÇAL LEMON TART

Serves 6 to 8

Lemons, round and yellow and so fragrant, seem to capture the flavor of the Mediterranean. You'll find lemons with savory or spicy food, squeezed onto salads or into soups, or made into cool refreshing drinks.

Meyer lemons, so fragrant and Provençal, are delicious made into this tart; so too are limes or at Christmas time, tangerines.

$1^2/_3$ to 2 cups flour

$^3/_4$ cup confectioners' (powdered) sugar

$^1/_4$ pound (1 stick) softened unsalted butter, plus extra for greasing pan

4 eggs

Pinch of salt

$^1/_2$ teaspoon vanilla extract

5 well-washed lemons, preferably Meyers, preferably unsprayed

$^1/_2$ cup sugar

$^2/_3$ cup ground almonds

$^2/_3$ cup heavy whipping cream

Sift $1^2/_3$ cups of the flour with the confectioners' sugar and work in the butter with a fork or your fingers.

Add 1 of the eggs, salt, vanilla, and grated zest of 1 of the lemons. Mix until it forms a smooth dough, then chill for at least 30 minutes.

Grease a 10-inch pan, then roll out the dough. Press into the pan and chill for 30 minutes or until firm.

Preheat the oven to 350°F. Place a piece of baking paper on top of the pie shell and line the shell with beans or pie weights. Bake for 10 minutes, then remove from the oven. Take out the paper and beans (save the beans for the next time you bake a tart) and return the pie shell to the oven for another 10 minutes.

Meanwhile, grate the zest of 2 of the remaining lemons and squeeze all of the lemons for juice. Beat the remaining eggs with the granulated sugar until it is thick enough to form a ribbon, then stir in the grated lemon zest, lemon juice, ground almonds, and cream.

Pour into the hot baked pie shell and return to the oven for 30 minutes. When it's done take the tart out of the oven, sprinkle it with sifted confectioners' sugar, and broil it for a few moments until the top lightly caramelizes. Serve hot, warm, or cool.

VARIATIONS

For lime tart, use 8 limes with the zest of 3 in the crust. For orange tart, use 3 oranges with the zest of 1 orange in the crust; for a tangerine tart, use 8 tangerines with the zest of 3 in the crust.

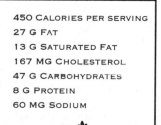

450 CALORIES PER SERVING
27 G FAT
13 G SATURATED FAT
167 MG CHOLESTEROL
47 G CARBOHYDRATES
8 G PROTEIN
60 MG SODIUM

Tarte aux Figues et Amandes

FRESH FIG AND ALMOND TART

Serves 6

This tart—its crisp crust filled with almond paste and a layer of fresh figs—was created during an autumn visit with friends in the hills behind Nice.

It was like visiting the garden of Eden, at least fruitwise: the persimmons were so sweet and ripe that we could hear their delicate splat as they fell from the tree. We laughingly suggested to lunch guests that for dessert, they had only to stand under the tree and open their mouths.

The figs, however, were much more versatile. We ate them drizzled with anisette, mashed with vanilla ice cream then refrozen, diced, and served on rich yogurt along with a spoonful of rose petal jam.

And we made the following tart.

1 cup ground almonds (almond meal)
$\frac{1}{2}$ cup sugar, or as desired, plus several more tablespoons for sprinkling
2 eggs, lightly beaten
Almond extract to taste
$\frac{1}{4}$ teaspoon cinnamon
Sweet dough for single pie crust
15 to 20 ripe figs, cut in half lengthwise
Jam such as strawberry or rose petal, for brushing

Heat the oven to 375°F. Combine the almond meal with the sugar, eggs, almond extract, and cinnamon. Set aside.

Roll out the dough into the bottom of a 9-inch baking tin. Spoon in the almond filling, then arrange a layer of figs on top. Bake for about 30 minutes, then remove from the oven.

Heat the jam with a tablespoon or two of water to thin it down, then brush it over the figs to glaze them. Serve either warm or cool.

450 CALORIES PER SERVING
23 G FAT
4 G SATURATED FAT
70 MG CHOLESTEROL
58 G CARBOHYDRATES
9 G PROTEIN
191 MG SODIUM

ICES, SORBETS, AND OTHER FROZEN SWEETS

Icy frozen treats are so refreshing in the Mediterranean lands, where the summer weather swelters, often climbing mercilessly into the 100's and staying there, impossibly and oppressively hot.

A mouthful of sweet ice, slithering down the throat and melting into a cooling balm, is often your only respite from the heat. This past summer, while walking back from the Roman metro, I stopped for a *granita* and was utterly amazed: not only was it delicious but it cooled me down, rehydrated me, and yes, put me in a much better mood.

Sweet ices come in a wide array: shaved ice topped with syrups in an Italian street, crushed fruit juice or sweet espresso served in a café, a cone of ice cream—*gelato* or *helado*—made of fruit, milk or cream, chocolate, nougat, nuts, and any variety of spices (a recent favorite of mine was *risotto gelato*—ice cream made from rice).

But it is the exotic ice creams and ices that for me typify the Mediterranean: almond and lemon ice; ice cream scented with orange flower water and vanilla beans; peaches steeped in red wine, made into an ice cream with ripe cherries or strawberries; and watermelon ice scented with rosewater.

Glace à la Lavande

LAVENDER AND HONEY ICE CREAM

Serves 4 to 6

The first time my daughter and I tasted this we spooned into it with dreamy looks on our faces, tasting the fragrant fields of Provence with every bite.

It makes a terrifically evocative and very sophisticated dessert, whether you're in your first childhood or your second.

$1/3$ cup honey
1 tablespoon lavender buds
2 cups milk
2 cups whipping cream

Gently heat the honey and lavender together. When the honey has melted, let it sit for about 5 minutes to absorb the lavender scent, then strain off the lavender buds.

Heat the milk and cream until bubbles form around the edge of the pan, then stir in the strained lavender honey.

Let the mixture cool, then freeze, either in an ice cream freezer or in an ice tray, scraping the icy edges every so often.

375 CALORIES PER SERVING
31 G FAT
19 G SATURATED FAT
118 MG CHOLESTEROL
21 G CARBOHYDRATES
4 G PROTEIN
73 MG SODIUM

Honeydew Melon Ice with the Scent of Flowers

Serves 4

I use a fork to lightly crush the juicy-ripe fruit in this recipe rather than a blender or food processor; these appliances make the task very easy but leave a uniformly boring texture.

1   very ripe medium-large melon, preferably an
    orange-colored honeydew
$1/4$ to $1/2$ cup sugar, or to taste
    Juice of $1/2$ lemon, or to taste
1   teaspoon orange flower water, or to taste

Cut open the melon and spoon out the seeds. Scrape out the ripe flesh with a fork and/or spoon and place in a bowl. Mash any large chunks and stir in the sugar, lemon juice, and orange flower water.

Place in the freezer and freeze until ice forms around the edges. With a fork, scrape the ice crystals into the mixture, which will become slushy or snowlike in consistency. Repeat this once or twice until a chunky sorbet forms. To serve, scrape portions into individual bowls and serve right away.

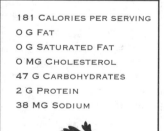

181 Calories per serving
0 G Fat
0 G Saturated Fat
0 MG Cholesterol
47 G Carbohydrates
2 G Protein
38 MG Sodium

Almond-Lemon Ice

Serves 4

This dessert is brightly refreshing, although I must warn you it is scented strongly with almonds and is not to everyone's taste. Those I tested it on either adored it or were less than enthusiastic. I loved it.

> 3 cups water
> 1 cup sugar
>   Pinch of salt
> 1 cinnamon stick
>   Several generous shakes of almond extract
>   Juice of ½ lemon

Combine the water, sugar, salt, and cinnamon stick in a saucepan and bring to a boil. Cook for several minutes until the sugar is well dissolved.

Let cool, then remove the cinnamon stick and add the almond extract and lemon.

Freeze, either in an ice cream maker or ice cube tray, scraping every so often.

---

182 CALORIES PER SERVING
0 G FAT
0 G SATURATED FAT
0 MG CHOLESTEROL
48 G CARBOHYDRATES
0 G PROTEIN
39 MG SODIUM

Sweets

Sorbet al'Ananas

PINEAPPLE AND VANILLA SORBET

Serves 4

You must make this with the sweetest, ripest pineapple you can find. A little pineapple juice added stretches the flesh and makes the lightest, most refreshing sweet.

1 ripe medium-large pineapple, peeled and diced (core removed; while many chuck it out, the core is probably my favorite part—I always save it for my own nibbling)

$\frac{1}{4}$ cup sugar, or to taste

$\frac{1}{2}$ cup pineapple juice, or more as desired

1 $\frac{1}{2}$ teaspoons vanilla extract

1 tablespoon cognac or brandy

Purée the pineapple with the remaining ingredients, adding more sugar to taste and more pineapple juice if the mixture seems too thick. If too sweet, add a few drops of lemon juice, but remember that cold dulls the tastebuds—it will need to taste sweeter than you want for it to freeze to the right flavor.

Freeze in an ice cream freezer or in a tray, removing every so often and scraping with a fork for a snowy texture. Alternatively, you can fluff up the frozen chunks in a food processor.

224 CALORIES PER SERVING
1 G FAT
1 G SATURATED FAT
0 MG CHOLESTEROL
54 G CARBOHYDRATES
1 G PROTEIN
4 MG SODIUM

Parfait aux Bananes et les Fruits Rouges

ICED BANANA-BERRY PARFAIT WITH BERRY COULIS AND CRÈME FRAÎCHE

Serves 4

The secret ingredient in this refreshing dessert is frozen banana chunks: they give body and an icy texture that is something between a milkshake and frozen sherbet, with a soft consistency that slips down your throat delightfully. Buy bananas when they are ripe and cheap and freeze them whole in their skins; the skins will blacken but the bananas remain fine inside. When ready to use, peel with a knife, cut into chunks, and use for whirling into frozen desserts such as this one, or defrost and use in cakes and breads.

1 cup raspberries or blackberries, fresh or frozen
1 tablespoon liqueur such as Fraise de Bois or Framboise
Sugar to taste
4 frozen bananas
2 cups milk
²/₃ cup *fromage frais* or plain yogurt
¹/₄ cup sugar, or to taste
Dash of vanilla or almond extract, to taste
2 tablespoons *crème fraîche,* sour cream (lowfat or nonfat is fine), or *fromage frais*

To make the berry coulis: Whirl one-half to two-thirds of the berries in a blender with the liqueur and sugar to taste. If desired, strain out the seeds. Set aside and chill.

To make the banana-berry freeze: Peel the frozen bananas and cut them into chunks (you may need to defrost them slightly to cut them). Place them in the blender with the remaining berries and the milk, *fromage frais* or yogurt, sugar, and vanilla or almond extract. Whirl until it forms a thick purée, much like soft frozen yogurt. If more liquid is needed, add a little more milk or yogurt.

Serve this icy fruit fluff in wine glasses or other appealing goblets. If using frozen berries the berry coulis will be sorbet-like in consistency and can easily be layered with the banana-berry freeze. If using fresh berries, the berry coulis will be at its best drizzled on top or puddled onto plates.

Serve topped with a dollop of *crème fraîche*, sour cream, or *fromage frais*.

270 CALORIES PER SERVING
5 G FAT
3 G SATURATED FAT
14 MG CHOLESTEROL
53 G CARBOHYDRATES
8 G PROTEIN
92 MG SODIUM

Sweets

Zuccotto Gelato

Serves 8 to 10

Zuccotto is a favorite Florentine sweet: a hemisphere filled with liqueur-soaked spongecake along with creamy custards or ice cream. It's gaudy and delicious, with no redeeming nutritional benefits—in short, everything that dessert should be.

There's a story about why this dessert is called *zuccotto* (meaning "soldier's helmet"): during one of the wars of the Renaissance, some soldiers kept their food in snow-filled caves deep in the Tuscan hills; the food stayed chilled even in the summer months. One day a soldier at the food-storage cave spilled some wine onto a pile of snow, had a taste, and found it quite delicious. Another soldier, slightly tipsy and gastronomically excited, exclaimed: "What else would be good mixed into this snow?" So the soldiers removed their helmets, filled them with snow, and mixed in all sorts of sweet ingredients. Soon word of these ice cream treats made in helmets spread to nearby Florence, where they have been enjoyed to this day. You'll often find them sold in pastry shops to be toted home for family dinners or other celebrations.

1 layer of sponge cake, sliced
1/2 cup rum
1/2 cup sweet liqueur such as Maraschino, Sweet Marsala, or other favorite
1 pint *each* slightly softened frozen yogurt or ice milk: rum-raisin or dark cherry vanilla, spumoni, pistachio, and chocolate
1/4 to 1/2 cup coarsely chopped or grated bittersweet chocolate

Use plastic wrap to line the inside of one large (12- to 15-inch diameter) or two smaller (6-inch diameter) stainless or temperature-resistant glass (such as Pyrex) bowls. Sprinkle the pound cake with the rum and liqueur and arrange the slices tightly together in the plastic-lined bowl(s).

Fill with the various ice creams and chocolate bits, arranged in a slightly haphazard manner, but pressed down so that it all fits together.

Cover tightly with plastic wrap and freeze until serving. Unmold, peel off the plastic, and serve in slices.

Sorbet au Coulis de Framboise

THREE-COLOR SORBETS IN RASPBERRY COULIS

Serves 6

Envision bright orange-colored mango sorbet, crisp green lime sorbet, and pale yellow pineapple or dark purple blackberry sorbet resting on a puddle of neon pink raspberry coulis. This is the lightest of desserts and amongst the most beautiful, with so little work required you might feel like laughing with sheer glee.

For further embellishment, you could decorate the plate with unsprayed edible flower petals that have a sweet scent, such as rose petals. Lacking that, a handful of blackberries would be very nice.

2 baskets fresh raspberries, picked over (about 12 ounces in total)
$^1/_2$ cup sugar, or to taste
1 tablespoon lemon juice
Optional: 1 tablespoon Frambroise liqueur, or to taste
1 pint *each:* lime sorbet, mango sorbet, and a third in a contrasting color/flavor

In a food processor or a blender combine the berries, sugar, and lemon juice and whirl until it forms a smooth purée. Add liqueur if desired.

Chill in a covered container until ready to use (this may be done up to 3 days ahead of time).

When ready to serve, cover the bottom of a plate with a layer of raspberry coulis, then add a scoop of each sorbet flavor. Serve right away.

239 CALORIES PER SERVING
0 G FAT
0 G SATURATED FAT
0 MG CHOLESTEROL
85 G CARBOHYDRATES
1 G PROTEIN
0 MG SODIUM

Mail-Order Sources

BALDUCCI'S
11-02 Queens Plaza South
Long Island City
New York, NY 11101-4908
(800) 225-3822 or in N.Y. (212) 673-2600

DEAN & DeLUCA
560 Broadway
New York, NY 10012
(800) 221-7714 or in N.Y. (212) 431-1691

LE MARCHE SEEDS
P.O. Box 190
Dixon, CA 95620
(916) 678-9244

RATTO'S INTERNATIONAL GROCERY
821 Market Street
Oakland, CA 94607
(415) 832-6503

SHEPARD'S SEEDS
30 Irene Street
Torrington, CT 06790
(203) 482-3638 or (408) 335-6910

ZABAR'S
85th Street and Broadway
New York, NY 10024
(212) 787-2000

Index